Precision Photoshop

CREATING POWERFUL VISUAL EFFECTS

Precision Photoshop

CREATING POWERFUL VISUAL EFFECTS

Lopsie Schwartz

CRC Press
Taylor & Francis Group
Boca Raton   London   New York

CRC Press is an imprint of the
Taylor & Francis Group, an **informa** business

AN A K PETERS BOOK

CRC Press
Taylor & Francis Group
6000 Broken Sound Parkway NW, Suite 300
Boca Raton, FL 33487-2742

© 2015 by Taylor & Francis Group, LLC
CRC Press is an imprint of Taylor & Francis Group, an Informa business

No claim to original U.S. Government works

Printed on acid-free paper
Version Date: 20140718

International Standard Book Number-13: 978-1-4665-9175-2 (Paperback)

Library of Congress Cataloging-in-Publication Data

Schwartz, Lopsie.
     Precision Photoshop : creating powerful visual effects / Lopsie Schwartz.
       pages cm
     Includes index.
     ISBN 978-1-4665-9175-2 (alk. paper)
       1. Adobe Photoshop. 2. Photography--Digital techniques. I. Title.

     TR267.5.A3S36 2015
     006.6'96--dc23   2014015774

Visit the Taylor & Francis Web site at
http://www.taylorandfrancis.com

and the CRC Press Web site at
http://www.crcpress.com

Contents

Preface

I work with Photoshop every day. I have since version 3. That is Photoshop 3, not CS 3. That was when I would work on a Mac one day, a Windows machine another, and follow it up with a Unix or Irix machine. (Yes—I worked on Photoshop on Silicon Graphics workstations.) So, Photoshop feels like that old friend I grew up with, that we have lived each other's secrets and developed and matured together. It feels exceptionally so now that Photoshop has integrated some video and three-dimensional (3D) capabilities. As the understanding friend who has already experienced 3D and Motion Graphics, I am patient while Photoshop learns the ropes and slowly improves on these capabilities. Already, PSCC (Photoshop CC) is so much better in that realm than when it first came out with 3D capabilities.

Like moving to a new area and trying to join people who grew up together, coming into Photoshop now can be daunting. There are so many ways to do the same thing, so many ways to obtain similar results, and all the options can be overwhelming. Even with experienced artists, I have never been on a project for which at least one person did not say, "Huh, I never knew that," about some Photoshop feature.

So, the question is, what information should I cover and how much? Do I assume you already know Photoshop? If so, then what parts are you going to know? I hope I struck a balance in this book so you will find clear instruction no matter what your level and yet will find something that makes you say, "Huh, I never knew that."

I have to admit, there are some tutorials that did not make it into this book. I hope to put some of them online as supplemental tutorials, so keep an eye out. Check in on www.LopsieSchwartz.com/PrecisionPhotoshop/ for updates. Additional material is available from the CRC website (http://www.crcpress.com/product/isbn/9781466591752).

While you are at it, please do contact me with feedback—I would love to hear from you.

Lopsie Schwartz

Acknowledgments

I would like to take a moment to thank a few people; without them, this book would never have seen the light of day. First and foremost, my editorial angel, Sarah Chow, whose patience and professionalism exceed all human boundaries and who believed in me and fought for me to get this book published. I feel like we just had a baby together.

I did not realize how ironic that statement was until Sarah went on maternity leave. I would also like to thank Judith Simon, Rick Adams, Scott Hayes, and Christopher Manion for helping me cross the finish line.

Speaking of which, I absolutely must thank my babies, my son, Xander, for understanding when not to bother Mommy when she was writing and my husband, Andy, who has always had that lifesaving sixth sense in that regard.

I also want to thank two lifesavers: Curt Clayson, my technical editor, and Dara Rochlin, the Book Doctor, who saved me from some embarrassing typos and technicalities and who helped crack the whip on me to deliver to Sarah.

I absolutely must also thank Bridget Gaynor, Manuel Prada, and Peter Rubin for their early support, and for having my back.

And last but definitely not least, I would like to thank CRC Press and the entire launch team for breathing life into the dream and for doing all the relentless work for which you really can never be thanked enough.

Love you all, every one of you.

About the Author

Lopsie Schwartz is a VFX and Animation veteran who has worked at such prestigious facilities as Weta Digital, Disney Animation, and Rhythm and Hues. Over the past 15 years, Lopsie has used Photoshop for projects ranging from commercials to major motion pictures, television shows to games, and photo retouching to fine art. She likes to share with others what knowledge she has gleaned over the years working in various capacities within the entertainment business and has taught at various college-level institutions for VFX and Animation.

You can follow her current journeys through her website www.LopsieSchwartz.com.

1

The Cheat

Introduction
Before You Start
The Tutorial

Introduction

My interview for my first major motion picture went something like this:

"Have you ever worked with the paint program Amazon 3D?"
"Um … no …."
"Have you ever worked on an SGI station?"
"Um … no …."
"Softimage?"
"No. … But I'm a very quick learner if you would give me a chance."

And that was how I got my first industry job. Why did they hire me? Because I knew Photoshop and had made a portfolio that matched the look of the movie, and they were going to pay me—oh wait—I can't say that. Anyway, I had one month to learn *everything*, not just learn, but be up to speed with the other artists. If I could not get up to speed, well then, I would have the experience and know what I needed to work on. But, if I could get up to speed with everyone else, I would have my first major motion picture credit.

So, this chapter is in honor of that first moment—the first project that launched me into my dream career and introduced me to some wonderful people that I still keep in touch with today (all of whom will be receiving this book just so they can laugh at the phrase "first major motion picture.")

This is *the* cheat. The premise is you do not know Photoshop at all—never touched it but need to know *everything, stat*. You will need to know it for some high-end work, and you do not have time to take a course or spend too much time going through five different books to glean the type of information you need. So, here it is: One lesson, one day, and you will know most of the features of Photoshop plus some impressive little tricks that will make it seem like you are a pro. And, I will take you there in baby steps. Oh, and you say that you cannot really draw—no worries. I also have that covered.

But, a crash diet will not keep off the pounds unless you follow up with some good nutrition and healthy habits, so after you are done with this chapter, check out the rest of the book: It's good for you.

Before You Start

There *is* one thing you'll need to do before you start this tutorial: Go to Chapter 2 and read the section on setting up Photoshop. That will ensure that your settings are at the default settings for Photoshop to give you the smoothest experience.

What should be painfully obvious is that you'll need specific files to do this tutorial. So, please download them at the website: http://www.crcpress.com/product/isbn/ 9781466591752 or www.LopsieSchwartz.com/PrecisionPhotoshop/Downloads.

The Tutorial

Go to **File > Open …**. Navigate like you would any other file browser to where you saved the Chapter 1 tutorial folder. Inside the folder, select Chameleon.CR2. This is a Canon RAW format (Canon RAW version 2), and Photoshop will automatically open this in Adobe Camera Raw (ACR) dialog. (If you are working with an older version of Photoshop, CS5 and older require you to install a plug-in.) The image is a little too blown out on the back of the chameleon for me, so let's bring down the exposure a bit. I brought it down just a tad to −0.75. Don't leave yet because we want to increase the details and obtain good texture on the chameleon. So, slide the **Clarity** slider all the way to the right, and while we are there, let's bring up the Vibrance to +33. You'll notice that the Shadow Clipping warning (that little symbol in the upper-right corner of the histogram) is lighting up a warning. Clicking on the symbol will highlight the areas in the image that are clipped. Try it. The areas are small specks in the darkest shadows, and although for our purposes that shouldn't be a problem, we'll get rid of it by bringing up the blacks a bit. Slide the **Blacks** slider up to about +28. Your settings should look like mine in Figure 1.1. If so, then go ahead and click **Open Object**. If your settings indicate "Open Image," then **Shift+Click Open Image** to open the image as a Smart Object. (You can go to Chapter 9 for an explanation and samples of Smart Objects if you are in search of enlightenment.) Had we clicked on "Done," then the ACR settings would be applied to our RAW image, but it will not open as a document in Photoshop.

The chameleon file is open and ready to edit. Because it is opened as a Smart Object, there is a small notation on the layer thumbnail's lower right-hand corner. Should you double-click the layer, ACR will reopen, and you can adjust the settings. Also, in the document title tab on top, you can see that this is in RGB (red, green, blue) mode and is 16 bit. The 16 bit will give us greater color depth but will limit some of the functions within Photoshop. We won't feel the limitations because so much is supported.

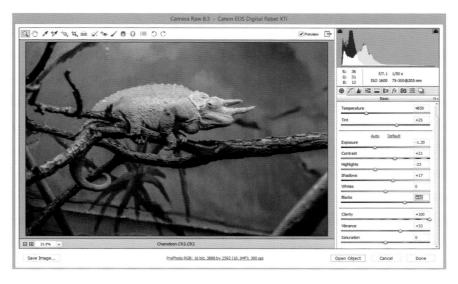

Figure 1.1

My ACR settings for the chameleon.

Let's start by isolating the chameleon and the branch from the rest of the image. Select the Magnetic Lasso Tool ![icon], which is in the Lasso Tool's ![icon] flyout menu, or shelf. If you press **Shift+L**, you will see the Lasso Tools circulate. Keep pressing **Shift+L** until you see the Magnetic Lasso Tool ![icon]. Carefully trace around the chameleon and some of the stick. When you have reached the starting point, the cursor will show a circle indicating closure. If you have a hard time getting it to pop up, you can hit **Enter/Return**, and the selection will close with a direct line from your last point to your starting point. Alternatively, you can simply double-click to have the selection close. If you need to add more to the selection, hold **Shift** and continue lassoing. If you accidentally select too much, you can hold **Alt/Option** and select around the areas you want deselected. Your selection should look something like Figure 1.2.

Figure 1.2

Select the chameleon and the stick.

My selection wasn't very exact, so I'll use the Quick Mask to help clean up the selection. Click on the Quick Mask Toggle ![icon] in the Tools palette. The parts that are masked are overlaid with red. Figure 1.3 shows that I need to clean up in a few areas. If your image is reversed from mine, get out of Quick Mask Mode so you have the crawling ants surrounding the selection and press **Ctrl+Shift+I/⌘+Shift+I** to invert the selection. Then, toggle back to Quick Mask Mode.

Select the Brush Tool ![icon] and choose the first option on the brush tip selection: Soft Round. Set the size to 100 and paint on the canvas. You will notice that painting with

Figure 1.3

The Quick Mask shows areas I need to clean.

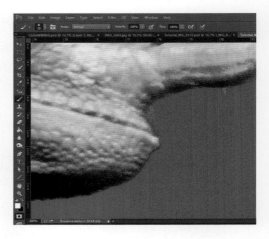

Figure 1.4

Zoom in and out of the mask while you paint.

black will give the red unselected designation and coloring in with white will make it clear, indicating the selection. You can press + or − to increase or decrease the size of your brush and press **X** to switch between the foreground color and background color. To ensure that you are painting with *pure* black and *pure* white, press **D**. Now, go ahead and paint out all the areas that are not part of the chameleon or the branch. Press **Ctrl++/⌘++** to zoom in closer and **Ctrl+-/⌘+-** to zoom out as you work (Figure 1.4).

When you are done, toggle off the Quick Mask Mode ▣, and in the Layers palette on your right, click on the Layer Mask button ▣. Photoshop will apply a layer mask using your selection to the currently selected layer. So, the gray-and-white checkered areas are actually transparent areas to your image (Figure 1.5).

Figure 1.5

The gray and white checkered areas are transparent parts of the layer.

Save your current project by going to **File > Save** and choosing PSD (Photoshop Document) for the file type. It's a good habit to save as you work, so I'm including occasional saves in this tutorial.

Now, we want to bring in a sky background for our chameleon. Go to **File > Browse** in **Mini Bridge.**

If you do not have Bridge already open, there is a button to **Launch Bridge** on the bottom where Mini Bridge pops up; go ahead and press it (Figure 1.6).

Using the file system on the left, navigate to the folder with all the Chapter 1 image downloads. Go into the backgrounds folder. Not sure which to choose? Select one and hit the **spacebar**. A full-screen preview will pop up so you can take a better look at it. Press **spacebar** again to toggle back. Select one and drag it over your chameleon. I chose one of the sky images, but you can choose a different one if you wish. The image appears over your chameleon with an *x* and little corner squares.

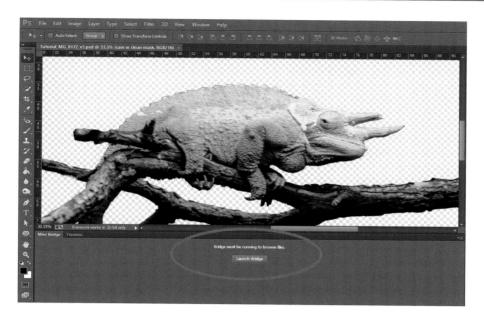

Figure 1.6

The Launch Bridge button.

These are handles to resize the image. Click and pull the image until it covers the entire canvas (Figure 1.7). When you are done, click on the check mark in the Options bar or hit **Enter/Return.**

Now, go to the Layers palette, click drag the background layer down until it is below the chameleon layer, and release the left mouse button (LMB). The chameleon is above your background. Hit **Ctrl+S/⌘+S** to save your file (Figure 1.8).

Now open the file with the orange in it. Since I didn't give you the name of the file and it has a non-descriptive name, you'll need to locate it visually. Look down in Mini Bridge and in the path indicator click up one level so you are no longer in the backgrounds folder. Find the file with the orange and double-click it so it opens in a new tab in Photoshop (Figure 1.9).

Figure 1.7

Resizing the background.

Figure 1.8

The background is moved behind/below the chameleon.

Figure 1.9

This is the image of the orange you are looking for.

Because this was not a RAW image, the photo immediately opens in Photoshop. This time we will select using the Quick Selection Brush ![]. The Quick Selection Brush ![] and the Magic Wand Tool ![] are on the same shelf, so if you see only the Magic Wand Tool ![], click and hold on the tool icon in the toolbar to have the drop-down menu appear and choose the Quick Selection Brush ![] (Figure 1.10).

Figure 1.10

Can't find the Quick Selection brush? Click and hold on the Magic Wand tool.

Make sure your settings in the Options bar have Auto-Enhanced selected, and you might as well have Sample All Layers selected (because we only have one layer, it doesn't matter, but generally we want the settings to sample all layers). Start brushing inside the orange. You'll see that, on release, the entire orange is selected. In the Options bar, select the Add to Selection button (see Figure 1.11 to see which one it is).

Brush along the inside of the big leaf. You'll see the leaf will also be selected. Make sure your brush is small enough to be inside an area but large enough to gather the right color information for the tool to use for selection; select the orange and its stem and leaves from the background. Should your tool select too much, just switch to the Subtract from Selection mode in the Options bar and brush on the background area that was selected. You can still use the Quick Mask Mode we just used for the chameleon. In the end, you should have a selection like you see in Figure 1.12.

We want to make sure we have this clean selection saved for future use, so we'll save it as a channel. Go to **Select > Save Selection ….**

In the dialog that pops up, make sure you have **New Channel** selected and give your Alpha Channel a name, such as "Orange Alpha." Click OK. If you go to your Channels palette right next to your Layers palette, you'll

Figure 1.11

Select the Add to Selection button.

Figure 1.12

Your selection should look similar to this.

Figure 1.13

You must click on the *thumbnail,* not just the layer while holding Ctrl/Option for this to work.

see that there is an extra black-and-white channel. This is your Alpha, Mask, or Holdout Matte—all names for the same thing. Click back to the Layers palette. You should still have the orange selected. Press **Ctrl+C/⌘+C** to copy the orange and press **Ctrl+V/⌘+V** to paste it back on a new transparent layer. You should see your orange on a new layer called Layer 1, but the selection is no longer there. We can bring back the selection in a few ways, but let's do a neat shortcut and hold **Ctrl/⌘** while clicking on the thumbnail of Layer 1 (Figure 1.13). The selection comes back. This shortcut selects by transparency.

With the selection active, go to **Image > Adjustments > Black and White …**. The Black and White dialog will appear. Adjust the settings until you obtain good texture across the orange, then hit **OK**. You now have a black-and-white orange floating on a separate layer (Figure 1.14). **Ctrl/⌘** click Layer 1 to load and activate the selection again. We're going to use the selection for another layer: go to **Layer > New Adjustment Layer > Curves …**. We want this orange to look like a metallic orange, so in the Curves dialog, make a squiggly line like I have done in Figure 1.15. Your orange should now look like a shiny chrome metal orange. For now, just save and close the file. We'll be bringing that back in further work. Go to **Save > Save As…** and make sure to save it as a PSD so we save all the layers and channels—all our hard work.

Go back to your chameleon file. I want to write, "Sky's the limit," but I feel there isn't enough canvas real estate for me to write it as large as I would like. So, let's first make this canvas larger. Hide the chameleon for now by pressing

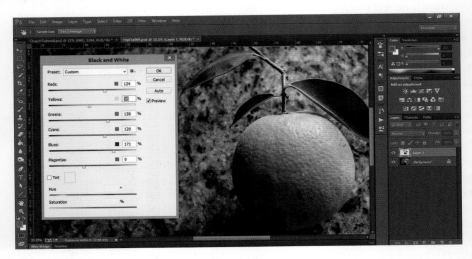

Figure 1.14

The black-and-white orange.

1. The Cheat

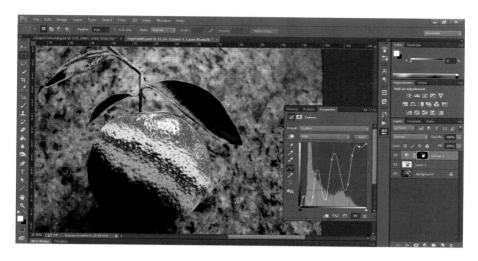

Figure 1.15

Adjusting the curves to achieve a metallic look.

on the Eye Icon 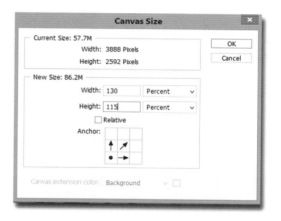 of the chameleon's layer. Then, select the background image layer, in my case "Sky." Next, go to **Image** > **Canvas Size ….**

In the Canvas Size dialog, you'll see input boxes for Width and Height. Before we enter any numbers, click on the units of measurement (by default, they will be in inches) and a drop-down menu should appear with several different choices. Choose Percent. The numbers in the Width and Height should automatically reset to 100 each, meaning 100% of the current width/height. Make Width 130 and Height 115, then click on the lower-left corner of the Anchor box. This tells Photoshop how the canvas should be increased. Left in the middle, it would increase the canvas all around, giving our image a framed look. We want to just have some extra space to the top and the right; hence, we anchor the image to the lower-left corner. Click on **OK** (Figure 1.16).

Figure 1.16

Anchor the image to the lower left corner.

Your canvas is now larger, but the additional space on the sky layer is blank/transparent. We need to fill in the photo image seamlessly, so let's let Photoshop do the work for us. Make a duplicate of the sky layer by dragging the layer into the New Layer Icon 🔳 on the bottom of the Layers palette. A duplicate of the layer is created, and it also is a Smart Object. But, our Fill action will not work on a Smart Object, so let's rasterize the new layer.

Select **Layer** > **Smart Objects** > **Rasterize**. The layer will show that it is no longer a smart image. Now, select the Magic Wand Tool 🪄 (remember it is behind the Quick Selection Tool if you can't find it) and click in the empty area. The Magic Wand Tool "magically" selects the entire new area. But, that's not all the magic; go to **Edit** > **Fill ….** In the dialog box, make sure that the Contents are using Content-Aware, and that the Blending Mode is

Figure 1.17

Make sure your Fill options match mine.

Normal with Opacity at 100%. Preserve Transparency should *not* be checked. Make sure your dialog box has the setting seen in Figure 1.17, then click **OK**.

Magic! The rest of the canvas is filled with some nice-looking sky and clouds, and there is little to fix. In my case, there is a little bit of cloud near the top that needs some cleanup; I'll use the Spot Healing Tool to clean up the cloud. Simply select the tool and brush over the offending area; the Spot Healing Tool will look at the surrounding area and intelligently fill it in (see Figure 1.18).

Unhide the chameleon by clicking the eye back on . Move the chameleon so that the branch is coming out of the right side. Use the Move Tool and simply click and drag the chameleon across the canvas. But, it looks odd because all the branches end at the same edge on screen left. Make sure you have the Matte selected (you'll see an outline around it) and use black to paint back some of the branches to make them seem shorter. It would be nice to be able to just paint white in the areas to extend the branches, but we can't do that because (1) there was no color information there in the first place and (2) this is a Smart Object and we can't paint on it this way.

Figure 1.18

Healing the sky.

So, we are going to create a new transparent layer by clicking on the New Layer button ▤ on the bottom of the Layers palette. Select the Clone Stamp Tool ▤ and make sure that Mode is Normal, Opacity and Flow are at 100%, Aligned is checked, and Sample is set to All Layers. Hold **Alt**/**Option** and click on the area you want to copy from. I'm choosing the large branch around the middle. I increase my brush side to be just smaller than the width of the chosen

Figure 1.19

Adjusting the branches via the Matte and by cloning on a separate layer.

branch, then go to the area I want to extend and paint away. You can reset the sampling point at any time by holding **Alt**/**Option** and clicking the new starting sample. If you need for the two pieces to blend a little better, you can use the Spot Healing Brush ▤ as you used for the sky (Figure 1.19).

Let's now create some text (Figure 1.20). Select the Type Tool ▤. Click anywhere on the canvas. You can set the font and size in the Options bar, and Photoshop makes it easy by showing you what the fonts look like. We will be writing "SKY's"—all caps, then an apostrophe and lowercase *s*. Choose a thick font with some heft. I chose Ravie because it looked a little whimsical. Set your font size to 200. The drop-down menu only goes up to 72, but you can input any number you wish. Different fonts size differently, so if 200 is too small or large for your font, then adjust accordingly. Don't worry about the color of the font. You just need to be able to see it; it doesn't matter what color it is right now. My text originally came in white, but for better visibility I double-clicked on the color swatch in the Options bar and chose a bright orange.

Right now our text is straight (and partly obscuring my chameleon); click on the Create Warped Text ▤ button next to the text color swatch. The Warp Text dialog appears. Currently, the Style

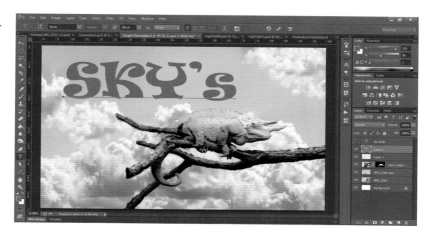

Figure 1.20

Check out my settings for the text and the relative size of the word to the image.

says **None**. Click on it and choose **Arc** instead. Adjust the bend and any of the sliders you wish and click **OK** (Figure 1.21).

Looking at it now, I see it is a little too large, and I don't like the spacing of the letters. I'm still in text mode, so I make sure I have the layer selected and change the font size to 170 pt. I click on the Character palette 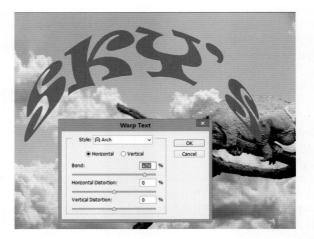 and adjust the kerning between the two characters. I set the tracking to −25 (Figure 1.22).

Figure 1.21

Warp Text dialog.

Figure 1.22

Changing the Text.

Press **Ctrl+T/⌘+T** to transform the text. Click and drag outside the handles to rotate the text. You can move, rotate, and resize; when you are done, hit **Enter/Return** or the check mark in the Options bar (Figure 1.23).

Let's add the rest of the line: "the limit!" Holding **Shift** while clicking on the canvas with the Text Tool will create a new text layer above the current one. Photoshop remembers the last text setting detail, so our font is currently set to the same font we used for SKY's. Change the color to black, the font to something simpler, and the size to fit between the last *s* and the edge of the image (Figure 1.24).

Figure 1.23

Click the check mark to confirm the transform.

Figure 1.24

Adding more text.

Figure 1.25

If you didn't want to use the menu, you could **right mouse button (RMB)/Ctrl+Click** on the type to obtain the pull-down menu so you can rasterize the type and adjust the shape.

Now, we will adjust the type a bit. Select the SKY's layer and go to **Type > Convert to Shape**. This will convert the type to a shape controlled with paths (Figure 1.25).

Before we start adjusting the paths, let's go over the parts of a path. Take a look at Figure 1.26 to see what each part is called.

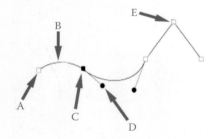

Figure 1.26

Breakdown of a path: A, unselected anchor point; B, path segment; C, selected anchor point; D, direction handle with direction point/controller.

Select the Path Selection Tool and click anywhere off the text shape. All the paths are deselected. Next, click on the lowercase *s*. The path is selected. We want to make this *s* a bit straighter for a nicer transition to the rest of the phrase, so press **Ctrl+T/⌘+T** to bring up the Transform Tool handles and rotate the *s* to be straighter. Click on the inside of the box and drag to move the *s* to a good location. Press **Enter/Return** to accept the Transform changes (Figure 1.27).

Let's switch to the Direct Selection Tool —you can do this by holding the pointer over an anchor point and press **Ctrl/⌘**—and select the lower-right corner anchor point of the letter *K*. Hold **Shift** and select the lower points controlling the bottom of the right leg of the *K*. See Figure 1.28 as an example. To deselect unwanted anchor points, hold **Alt/Option** and click on the unwanted vertex. Once you have them selected, click drag any one of the anchor points and all the selected ones will move; the shape is adjusted accordingly.

Move the leg out to be closer to the base of the letter *Y*. You can deselect by clicking off the path then adjust singly as needed. Press **Ctrl++/⌘++** to zoom in while you are working to better see the anchor points. Hit **Enter/Return** when you are done (Figure 1.29).

Now that the letters are exactly as we would like them, we are going to use them as a clipping mask. Open Mini Bridge by double-clicking on the Mini Bridge tab on the

Figure 1.27

Last time we clicked on the check mark; this time we'll just hit **Enter/Return** to accept the transform.

bottom of the workspace. If for any reason it is not there, simply go to **Window > Extensions > Mini Bridge** to bring it back. Go back to the Backgrounds folder and choose a sky image; if you chose a sky image for your background the first time around, make sure you use a different and contrasting cloud/sky. I chose the sunset sky for this. Click and drag into your current file. Hit **Enter/Return** to accept the image. Click drag the layer so it is directly above the SKY's text layer. **Right-Click/Ctrl+Click** to obtain the layer pull-down menu and select **Create Clipping Mask**. You will see that your chosen sky is now held within the letters of Sky's, as you can see in Figure 1.30.

You can use the Move Tool ![move tool icon] to move the sky around until you have something pleasing in the letters. You can see that even with the best positioning, the letters still seem to be lacking something. We'll use some layer effects to make it pop (Figure 1.31).

With the SKY's layer selected, click on the Layers

Figure 1.28

Selecting multiple points on the K path.

Effects ![fx icon] button on the bottom of the Layers palette and select **Drop Shadow....**

In the Layer Style dialog that comes up, increase the Distance, Spread, and Size with the sliders. Adjust the Angle by click dragging the light direction (it's that line that looks like a clock hand). You can see instant feedback on the look of the drop shadow on the canvas. If you do not see it, make sure the Preview box is checked. Click **OK** when you are done (Figure 1.32).

The Tutorial

Figure 1.29

Zoom in to see anchor points clearly.

Figure 1.30

The clipping mask in action.

Remember that orange we worked with? We'll be bringing that in now. Open your Orange.PSD. You can either go to **File > Open ...** or use Mini Bridge and double-click the thumbnail. Go to **Select > Load Selection**. In the dialog that ensues, select your Orange Alpha and click **OK**.

Your metal orange and leaves are selected from the background. Now, go to **Edit > Copy Merged** to copy the orange to your virtual clipboard. Click back to your chameleon

Figure 1.31

The letters need to pop more.

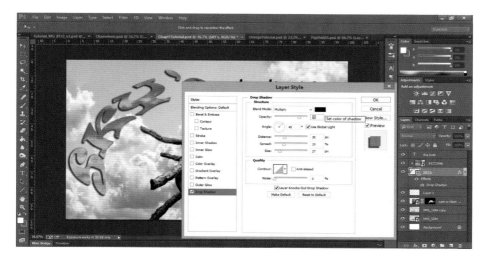

Figure 1.32

Drop Shadow dialog.

document and press **Ctrl+V/⌘+V** to paste the orange into your document. You'll see it is quite large and is placed in the middle of your canvas (Figure 1.33).

Press **Ctrl+T/⌘+T** to transform and resize your orange to fit your branch. While still in transform mode, move your orange to the location you want it and hit **Enter/Return** when you are done.

Figure 1.33

My, what a big orange you have there.

The metal is grayscale and needs some reflections from the world around it, even if this is a fantastic image ("fantastic" as in fantasy, although I also think it's pretty fabulous). Select your sky background layer, then choose the Rectangular Marquee Tool ▦. Select a good rectangular area larger than your orange by **click dragging** across an area. Press **Ctrl+C/⌘+C** to copy and, after clicking on the orange Layer, press **Ctrl+V/⌘+V** to paste into a new layer above. We'll use this as a reflection, but first let's get a round bulge happening: go to **Filter > Liquify …**.

In the dialog, make sure you have Bloat Tool ◈ selected and create a round bulge near the bottom of the rectangle; we'll use that area for the orange, and the rest will cover the leaves (Figure 1.34). Click **OK**.

Use the Move Tool ▶ to move your piece of sky to fit over the orange. Change the layer mode to Hard Light on the top of the Layers palette. Now you can see how your sky fits over the orange. Use the Free Transform again if you need to and don't worry about anything that is outside the orange; we'll matte that out. In fact, let's do that now. **Ctrl+Click/⌘+Click** on the thumbnail of the orange. Make sure you are on the piece of sky layer and click on the Quick Mask button ⬚ on the bottom of the Layers palette. Click on the link between the mask and the layer thumbnail so that it is off. That way, you can move the sky piece to fit the orange better. Continue tweaking until you are happy with the reflections placement. Once you are there, reduce the opacity of the Hard Light layer to about 75%. Click back down to your metal orange and duplicate it with **Ctrl+J/⌘+J**, then drag it up above your Hard Light layer. Set that layer to Overlay and reduce the opacity to 45%. Now, the orange looks a little more integrated. Press the New Layer button ⬒ on the bottom of the Layers palette to create an empty layer above your Overlay layer. With a white brush, paint in a couple of hot hits for highlights and you are done (Figure 1.35).

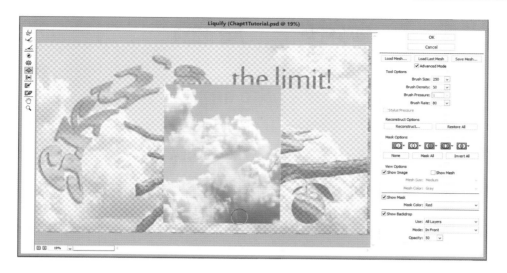

Figure 1.34

Creating the reflection.

Did I say done? I only meant for the orange.

First, let's let the chameleon do his thing. Create a copy of the sky background layer (we've done this multiple times, so the **Ctrl+J/⌘+J** command should almost be automatic now). Drag the sky layer above the chameleon layer. Change the layer blend mode to Color. Your chameleon and the stick it is on will be somewhat blended into the sky, but the colors need a little more punch. Duplicate the Color layer and this time set the layer blend mode to Overlay. You will now have something like Figure 1.36.

Ctrl+Click/⌘+Click on the matte of the chameleon to load the selection, then use the quick mask 🔘 to hold out the two sky layers you just added. Now, with a small paintbrush brush away at the mattes of the sky so that only the chameleon is affected—and not the entire chameleon—let some of his colors come through (Figure 1.37).

Figure 1.35

Orange completed.

Before we move on, save your project, **File > Save**. We want to simplify the image before we add the final finishing touches: Go to **Image > Duplicate…** and in the Duplicate Image dialog make sure you have Duplicate Merged Layers Only checked. Name your image something like ChameleonMerged and hit **OK**.

A new window will pop up with a merged image. This comes in handy when you know you want to have a flattened image but want to save all the layers in a separate file. Now, we'll give this a happy ending—and put a smile on the chameleon's face. Make a selection around the chameleon's head, giving plenty of room around it, like in Figure 1.38.

Figure 1.36

Your progress should be similar to this.

Figure 1.37

Giving the chameleon some camouflage (make sure that the matte thumbnail is selected, An outline should appear around the thumbnail of the matte in the Layers Pallet).

I used the Lasso Tool , but you can do it whatever way you want. Then, duplicate that area (again, your choice; we've done this so many times, I'll let you choose your method) into a new layer. With that subsection selected, choose **Edit > Puppet Warp**.

A mesh appears around the head; click to pin the areas we do not want to move. Then, click to put a pin in the curve of the mouth. If you accidentally put a pin where you don't want it, **Right-Click/Ctrl+Click** to delete a pin. Sometimes, it is a bit difficult to see with

Figure 1.38

Make a selection with room to spare.

Figure 1.39

Making the chameleon smile.

the mesh in the way. You can hide the mesh by unclicking the Show Mesh box in the Options bar. Move the pins along the mouth line to make our chameleon smile (Figure 1.39). Either hit the check mark in the Options bar or hit **Enter/Return** to bake the warp.

There we go! Whew! All done, but do you have more questions? For instance, what is a Smart Object? What do I mean by RAW? What kind of three-dimensional (3D)

Figure 1.40

Congratulations! You have now touched on just about all the most commonly used tools of Photoshop, and can blend in with the Pros!

capabilities does Photoshop have? Answers will be in Chapters 7, 5, and 9, respectively. Really, you should have a balanced diet of Photoshop; go through the Contents and gorge to your heart's delight (Figure 1.40).

Oh, and what happened with that first job? I made it. I was overjoyed, and it was a great if *interesting* experience in the Chinese interpretation of "May your life be interesting." I learned who Alan Smithee is and made a lot of great friends that I know to this day—all named Alan/Allen Smithee.

2

Photoshop Setup and Overview

Starting/Setting Up Photoshop
Setting Adobe Photoshop to the Default Preferences
Work Area Overview

Starting/Setting Up Photoshop

It is assumed you are computer literate enough to know how to launch the program. You may be launching from a shortcut on your desktop, an icon on your Mac's dock, through the applications or programs menu, or via an app square on Windows 8. With the variety of environments and settings available, it becomes even more important to make sure that your Photoshop is set to the manufacturer's default settings.

Photoshop saves information from your last session in a preference file. Positions of the panels, certain settings, and any selections you make in the Preference dialog box are all recorded in this preference file. You need to make sure there are no customized preferences because customization may thwart your progress if what you see on screen does not match the images or instructions in this book.

It is not an absolute necessity to reset the settings. So, if you need to keep the current preferences, just be aware that the settings of workspace, panels, and tools may be different from this book. You will still be able to do the tasks, but you may have to work around the existing settings. That said, if you are using a friend's computer or a computer at work, you should talk to your friend or your work's information technology person to make sure it is all right to reset the settings.

Also note, if you *reinstall* Photoshop, that does not mean you have the default preferences. Reinstalling Photoshop does not reset the preference file, as odd as that may seem. So, you will still need to reset your preferences to ensure the default settings.

Setting Adobe Photoshop to the Default Preferences

Figure 2.1

If you are resetting Photoshop, you should get this dialog box. If you don't, you haven't reset.

1. Launch Adobe Photoshop. Immediately hold down **Alt+Ctrl+Shift/ Option+⌘+Shift** while Photoshop is still launching. A dialog window like the one seen in Figure 2.1 should pop up. If it does not, then you probably didn't hold down the keys long enough or at the right time. Close Photoshop and try again until the warning dialog window appears. If you are using a wireless keyboard, you may need to attach a wired keyboard for this to work. Alternatively, you may find success in holding down the keys as you launch Photoshop.
2. Click **Yes** to confirm that you want to delete the Adobe Photoshop Settings file. Photoshop will complete the launch, and you are now ready to start any tutorial.

Alternate Methods to Reset

If you are having a hard time getting the keyboard shortcut to work, you can re-create the default preferences by deleting the Adobe Photoshop Settings file. Because preference files vary by name and location for each version of Photoshop, you can go online to Adobe's website (http://www.Adobe.com) and do a search of "Photoshop Preference File Locations," and the locations for each version and platform of Photoshop will be listed in the search results.

If you are on a **Mac running OSX 10.7** or later, the user library is hidden by default. You can easily circumvent this by choosing **Go > Go To Folder** in the Finder. In the Go To Folder dialog, type

```
~/Library
```

and click **Go**.

Just remember: If you choose this route, make sure that you delete the correct file and *only* that file.

Color Settings

Often, people are unaware of their color management. But, ignorance of the subject does not mean that the subject does not exist. Color data have to be interpreted throughout the workflow. Your camera captures with a specific range of color. This must be interpreted in Photoshop and manipulated. Afterward, the file format and other output considerations will also translate that color data.

Before we set our color settings, we will check and save any customizations for retrieval later. Most people can just manually reset their color settings to their particular preferences, but it's a good idea to know how to save settings in case you are using someone else's license, if you are upgrading and want to save just in case, or if you are in a company setting where there might be specific custom settings.

How to Save Your Current Color Settings

In Adobe Photoshop, go to **Edit** > **Color Settings** (**Photoshop** > **Color Settings**). A dialog window such as that in Figure 2.2 should appear. If the name of the settings is anything other than "Custom," write down the name of the setting. Nothing more needs to be done, as it is a saved color setting that you can access later.

If the name of the setting is "Custom" (as it is in Figure 2.2), we will need to save out the customizations. Click **Save** (notice I said "**Save**" not "**OK**"). The Save dialog window will open. Note the location of where it is set to save the color setting so you know where to find it later when you need it.

In the **File Name** field or **Save As** field, give your settings a descriptive name with the .csf file extension. Click **Save**.

In the Color Settings comment dialog box, you can type any descriptive text that will help you identify the color settings later. Click **OK** to close the Color Settings comment dialog box and again to close the Color Settings dialog box.

You have now successfully saved your color settings.

Figure 2.2

Color Settings dialog.

Restoring Color Settings

Restoring color settings is rather straightforward and easy. Choose **Edit** > **Color Settings** (**Photoshop** > **Color Settings**). In the Settings Name field in the Color Settings dialog box, select the settings file you wish to import and click **OK**.

Work Area Overview

General Overview

Photoshop is an ideal cross-platform application because it has so few user interface differences between the OSX and Windows versions. If you are using a Mac, there will only be a slight difference in the top menu and an extra bar between the top menu and top tool options indicating the application frame as shown in Figure 2.3. The Mac has the ever-present Apple menu at the far left, followed by the Photoshop menu option before the File menu option.

Some people find the current incarnation of the interface to be too dark. This, for some strange reason, was such an issue to users (usually legacy users who preferred the lighter tone used in older versions of Photoshop) that Photoshop CS6 made sure there was a keystroke shortcut **Shift+F1/Shift+F2** to lighten and darken, respectively, the interface. Mac users, however, ran into issues because this shortcut interfered with the system shortcut "Move Focus to the Menu Bar"—a commonly used shortcut for many Mac Users. Windows 8 users and laptop users found the shortcut did not work for them either, even with the function key included. As of this printing, Adobe's help documents show that for Photoshop CC, you can lighten or darken the interface with **Shift+1/Shift+2**—this has not worked for anyone I know so far. All I can say is that if this feels like a crucial issue to you, your best bet is to follow the forums and lend your voice toward a working shortcut. In the meantime, you can still adjust the interface colors the old fashioned way – via the top pull-down menus: **Edit** > **Preference** (Windows) or **Photoshop** > **Preferences** (Mac OS). Go to the Interface section and choose a Color Theme swatch in your favorite shade of gray.

To follow any of the tutorials, you will need to know some basic terminology that defines the workspace. These are labeled in Figure 2.4. At the very top is the **Menu bar**, with the **Tool Options bar** directly below it. If you are on a Mac, there will be the application frame's header bar in between. At the far right end of the **Tool Options bar** is a drop-down **Workspaces menu**. Underneath the **Workspaces menu**, by default, Photoshop docks a few select panels. Panels are a way that Photoshop keeps tools and settings organized. There are many different panels that help edit and monitor various elements of your image. You can change, undock, move, or remove the panels as you customize to your taste. By default, a select few panels are grouped and docked to the far right of the screen. Some panels have others grouped with them. These appear as tabs alongside the visible panel's name.

At the bottom, you will see two tabs minimized: the Mini Bridge tab and the Timeline tab. Those familiar with video editing, animation, or even sound editing are already familiar with the concept of a timeline. Most people using Photoshop just for photo manipulation, however, will not ever need to use it. (Although I hope you get inspired by Chapters 10 and 11 and find how useful it can be.) MiniBridge, on the other hand, is a convenient access point to an integral aspect of any Photoshop workflow: Bridge. Photoshop ships with an asset management system called Bridge; this is discussed

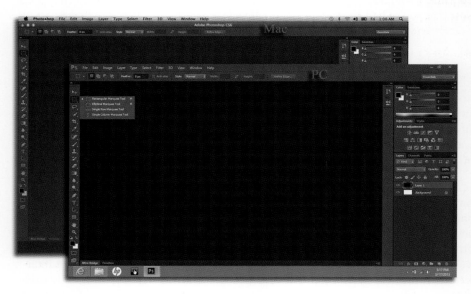

Figure 2.3

There is little difference between platforms and versions.

2. Photoshop Setup and Overview

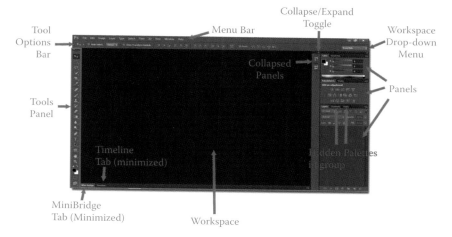

Tool Options Bar

Menu Bar

Collapse/Expand Toggle

Workspace Drop-down Menu

Collapsed Panels

Tools Panel

Panels

Timeline Tab (minimized)

Hidden Palettes in group

MiniBridge Tab (Minimized)

Workspace

Figure 2.4
Workspace with areas defined.

further in Chapter 3. The last panel, the **Tools panel**, sometimes called the Tools palette or Toolbox, is at the far left. The blank area in the middle is called the Workspace.

Images opened are by default docked into the workspace with tabs on top indicating the file name, magnification, current selected layer, image mode, and bit depth. Click dragging this tab will undock the window to be a floating window. Dragging a floating window near the top edge of the workspace until the workspace area is highlighted with a blue outline, then releasing the left mouse button (LMB) will redock the image.

Now that you've had an overview of the interface, let's take a closer look at some of its main components.

Menu Bar

The Photoshop Menu bar works like the menu bar in any other standard application. So, for example, the "Save" and "Save As" operations will be found under the File menu item: **File > Save** or **File > Save As…** and **Ctrl+S/⌘+S** and **Shift+Ctrl+S/Shift+⌘+S** are their respective keyboard shortcuts.

Of course, there are a few nonstandard menu items, such as "Image" and "Filter," but these are explained in detail as we use them in the tutorials. For now, let's just get the overview.

The **Menu bar** consists of 11 menus: File, Edit, Image, Layer, Type, Select, Filter, 3D, View, Window, and Help. It helps to take a few moments to look at each of the menus and familiarize yourself with their contents. Figure 2.5 shows an exploded view of the **Menu bar**.

You may notice that some menu commands are followed by ellipses (…). This indicates that additional input is needed from the user; therefore, a dialog window/box will appear for you to enter additional settings. Some menu commands are followed by a right-pointing triangle/arrow to the far right of the drop-down menu ▶. This indicates a submenu of related commands.

Throughout this book, I use the following syntax for instructions that involve navigating menus in Photoshop: **File > New**. A three-deep navigation would look like this: **Edit > Transform > Scale**.

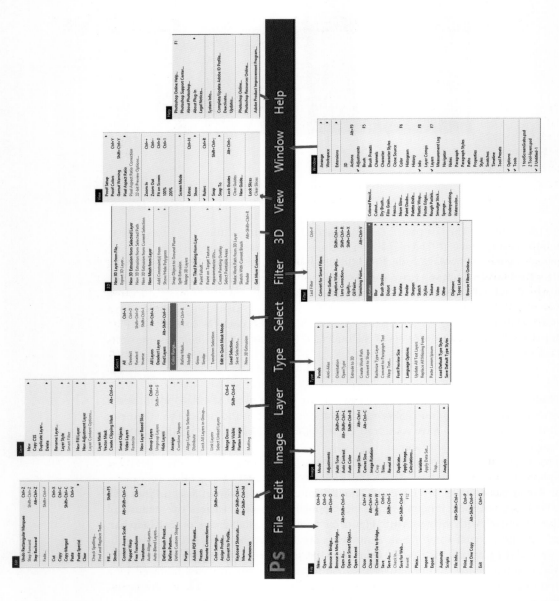

Figure 2.5
Menu bar exploded.

2. Photoshop Setup and Overview

You'll also notice that many commands are followed by keyboard shortcuts. Over time, you will find which of these shortcuts are most useful in your workflow, and you can edit and create shortcuts for those menu items that do not have a shortcut by default. All keyboard shortcuts, including these menu shortcuts, are listed in **Edit** > **Keyboard Shortcuts**. It is here that you can also create custom shortcuts, which we will cover in Chapter 11. I've also included a handy keyboard quick reference at my website for those who prefer a more visual reference: www.LopsieSchwartz.com/PrecisionPhotoshop/KeyboardShortcuts.

Options Bar

Below Photoshop's menu bar is the **Tool Options bar** (or, in the case of Mac, right under the application window header). The **Tool Options bar** gives easy access to the settings for the currently active tool. It is a context-sensitive toolbar, meaning that it changes according to which tool you have selected. Figure 2.6 shows a couple of different settings that come up for different tools.

The **Tool Options bar** also enables you to create Tool Presets, essentially saving the particular preference settings of any particular tool so that you can retrieve and use them later.

The **Tool Options bar** can be pulled away from the top of the window and moved around in the workspace by clicking on the small line on the far left of the toolbar and dragging it to a new position. Most likely, you'll want to leave it right where it is.

If your **Tool Options bar** has mysteriously disappeared, you can easily bring it back by simply choosing a tool and hitting **Enter**/**Return**.

Tools Panel

The long, thin panel on the far left side of the workspace is central to Photoshop and is called by many different, yet similar, names: Tools panel, the Toolbox, or the Tools palette. I believe the official name is Tools panel, as is the most recent nomenclature used on the Adobe websites and help sections. Some others prefer to keep consistency in calling all the floating windows "palettes," therefore Tools palette. Whatever you decide to call it yourself, it is rather efficient. Adobe has developed so many tools that Photoshop had to hide most of them. A small triangle at the lower-right corner of a tool's button indicates the existence of a flyout menu ◢. Holding down the LMB when selecting the tool, or just **Right-clicking**/**Ctrl+clicking** on the tool button, will reveal the flyout menu. The flyout menu lists hidden tools and the keyboard shortcut of the tool—convenient for when you need to know the shortcut or have forgotten it. Figure 2.7 shows an exploded view of the Tools palette. I recommend making a photocopy and keeping it handy for reference (or you can just bookmark this page) until you intuitively know where all the tools are located.

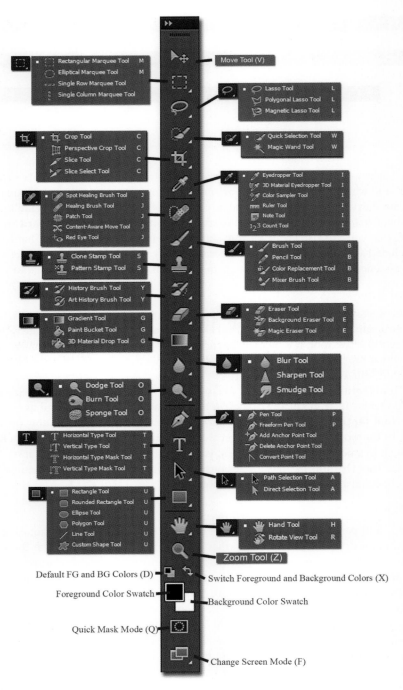

Figure 2.7

Tool palette exploded.

Pressing **Shift** while hitting the tool's shortcut letter will cycle through the hidden tools unless the tool flyout menu shows no letter next to the tool. Notice, for example, the Pen Tool has a **P** next to the Pen Tool and next to the Freeform Pen Tool Pressing **Shift+P** will cycle between those two, but you would not be able to cycle to the Add Anchor Point Tool . You would have to specifically choose it from the Pen's flyout menu. You can easily customize a shortcut if you would like to, but by default **P** is assigned only to the Pen Tool and Freeform Pen Tool .

The best way, really, to learn how to use the tools is to use them in context. Nonetheless, I think it is nice as a reference to have a basic overview of the tools. Remember, any time you choose a tool, the **Tool Options bar** changes to display the basic modifiable attributes for that tool. The cursor, for most of the tools, also changes to reflect the tool. The tools in this palette are generally tools that allow you to work directly on an image. The actions of those tools rely on your ability and sense, and they generally require you to place and drag your cursor to enact the action of the tool.

The Double Arrow Toggle will toggle the Toolbox from single to double column. A list of tools in the order they appear in the Tools panel, with a brief description, is presented next.

The Move Tool

 Move Tool (keyboard shortcut: **V**): The Move Tool (Figure 2.8) moves selections, layers, and guides. You can move layers not only inside a document but also from one document to another. This will be one of your most-used tools, hence its primary position in the Toolbox.

Figure 2.8

Move Tool.

The Marquees: Geometric Selection Tools

 Rectangular Marquee Tool (keyboard shortcut: **M**): This makes, you guessed it, rectangular selections (Figure 2.9). Holding down **Alt**/**Opt** will enable you to draw a section from the center and holding the **Shift** key at the same time as dragging will constrain your selection to a perfect square.

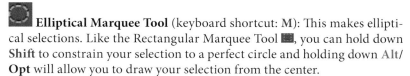

Figure 2.9

Marquees.

 Elliptical Marquee Tool (keyboard shortcut: **M**): This makes elliptical selections. Like the Rectangular Marquee Tool , you can hold down **Shift** to constrain your selection to a perfect circle and holding down **Alt**/**Opt** will allow you to draw your selection from the center.

 Single Row Marquee Tool (no default keyboard shortcut): Use this tool to quickly create a single-pixel horizontal selection.

 Single Column Marquee Tool (no default keyboard shortcut): This tool quickly creates a single-pixel vertical selection.

The Lasso Tools: Freeform Selection Tools

 The Lasso Tool (keyboard shortcut: **L**): The Lasso Tool is used to make freehand selections (Figure 2.10). A circle appears when you have

Figure 2.10

Lasso tools.

completed a loop. If you release your LMB before you close the selection, it will draw a straight line from that point to the beginning. To continue adding to the selection, hold **Shift** and drag out another selection. The additional selection will be joined to the first one (even if they are physically separate). To subtract sections, hold **Alt/Opt** and drag around the area you do not want selected.

Polygonal Lasso Tool (keyboard shortcut: **L**): This tool allows you to make straight-edged selections. LMB click to set points and the tool draws a straight line between the points. When you hover over the first point, a little circle will appear to indicate that this closes the polygon. Alternatively, you can double-click at any stage to automatically complete the selection. The same idea of **Shift** and **Alt/Opt** hold for adding to and subtracting from the selection apply to all the selection tools (see Lasso Tool).

Magnetic Lasso (keyboard shortcut: **L**): This snaps to the outline of an object as you trace around it. The tool will place points for the selection based on contrast/edge. If you are using a tablet, you can use the tablet pressure to alter the detection width used to determine the width from the cursor in which to detect edge contrast.

The Auto Selection Tools

Quick Selection Tool (keyboard shortcut: **W**): This selection tool uses a brush-based approach to selections, letting you quickly "paint" a selection using a round brush tip, and it intelligently expands to the edges as you go (Figure 2.11). Should you overselect, you can hold **Alt** and paint out the areas you don't want selected.

Magic Wand Tool (keyboard shortcut: **W**): Another selection tool, this tool selects pixels based on color. You can point sample or choose a larger sample size, up to 101 x 101 average. These options are listed in the **Sample Size pull-down menu** in the **Tool Options bar**. Alternately, you could change the Tolerance in the **Tool Options bar** to set a range around the color sampled.

Figure 2.12

Cutting tools.

The Cutting Tools

Crop Tool (keyboard shortcut: **C**): The Crop Tool trims an image (Figure 2.12). By default, a *rule-of-thirds* overlay is shown when you use the Crop Tool for ease of composition, but other options can be found in the **Tool Options bar**. Also, you now have the option to crop nondestructively. Simply make sure the **Delete Cropped Pixels** option in the **Tool Options bar** is unchecked.

Perspective Crop Tool (keyboard shortcut: **C**): This allows you to trim an image and flatten out perspective at the same time. This is useful for creating tiles from a photo with perspective.

Slice Tool (keyboard shortcut: **C**): This tool is used to "slice" an image for faster loading for the web.

2. Photoshop Setup and Overview

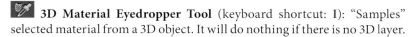 **Slice Select Tool** (keyboard shortcut: **C**): This is used to select a slice for further editing.

Annotation Tools

Eye Dropper Tool (keyboard shortcut: **I**): Use this tool to "grab" a color from an image (Figure 2.13). The selected color replaces the foreground color in your foreground color palette. You can also select between a point sample or an average of colors in an area, up to 101 × 101 pixels square.

3D Material Eyedropper Tool (keyboard shortcut: **I**): "Samples" selected material from a 3D object. It will do nothing if there is no 3D layer.

Color Sample Tool (keyboard shortcut: **I**): This samples and marks up to four areas from your image and displays the color information in the information panel. It is useful for comparing colors numerically or for adjusting colors numerically.

Ruler Tool (keyboard shortcut: **I**): This allows you to measure distances and angles in your image. When you click and drag between two points, the information panel will display the length and angle of the line drawn.

Note Tool (keyboard shortcut: **I**): This tool attaches nonprintable notes to an image. It is useful for giving feedback or direction.

Count Tool (keyboard shortcut: **I**): This is an aid to help count objects in an image; it numbers consecutively as you click. Like guides, these numbers do not show up in your final product.

Healing Tools

Spot Healing Brush Tool (keyboard shortcut: **J**): This quickly removes small imperfections without a sampling source (Figure 2.14). It intelligently replaces pixel information based on proximity, texture, or content. You set the method used in the **Tool Options bar**.

Healing Brush Tool (keyboard shortcut: **J**): This is like the Spot Healing Brush 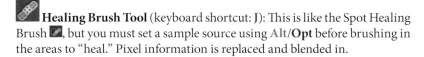, but you must set a sample source using **Alt**/**Opt** before brushing in the areas to "heal." Pixel information is replaced and blended in.

Patch Tool (keyboard shortcut: **J**): This tool allows you to lasso a selection you want to replace and drag the selection to an area you would like to sample. The tool will blend the edges automatically on release of the mouse button.

Content-Aware Move Tool (keyboard shortcut: **J**): This fills and blends pixels automatically for you when you cut out and move a selection from one part of an image to another.

Red Eye Tool (keyboard shortcut: **J**): Use this tool to quickly remove red eye from flash photography in one click. It is one of those tools that existed in a lot of smaller and simpler photo-retouching packages, including Adobe's own Elements, but it took a while for it to be accepted as a "professional tool."

Painting Tools

Figure 2.15

Painting tools.

Brush Tool (keyboard shortcut: **B**): The Brush Tool is the most versatile and used tool in Photoshop. It is the main painting tool and has a variety of tips and effects (Figure 2.15). See Chapter 7 for an in-depth look into the Brush Tool.

Pencil Tool (keyboard shortcut: **B**): This is a painting tool with harder edges and slightly harder strokes. You can control the Pencil Tool in exactly the same way as the Brush Tool, but hardness is calculated differently internally. Therefore, at 100% hardness, the brush and pencil behave slightly differently.

Color Replacement Tool (keyboard shortcut: **B**): This substitutes a specified color for another as you paint over an image. Only the specified color is changed, and all the image detail is retained.

Mixer Brush Tool (keyboard shortcut: **B**): This blends colors together for painting, mimicking real-world painting. You can push colors together, choose to load or clean your brush, as well as change the wetness and flow.

Stamping Tools

Figure 2.16

Stamping tools.

Clone Stamp Tool (keyboard shortcut: **S**): This paints using a selected source, but without the blending that is calculated with the Healing Brushes (Figure 2.16). **Alt/Opt** click to select your source, then paint on the area you want to clone over. You can also clone across documents and have the clone source be from a different document than the document into which you are painting.

Pattern Stamp Tool (keyboard shortcut: **S**): This is a tool that allows you to paint with a tileable pattern on your images, essentially stamping on a pattern.

History Brushes

Figure 2.17

History brushes.

History Brush Tool (keyboard shortcut: **Y**): This enables you to paint your image back to a previously stored state (Figure 2.17). This, in effect, is a "selective undo."

Art History Brush (keyboard shortcut: **Y**): This also allows you to paint back to a specific history state, but it paints stylized strokes that simulate a paint style.

Erasing Tools

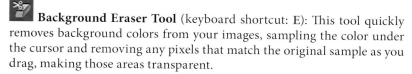

Eraser Tool (keyboard shortcut: **E**): This erases pixels in an image to transparency, the background color, or a specific history state (Figure 2.18).

Figure 2.18

Erasing tools.

Background Eraser Tool (keyboard shortcut: **E**): This tool quickly removes background colors from your images, sampling the color under the cursor and removing any pixels that match the original sample as you drag, making those areas transparent.

Magic Eraser Tool: (keyboard shortcut: **E**): This erases solid-color areas to transparency with a single click.

Fill Tools

Gradient Tool (keyboard shortcut: **G**): This tool creates smooth blends from one color to another or from a solid color to transparency (Figure 2.19). Click and drag to create a gradient. Different styles are available in the **Tool Options bar**, so you can easily switch from linear to radial, for example.

Figure 2.19

Fill tools.

Paint Bucket Tool (keyboard shortcut: **G**): This fills areas with either the foreground color or a pattern.

3D Material Drop Tool (keyboard shortcut: **G**): This "fills" a 3D object with a loaded material.

Adjustment Tools

Blur Tool (no default keyboard shortcut): This allows you to "paint on" a blur (Figure 2.20). You can adjust the size and strength in the **Tool Options bar**.

Figure 2.20

Adjustment tools.

Sharpen Tool (no default keyboard shortcut): The tool sharpens soft edges with a brush-based approach, essentially the opposite of Blur.

Smudge Tool (no default keyboard shortcut): This smudges by "pushing" and "pulling" existent pixels in an image. The fingerpainting option allows you to introduce the foreground color into the smudge.

Photography Tools

Dodge Tool (keyboard shortcut: **O**): This lightens areas selectively with a brush-based approach (Figure 2.21).

Figure 2.21

Photography tools.

Burn Tool (keyboard shortcut: **O**): This tool enables you to darken areas with a brush, essentially the opposite of the Dodge Tool .

Sponge Tool (keyboard shortcut: **O**): The tool changes the color saturation of an area.

Pen/Curve Tools

Figure 2.22

Pen/Curve tools.

Pen Tool (keyboard shortcut: **P**): This is used to draw vector paths and custom shapes that can be adjusted using Bézier curves (Figure 2.22). These paths are resolution independent.

Freeform Pen Tool (keyboard shortcut: **P**): This is like the Pen Tool, but instead of a Bézier curves approach, it calculates the best anchor points as you draw freehand. You can choose the magnetic option that will have the path stick to edges of an area, like the Magnetic Lasso Tool.

Add Anchor Point Tool (no default keyboard shortcut): This enables you to add anchor points to existing paths.

Delete Anchor Points Tool (no default keyboard shortcut): This tool enables you to delete anchor points along an existing path and keeps adjacent points connected.

Convert Point Tool (no default keyboard shortcut): This enables you to edit the point and path for fine-tuning.

Type Tools

Figure 2.23

Type tools.

Horizontal Type Tool (keyboard shortcut: **T**): This tool creates editable text on a separate layer (Figure 2.23). You can choose the font weight, size, and color as in most text editing programs. Text appears as horizontal rows by default. You can warp the type with tool options, and you can type along a path by clicking on the path and typing.

Vertical Type Tool (keyboard shortcut: **T**): This creates editable text on a separate layer, but text appears in vertical columns.

Horizontal Type Mask Tool (keyboard shortcut: **T**): This creates a mask or selection based on the text size and font you have chosen.

Vertical Type Mask Tool (keyboard shortcut: **T**): This too is the same as the Horizontal Type Mask Tool but with vertical type.

Path Selection Tools

Figure 2.24

Path Selection tools.

Path Selection Tool (keyboard shortcut: **A**): This tool enables you to select a path or multiple paths and move around or combine (Figure 2.24).

Direct Selection Tool (keyboard shortcut: **A**): This enables you to directly select points on a path for adjustments.

2. Photoshop Setup and Overview

Shape Tools

Shape Tools draw vector shapes on their own shape layer. The flyout indicates the type of shapes available (Figure 2.25).

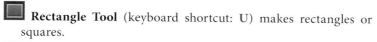

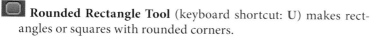

Figure 2.25

Shape tools.

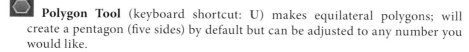 **Rectangle Tool** (keyboard shortcut: **U**) makes rectangles or squares.

Rounded Rectangle Tool (keyboard shortcut: **U**) makes rectangles or squares with rounded corners.

Ellipse Tool (keyboard shortcut: **U**) makes ellipses or circles.

Polygon Tool (keyboard shortcut: **U**) makes equilateral polygons; will create a pentagon (five sides) by default but can be adjusted to any number you would like.

Line Tool (keyboard shortcut: **U**) makes lines; can add arrowheads to either side of the line to create arrows.

Custom Shape Tool (keyboard shortcut: **U**) includes different shapes such as hearts, paw prints, trademark symbol, and so on, available from a shape list.

Navigation Tools

 **Hand Tool** (keyboard shortcut: **H**): This pans the image relative to the viewable window area (Figure 2.26). This is used to navigate around an image when zoomed in. Holding down the **space bar** will activate the Hand Tool no matter what other tool you are using (unless, of course, you are typing text). **Double-clicking** on this tool is a shortcut to fit the current canvas to the screen.

Figure 2.26

Navigation tools.

Rotate View Tool (keyboard shortcut: **R**): This nondestructively rotates the canvas. This is handy for obtaining a better angle for painting with a Wacom tablet. The document itself does not change orientation; it is just the view that is rotated.

Zoom Tool

Zoom Tool (keyboard shortcut: **Z**): This tool magnifies and reduces the view of the image (Figure 2.27). Double-clicking on this tool will jump your canvas to 100% or 1:1 magnification.

Figure 2.27

Zoom tool.

More Tools

After the Zoom Tool 🔍, there are a few more useful options listed in the Tools palette (Figure 2.28), including the ■ **Default Foreground and Background** (keyboard shortcut: **D**) (pure black and pure white).

Switch Background and Foreground Colors (keyboard shortcut: **X**): Clicking on this will switch the two color swatches.

Figure 2.28

More tools.
1. Default FG/BG colors
2. Switch FG/BG
3. FG/BG swatches
4. Quick mask mode toggle
5. Screen mode

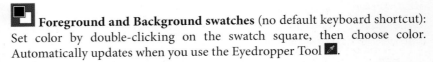 **Foreground and Background swatches** (no default keyboard shortcut): Set color by double-clicking on the swatch square, then choose color. Automatically updates when you use the Eyedropper Tool .

Edit in Standard or Quick Mask Mode (keyboard shortcut: **Q**): This allows you to speedily work on a selection with any of Photoshop's tools, such as a brush or a filter. The selection shows as a red overlay and can be adjusted the way any painting can be adjusted, but all effects are on the selection only.

Change Screen Mode (keyboard shortcut: **F**): You can choose to go to full screen by pressing **F**, and continuing to press **F** will rotate through the three modes of Full Screen, Standard Screen, and Full Screen with Menu Bar.

The Palettes

In Photoshop, palettes are used to help modify and monitor your documents. An understanding of how to use, organize, and adjust palettes is essential in learning how to use Photoshop.

When you first open Photoshop, the palettes are stacked along the right edge of your screen in palette groups. The default workspace mode is Essentials. Take a look at the Essentials palette setup as shown in Figure 2.29; there are four (technically five, but we'll get to that) groupings.

The first group contains the Color and Swatches palettes. Directly below are the Adjustments and Styles palettes grouped together. Below that are the Layers, Channels, and Paths palettes docked together into another group. These three groups are docked together such that you can collapse the entire stack to icons in a palette bar. To the left of this stack of palettes is a collapsed stack holding the History palette and the Properties palette. This may seem like one group, but it is one stack with two groups.

If you were to change the workspace setting to 3D, for example, then Photoshop will display different palettes (but still grouped to the right of the screen). Are the palettes not where you would like them to be? Have a hard time seeing one because it is too small? Luckily, all of these aspects are adjustable.

Arranging Palettes

It is possible to position palettes to your personal taste. Doing so can help increase your efficiency as you can make your most frequently used palettes easily accessible in the workspace.

Both individual palettes and palette groups can be moved around by clicking the top of the palette window and dragging the palette to a new position. When dragged away from their default docked positions, the palettes can be placed anywhere within the main Photoshop window or on the Windows desktop. (Yes! That

Figure 2.29

Essentials workspace.

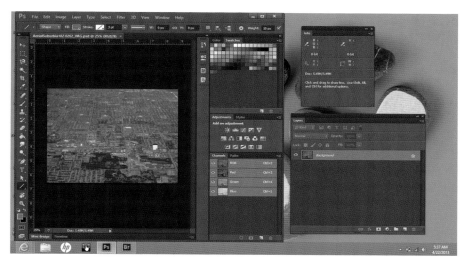

Figure 2.30

Palettes outside the workspace.

means they can be *outside* the Photoshop workspace. Figure 2.30 shows an example.)

To dock a palette to any side of the Photoshop workspace, just drag your free palette onto the edge of the window until a blue line appears, as in Figure 2.31. The palette will be docked to that side on release of the mouse button.

Hiding Palettes

All these different palettes do take up a good chunk of workspace real estate. If you wish to hide *all* the currently opened palettes, simply hit **Shift+Tab.** This does not close them. It merely hides them. You can even temporarily hide the Tool palette with the other palettes so you can maximize canvas space. Just tapping **Tab** will hide all the palettes and the toolbar. Both of these methods are toggles and tapping them again brings it all back.

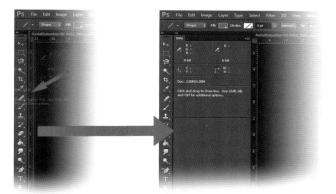

Figure 2.31

Moving palettes.

Adjusting and Closing Palettes

Palettes can be resized either by holding your cursor over an edge and dragging when the cursor changes to a double-ended arrow (↔) or by clicking and dragging on the right corner.

The height of docked palettes can be adjusted by positioning your mouse over the line where two docked palettes meet. The mouse pointer changes to a double-ended arrow pointing up and down ⬍, and you simply click and drag to change the height of the two groups.

Each palette group has a collapse ⏩ and a close ❌ button in the title bar area. The collapse button ⏩ works as a toggle; clicking the button a second time after the palette is collapsed will expand the palette again. You can also collapse a group by double-clicking on the palette group's header bar. To display a collapsed palette, just double-click again.

Palettes are closed by clicking the **X** in the upper-right corner of the palette. Docked palettes must be undocked before the **X** appears. Right-clicking the top bar of the palette and selecting the Close option will also close a palette. When you click the Close option on a palette group, it closes all the palettes in the group.

Showing Palettes

To display a palette that is not shown, you can either choose the command from the Windows menu (for example, **Window > Brush**) or display the palette using its keyboard shortcut. New palettes appear undocked, although they can be docked to either side of the Photoshop window if you wish.

Not all palettes have a shortcut by default, but the most commonly used ones do. They are

- **F5** = Show/Hide Brushes palette
- **F6** = Show/Hide Color palette
- **F7** = Show/Hide Layers palette
- **F8** = Show/Hide Info palette
- **F9** = Show/Hide Actions palette
- **Tab** = Show/Hide Toolbar and all palettes
- **Shift-Tab** = Show/Hide all palettes

To bring a grouped palette to the front of the group, click on the palette's tab. You can also ungroup and rearrange the palettes by clicking on a tab and dragging it outside the group or to another group.

Resetting Palettes

If you are having trouble getting your palettes back into place and simply want to revert to the default palette layout, go to **Window > Workspace > Reset (workspace)** in your **Menu bar**, where **(workspace)** is whatever workspace you are currently in. This will reset everything back to the default settings for that workspace.

3

The Visual Bridge: Accessing and Organizing Files

Introduction

Whatever your occupation, if you are using Photoshop, you will inevitably have a time when you come across a slew of references that you will need to access and work with. Photoshop comes with an organizational viewer called Bridge (see the side note, "Adobe Bridge CC," p. 42). With a customizable layout and fast thumbnail views, this is beyond any standard file browser that our increasingly visual operating systems might offer, and because Bridge is used with more than just images and Photoshop, it goes beyond the sphere of Lightroom (another excellent program offered by Adobe for photo management).

Bridge is a visual *asset management system* that can be accessed from any other Adobe application. Notice that I said asset management—not *image* management. Bridge allows you to quickly access multiple assets—document text files, videos, three-dimensional (3D) files, HTML files, or anything else you might access with any of Adobe's other programs. You'll get a chance to see how to manage these heaps of files using collections and cataloging all the information in a way that makes sense to you.

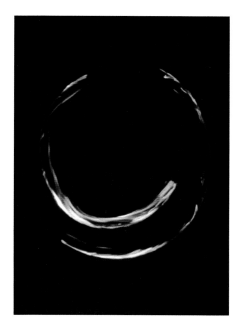

Adobe Bridge CC

Adobe Bridge CC uses a separate installer, whereas previous versions of Adobe Photoshop automatically installed Bridge with Photoshop. This decoupling from Photoshop is in part because other CC applications now use this file management system.

Installing Bridge CC

If you are working with a previous version of Photoshop other than Photoshop CC, Bridge was already installed when you installed Photoshop. So, you can skip this section with impunity.

The first time you try to access Bridge from Photoshop CC, you'll be asked to download and install it separately. With the Creative Cloud subscription, all the Adobe applications are included in your subscription price, so there is nothing extra you need to do other than install it.

Download and Install Bridge from the Download Center

To download and install Bridge from the Download Center (Figure 3.1), sign in to the Creative Cloud. I have the app installed and a shortcut on my desktop, but you can also access the Creative Cloud at https://creative.adobe.com. Please note that you will need Internet access (obvious, you would think, but you'd be surprised).

In the top bar, click Apps. Find the Bridge Icon and click Download. Now that you have it installed, let's take a look at Bridge.

Workspace Overview

Let's start with a basic workspace overview. When you first launch Bridge, Bridge's default Essentials workspace will display five frames arranged into three columns. The leftmost

Figure 3.1

Creative Cloud Download Center.

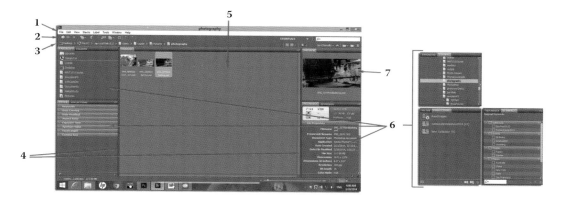

Figure 3.2

Workspace overview exploded view. 1. Menu Bar, 2. Application Bar, 3. Path Bar, 4. Division Bars, 5. Content Panel, 6. Dockable Panels, 7. Preview Panel.

column will have two sections, or frames, with a couple of panels docked into it. The middle frame will show thumbnails of the contents of the currently selected folder, and the right-most column will show a preview in one frame and a couple of other panels docked below that. You can adjust the Adobe Bridge workspace by moving, docking, or resizing panels and create your own custom workspace, or you can just use one of the preset workspaces as is.

You should know that I love exploded and dissection views, so here you go: Figure 3.2 shows this very thing.

Main Components

The following are the main components of the Adobe Bridge workspace:

The **Menu bar** has all the possible options for you to navigate.

The **Application bar** has a graphical representation of essential tasks in easy-to-use buttons, such as navigating the folder hierarchy and switching workspaces. A handy search field is also included.

The **Path bar** shows the path for the folder you are viewing and allows you to navigate the directory.

With the **Division bars** you can increase or decrease the size of the panels docked in the frame by moving the division bars. Moving this bar to the far right or left (or top or bottom) will make a frame "disappear." Pulling it back out will reopen the frame.

The **Content panel** displays the assets specified in the area navigated.

All other **dockable panels** can be moved to any other frame in Bridge. Their only limitation is that they cannot be popped out individually.

The **Preview panel** displays a preview of the select file or files if it is an image or video. The preview is a useful way to quickly view details of an image without having to open the file. Previews are separate from, and typically larger than, the thumbnail image displayed in the Content panel.

Figure 3.3

Adjusting panels.

Adjusting Panels

You can adjust the Adobe Bridge window by moving and resizing its panels (Figure 3.3). However, you cannot move panels outside the Adobe Bridge window.

The following are ways you can adjust panels:

- Drag a panel by its tab into another panel.
- Drag the horizontal divider bar between panels to make them larger or smaller.
- Drag the vertical divider bar between the panels and the Content panel to resize the panels or Content panel.
- Press Tab to show or hide all panels except the center panel (the center panel varies depending on the workspace you've chosen).
- Choose Window, followed by the name of the panel you want to display or hide.
- **Right-Click** or **Ctrl-Click** a panel tab and choose the name of the panel you want to display.

There you go—pretty basic. Now we will look at the more interesting parts.

Basic Navigation

If you've had any experience with computers at all, you could probably figure out that double-clicking a folder in the Content panel will open that folder and display its contents. And, double-clicking on an image in the Content panel will open up that image in Photoshop. Or, if you tend to favor Windows Explorer, you might like navigating using

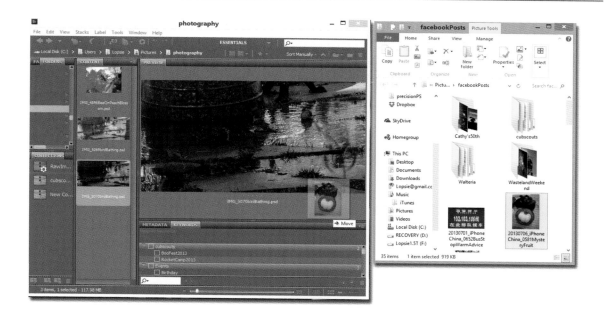

Figure 3.4

Ignore the "move" displayed. It will not actually be moved.

the folder hierarchy in the Folders panel. But, there are some nifty ways to navigate and open files that not only are fun to do but also save time.

Click drag a folder from **Windows Explorer (Windows)** or the **Finder (Mac OS)** to the path bar to go to that location in Adobe Bridge.

Drag a folder from **Windows Explorer (Windows)** or the **Finder (Mac OS)** to the Preview panel to have Bridge jump to display that image and directory. (Do not let the "move->" displayed scare you. It will not move the file from its folder. Bridge will just jump to the directory where the image is stored; Figure 3.4.)

In Mac OS, you can also drag a folder from the Finder to the Adobe Bridge Icon to open it.

Ctrl+Double Click/⌘+**Double Click** a folder in the Content panel to open that folder in a new Bridge window. You can open multiple images by pressing **Shift** to select contiguously or by holding **Ctrl**/⌘ and highlighting multiple noncontiguous files before double-clicking (any one of them).

A full-screen preview is just a button away as pressing the **spacebar** while having a thumbnail selected will bring the image to full screen. Pressing the **spacebar** again will return back to Bridge. But, that is just one image (selecting more than one image will still only give you a full-screen image of the first image). So, that brings us to **Review mode**, a neat method to view a group of images. Select the images you want to view and press **Ctrl+B**/⌘+**B**. A carousel of all the images comes up full screen (Figure 3.5).

Note that this shortcut is *Bridge specific*; this shortcut does not work in Photoshop as it is assigned to another function by default.

Figure 3.5

Review carousel.

Once in Review mode, you can do any of the following:

Click the **Left Arrow** or **Right Arrow** buttons to go to the previous or next image.

Drag the foreground image right or left to move around the carousel.

Click any image in the background to bring it to the front.

Press **H** to display keyboard shortcuts for working in Review mode.

Right-Click/Ctrl+Click any image to rate it, apply a label, rotate it, or open it.

Press] to rotate the foreground image 90° clockwise. Press [to rotate the image 90° counterclockwise.

To remove an image from the selection, drag the image off the bottom of the screen or click the **Down Arrow**.

Press **Esc** or click the ✖ button in the lower-right corner of the screen to exit Review mode.

Click the New Collection button in the lower-right corner of the screen to create a collection from the selected images and exit Review mode. Nifty, eh?

Finding Your Keys

Part of asset management is the ability to find the necessary assets at the time you need them—easily. One of the (ahem) *key* ways of doing this is to use keywords. The creation and tagging of images with keywords is a laborious task, but it is (dare I say it again?) *key* to a well-organized image library. It's important not only to have keywords tagged but also to have a robust list of keywords with some kind of hierarchy. Rather than just having keywords such as Xander, Andy, Lopsie, Calvin, Cindy, and so on, you

3. The Visual Bridge: Accessing and Organizing Files

can have Family|Schwartz|Xander. Another example of a robust hierarchy would be Materials|Metals|Corrosion|Rust

Keywords are descriptive labels that help organize your files. You can attach one or more to any asset and use them later to organize your view in Bridge. Do you want to see all the images of your dog? If you had assigned the keyword *dog* to each of the dog image files, you could easily find and display them. Click the Keywords tab in the bottom-right frame. Adobe provides a few default categories. You can leave, hide, or delete these. For now, leave them.

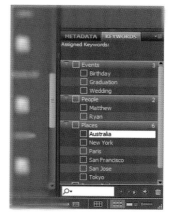

Do you want to create a new keyword? Follow along:

1. Go to the level at which you want the new keyword. For example, I have pictures from Australia that I want located under one of the default category keywords: Places.
2. Click **Places** to select it.
3. Click the New Sub Keyword icon ▣ at the bottom of the Keywords palette. Alternatively, you could have had Place selected and clicked on the New Keyword icon ▣ to create a keyword on the same level as Place.
4. A field entry window will appear in the proper level; go ahead and type in your keyword (Figure 3.6).

Figure 3.6

Creating a new keyword.

Script Your Keywords

You say you want to become even slicker with your keywords? Here's a little quick cheat:

Use a text editor to create a plain text file such as shown in Figure 3.7

To create subdirectory keywords, press the Tab key and write each keyword in its own line after the "parent."

Use the Keyword panel menu to load your text file: click on the pull-down menu in the far-right corner of the panel and choose **Import…**.

Note that if you want to get rid of the existing keywords, including the default keywords that Adobe includes, choose

Clear and Import…

Instead of just

Import…

Figure 3.7

A simple text editor can be a powerful weapon.

Tada! Mind you, you'll still have to assign the keywords (Table 3.1), but hey, I have to leave *something* for you to do, right?

You can see what keywords are assigned to an image by looking for the check marks next to the keywords in the Keywords palette when you have the image thumbnail selected, as shown in Figure 3.8. You can toggle the check marks to assign or unassign keywords to the image. If you already have a keyword assigned to an image, don't worry: Assigning a keyword simply adds the keyword to any existing keywords.

Table 3.1 Keyword Essentials

What Do You Want to Do?	Here's How
Assign the keyword to the image you have highlighted	Click the picture thumbnail and then click the keyword check box in the Keywords palette.
Give all the images in this file the same keyword	Go to the file browser's bar menu at the top of the dialog box and click **Edit > Select All** (or press **Ctrl+A/⌘+A**, then click the keyword check box).
Remove a keyword from one or more images	Just choose the image thumbnails and click the check mark next to the keyword to deselect the image's assignment to that keyword.
Add a keyword to the new keyword set	Highlight the folder before creating the keyword.

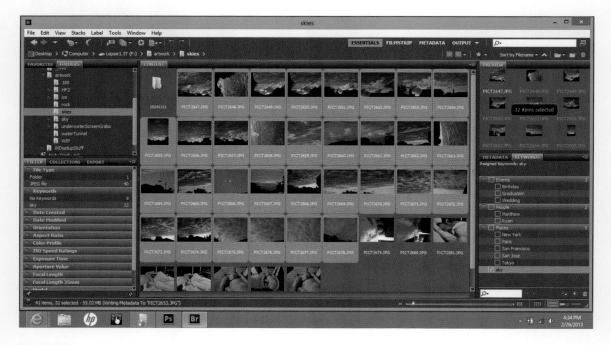

Figure 3.8

Check marked keywords are assigned to image.

Caution

Now, a few disclaimers and small print (enter deep lawyer voice): If you rename a keyword after applying it, Photoshop does *not* update the keyword on images to which you previously assigned it. You have to reapply the keyword. Likewise, deleting a keyword does not take the keyword off images to which you previously applied it; you have a dangling keyword that just uses space.

Using Your Keys

That little field in the Keywords palette with a magnifying glass is the search field. As you start typing in a word, the keywords that fit will be highlighted in the palette. So, typing in "W" will highlight "WIP," "Will," and "work," but "Wi" will narrow the highlights to the first two. Should you type in "Witty" and hit Enter, Bridge will create that keyword under Other Keywords. This comes in handy when you are trying to remember what keywords you might already have or you want to quickly reach an existing keyword to assign it to the currently selected files.

You can do a search on all of your images by keyword, name, date, rank, and many other options.

Rank and File Labeling

I remember the days of Photoshop's File Browser. At that time you were given the option to create your own ranking system. You could assign any alphanumeric rank to any of your pictures. But, you would have to understand that whatever you type in the Rank box was ordered; numbers had a higher value than letters, and values were evaluated from left to right. So, 1 came before 2, but 10 also came before 2, and mango came before mangosteen. I guess I was the only one to have a ranking system based on fruit names and constellations. Now in Bridge, you have two options: the 1- to 5-star option and the Select, Second, Approved, Review, and Reject rating. The second option also comes with a color code so you can see at a glance what rating you gave it. And, for those of us who insist on unconventional labels, you can change those colored labels to different words of your choice. For example, you could have red labels be for appetizers, yellow for drinks, and so on—but of course you could use keywords for that, and there is no implied rank to the colored labels.

Remember to refresh after sorting [**View > Refresh**]. This is worth repeating because it's a detail that people forget. Photoshop doesn't seem to reliably refresh, so pressing the Refresh button **F5** will ensure that you are looking at the proper results of your change. Occasionally you need to refresh for that changed image to pop into place in its rank. So, to be on the safe side, get into the habit of **F5**.

Any rank or labeling of your assets is always visible no matter what view you choose. If you go to **View > As Details** to display your thumbnails in Detail form that displays data next to the thumbnail, you will see the rank or label to the right of the thumbnail under the file name. If you go to **View > As Thumbnails**, you will still see the rank right under the thumbnail image and on top of the file name. Now, if you think you really messed up, you can get rid of all the rankings and start over: Select all the images and go to Bridge's menu bar; select **Label > No Label** or **Label > No Rating**.

Say you don't need such a complex ranking. All you want to do is flag the images you like out of the virtual pile that was thrown at you. At one point, there was a flag symbol so you could "flag" a picture. The flagging capability is gone now, but you can just label it with a label and filter using that label. You can change the name of the label to actually be *flag* if you want. Another option is to negative mark (to mark the ones you reject with the reject label). This is great if you have to sort through a plethora of images and just need to make a yea or nay pile.

Collections

At one time, you probably organized all your assets into different folders: There were documents, pictures, and videos, then subfolders for work, play, family—and what happens when you cross the streams? (Ghostbusters reference: I give away my age, don't I?)

Often, we had to duplicate or create shortcuts or some other form of messy organization to deal with multiple overlapping references. Luckily, now Bridge will support Collections (Lightroom users have been using this handy organization aspect for some time). A Collection contains a pointer reference to any asset, so no files are moved or copied; they are simply referenced no matter where they are physically. A single file can belong to many Collections, and a Collection can contain files from multiple directories.

As if that weren't awesome enough, there are also Collections that are "smart." Smart Collections will automatically build your content based on user-defined criteria. So, if new images are added that match the criteria, they are automatically included in the Smart Collection. For example, if you wanted to create a collection of only your best photography, you could create a Smart Collection that contains anything you rate as five star.

Manage Color

Synchronizing color settings ensures that colors look the same in all color-managed Adobe products. Make sure that you have your correct color settings: go to **Edit > Color Settings** and make sure you have chosen the proper settings for your needs (Figure 3.9). With Adobe Bridge CC, color settings are synchronized across all color-managed apps and components. When you specify color settings using the **Edit > Color Settings** command, color settings are automatically synchronized.

If you are primarily working with digital files and not going to print, you may be tempted to choose Monitor Color or Web Internet. Know that choosing those color profiles may reduce your color gamut irreversibly for your pictures. If you don't know anything about color management, just stick to your local defaults, in my case, North America General Purpose 2.

But, if you are working in motion pictures or with some other precise and specific color lookup table, you can choose the saved color profile from here. Ask your network administrator to make sure that the color profile is saved in Adobe's Color Settings directory.

Figure 3.9

Color Settings dialog.

Batch Renaming Your Files

I don't know about you, but I hate the camera's generic image names: DSCF0459 or img2356. It would help on so many different levels if I could just rename all of them to Hawaii0001 through Hawaii1234. Luckily, Photoshop makes this a lot easier with its **Batch Rename** function. This can also help with, say, a hypothetical situation such as renaming all of Chapter 1 figures to Chapter 2 figure nomenclature because the order

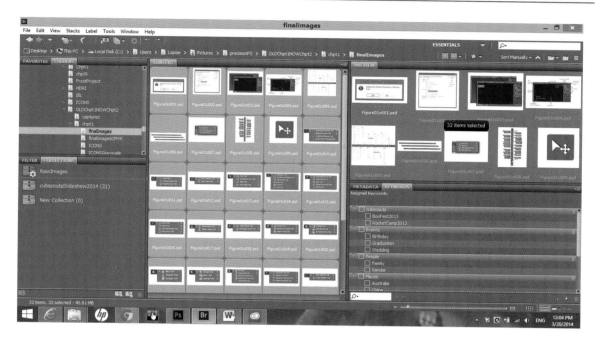

Figure 3.10

Selecting all the files to Batch Rename.

of your book is changed around and you need to deliver these images under a time crunch—hypothetically, of course.

1. Go to your folder in Bridge's file browser.

2. Choose **Edit** > **Select All**, as shown in Figure 3.10, or press **Ctrl+A**/⌘**+A**.

   This selects all the image thumbnails in the folder. (This is the same keyboard shortcut for **Select** > **All** that you use when selecting all the content on a layer in an image in Photoshop.)

   You don't have to select all of the files. You could do a noncontiguous selection by holding the Ctrl/⌘ key and selecting images.

3. Go to Bridge's bar menu and choose **Tools** > **Batch Rename**.

   The Batch Rename dialog box will appear. Take a look at my settings for renaming the Chapter 1 images to Chapter 2 in Figure 3.11.

4. You can choose the Rename in Same Folder option since you already have your images in a separate folder, but to avoid a possible "infinite loop" and to be on the safe side, I created a new folder for placing my renamed images.

Figure 3.11

Batch Rename dialog box.

Move to New Folder does *not* **copy** the renamed files to the new folder. Instead, this option moves the image files to the new folder after renaming them.

Figure 3.12

My renumbered images.

5. Under the File Naming area, choose your type of input from the pull-down menu; in this case, I wanted to start with the text Fig02x to indicate Chapter 2 figures. Then, I wanted a numerical sequence to follow in order with a padding of three digits. I could have had the numbers start from 67 (to match the previous numbers, say), but since I want this to start with 1, I enter 1. At the bottom of the File Naming area, a sample of what the name looks like reflects your selections.

6. Click **OK** and you see that all of your selected images have been renamed. Figure 3.12 shows my renumbered images. If you navigate through a system window, you will see that the actual files have been renamed. This is not an Adobe-application-specific change like rotation of the image or labels. Renaming changes are permanent to the files.

Creating a Custom Layout

You don't need to create your own layout, but most likely you have a particular ritual that sets up your workspace just so. Bridge will remember your last setup, but occasionally you might either reset or change and wish you could go back to a favorite setup. Make it easy on yourself and save your favorite layout so it will be an easy one-click setup whenever you need it.

1. Move your palettes and adjust your panels to how you would like to have them saved. In my case, I have adjusted the thumbnail size with the slider on the bottom of Bridge; moved the palettes so I can see Metadata, Keywords, and Folders at the same time; and dragged the panel bars until I had a nice, large-size preview like that in Figure 3.13.

2. Save this setup using **Window > Workspace > New Workspace**.

3. Type a name in the Save Workspace dialog box that appears and click Save.

I like the name Andy, but thought Lopsie's Favorite was more descriptive for the workspace. Remember, saving a workspace is just that: saving a complete workspace, including the location of all of your other palettes. Keep this in mind when you go to save your workspace; double-check the entire screen for the location and visibility of the other palettes.

Figure 3.13

I like my previews to be fairly large.

Bridge will remember whatever changes to the workspace you have made and assign them to the current workspace profile, but you can always revert to the original profile by going to **Window > Workspace > Reset Standard Workspaces**.

Exporting Bridge Adjustments

You have rotated, renamed, annotated, and made a few other spiffy changes, all in Bridge. Now, you want to make sure that anyone else on the network can see the image modifications the way you do. Or, you want to burn it all to a CD. How do you ensure that others have all that information? If you're like me, you just burned it to a CD and found out the hard way that none of this information was passed on.

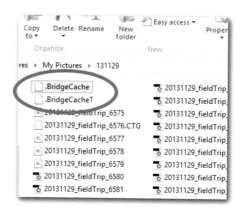

It is pretty easy to remedy the situation: Go to your file browser's bar menu and choose **Tools > Cache > Build and Export Cache**. A dialog box lets you know the cache has been exported.

These files are in the same folder/area in which the images appear (see Figure 3.14). As long as they are there in the same folder as the images, anyone using Bridge to view the folder contents will see the rotation changes you made, and the picture thumbnails will load more quickly. If you burn the

Figure 3.14

The cached files that convey Bridge adjustments.

folder of images to a CD, all will be well if you include the three cache files in the folder with the images.

Search for Files and Folders

You can search for files and folders with Adobe Bridge by using multiple combinations of search criteria. You can save search criteria as a Smart Collection, which is a collection that stays up to date with files that meet your criteria.

1. Choose **Edit > Find**.
2. Choose a folder in which to search.
3. Choose search criteria by selecting options and limiters from the **Criteria** menus. Enter search text in the box on the right. To add additional search criteria, click the plus sign (+). To remove search criteria, click the minus sign (–).
4. Choose an option from the **Match** menu to specify whether any or all criteria must be met.

   If you want to expand the search to any subfolders in the source folder, then select **Include All Subfolders**.

   If you would like to specify that Adobe Bridge search uncached as well as cached files, then select **Include Non Indexed Files**. Searching uncached files (in folders that you have not previously browsed in Adobe Bridge) is slower than searching just cached files.
5. Click **Find**. All those files matching your criteria will be displayed.
6. You can save the search criteria by clicking the **New Smart Collection** button in the **Collections panel**. The Smart Collection dialog box automatically includes the criteria of your search. You can refine the criteria if you wish, before you click **Save**. Type a name for the Smart Collection in the Collections panel and then press **Enter/Return**.

Stacks

Again, in a lesson learned from big brother Lightroom, Bridge offers a way to view more efficiently by stacking images (Figure 3.15).

To Stack

Select several related images. Choose **Stacks > Group** as Stack or use the shortcut **Ctrl+G/⌘+G**.

A number in the corner tells you how many images are in the stack and clicking the number will expand or collapse the stack. Hovering your cursor above the thumbnail will show a play button that you can click to view all the images in a stack. You can adjust some of the settings, such as the rate of playback in your Bridge Preferences.

This should not be confused with Photomerging in Photoshop.

Mini Bridge

Bridge is wonderful, helpful, and so on and so on. Then, what's up with the mini-me? Why have a Mini Bridge?

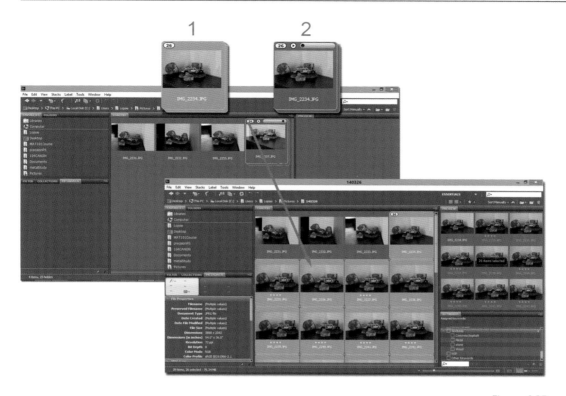

Figure 3.15

You can see the stacked images. 1. stack, 2. stack with play button, 3. stack expanded.

When you first open Photoshop, there are little tabs on the bottom, and one of them is the tab for Mini Bridge. I used to avoid Mini Bridge. I mean, why would I use Mini Bridge if it has to open regular Bridge to function? There are definite speed and ease benefits to Mini Bridge, and it has come quite a distance from its original meek file browser start.

First, click on the Mini Bridge tab and a panel will expand on the bottom of the screen. If you do not have Bridge already open, then there will be a Launch Bridge button (Figure 3.16). If you do not see the Mini Bridge tab on the bottom, then you can access Mini Bridge by going to **File > Browse in Mini Bridge…**.

Click on the button for Bridge to open in the background. There is a folder navigation panel on the left. Navigate to the directory where your image is, then double-click on the image in the thumbnail preview panel on the right to open it in Photoshop. That is straightforward, right? And, if you were looking for an image to match your opened image, it's faster and easier to do it via Mini Bridge because you would still have your first image right above it.

Now, if you had to go five folders back, it could be a pain to have to double-click back five times. Mini Bridge keeps it simple by giving you a path that you can click on to jump back to a particular directory within a path at the top of the panel. Or, if you **left-click** on

Figure 3.16

The Launch Bridge button.

the arrow of the deviation, a drop-down menu will appear with all possible directories listed for you to choose from. If there are a lot of subfolders, the drop-down will scroll (see Figure 3.17). After you click on the directory of choice there, you can either use the standard folder navigation on the left panel or left-click on the path arrow to choose the next directory from the pull-down menu.

By default, Mini Bridge is docked on the bottom of the workspace. But, Mini Bridge can be undocked and resized like most floating panels. To undock, click and drag the tab into the workspace much like you would for any other panel. To reap the maximum benefits from Mini Bridge, however, I would keep it docked on the lower edge.

I used Bridge because I wanted to identify files by images rather than by file name. But, now you can see a small thumbnail for most image formats in the standard operating system file browser, so the point of using Bridge is seeing information such as camera settings or seeing a larger preview image. To resize or see larger images, you have to drag the panel window larger by taking an edge and click dragging it to the size you want. This is precisely why I didn't like Mini Bridge before: If it takes up too much screen space, then why use Mini Bridge instead of Bridge? Well, that was then, and this is now.

You can obtain an instant full-screen preview by clicking on a thumbnail and pressing the **spacebar** (much like Autodesk's Maya for toggling between a single panel and multiple panels) (Figure 3.18). Using the right and left arrow keys will slide you to the next or previous image respectively.

Another cool aspect of Mini Bridge is the review option. Bridge also has the review option, but it's so much more convenient in Mini Bridge.

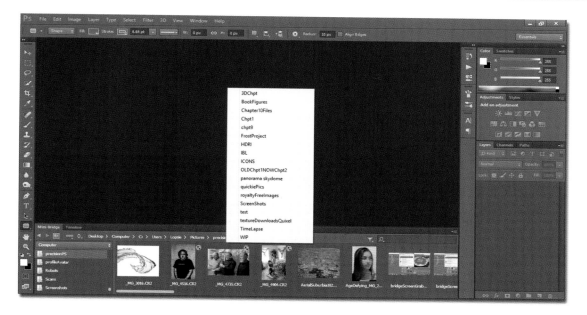

Figure 3.17

Clicking on the arrow brings a drop-down menu of subdirectories or files.

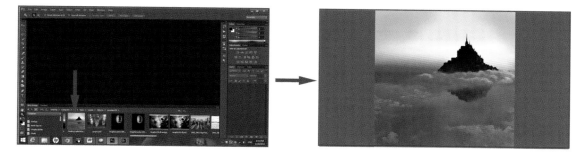

Figure 3.18

Full screen at a touch of a button—or rather bar, spacebar.

How to Review Images with Review Mode

To review images with Review mode, choose more than four images; it can be several in a folder. If you do not select any, all the images in the current folder will be selected.

If you do not choose at least five images, you will not get the carousel effect. The images will simply be tiled. So, you do not *need* to have at least five images to review; you just don't get the nifty carousel effect.

Go to the **View Icon** ▦ (two rows of squares; image) and click to get the pull-down menu. Choose **Review mode**. This will give you a review carousel that is reminiscent of the Apple/Mac file viewer interface. Press **H** to obtain a selection of available commands.

The reason this is called Review Mode is that presumably you are either reviewing similar images or culling from a group of multiple various images.

- To cut one out, press the **down arrow** key.
- To flag/mark, press **Ctrl+1/⌘+1** for 1 star and **Ctrl+5/⌘+5** for five stars.
- **Alt+Delete/Option+del** will mark the photos to "reject."
- Was that an "oops"? Then, **Ctrl+0/⌘+0** to remove any label. Just be careful because **Ctrl+Delete/⌘+Delete** will move the file to the trash.

If you already have an image open, you can drag and drop an image from Mini Bridge and the chosen image will appear as a Smart Object in your layers—just like if you drag an open image to an another—allowing you to skip the step of opening it and then closing it.

4

Quickies

Introduction

The "quickies" are the top 10 questions I am asked by non-Photoshop users. The questions usually start with them saying to me: "I just need to …." These are the questions that I have been asked by my father-in-law, my neighbor, my cousin's best friend, and those morning coffee regulars that visit Panera, to name a few. You know when they finally hear that my book is out, they are going to browse through to see if they "can just …." Yeah, you get the gist. So, I felt I had to include these quickies.

Although this book is considered an advanced book on Photoshop, in my teaching experience I have found many professionals who have found ways of avoiding Photoshop, in part from fear. Photoshop can be intimidating for those who are aware of the capabilities but overwhelmed by them at the same time. Treat this as your gentle introduction—the single small step onto the path of Photoshop proficiency—and remember, the first one is free …;)

Figure 4.1

What do you mean by "make this smaller"?

1. I Just Need to Make This Picture Smaller

One of the most common questions relates to "just making this picture smaller," and usually the person asking doesn't realize that there are different interpretations of this question (Figure 4.1): Do you mean you need the file size to be smaller? Or do you mean that you want the dimensions to be smaller? Do both apply? Luckily, it's easy to address both.

Making the Dimensions Smaller

Open the file you would like to reduce in size:

> **File > Open.**
> Go to **Image > Size**.

Figure 4.2

Image Size dialog. Notice that making the dimensions smaller also makes the file size smaller.

A dialog appears like the one shown in Figure 4.2. The dialog that appears will show the pixel size and the approximate file size in megabites at the top. Most likely, you are reading this section because either you need the pixel dimension to be a certain size or you need the file size to be within a certain range.

The **Constrain Proportions** box should be checked by default, so as you adjust the pixel dimensions of the width, the height should change accordingly. Adjust the width to the dimension you need it to be, or until the file size shows an acceptable size, then left mouse button (LMB) click on **OK**. Alternatively, if you want to "make an image smaller" because you want it to fit to a certain paper size, you can see if your paper size is listed in the **Fit to** pull-down menu in the Image Size dialog. But, if you know the dimensions you need, you might as well input the size yourself.

Making the File Size Smaller

Ctrl+S/⌘+S will save your file, but if you want to keep the original intact, then **Ctrl+Shift+S/⌘+Shift+S** will bring up the Save As dialog window. You can then navigate to the location where you would like to save the file, in the top Save In field, and rename your file in the File Name field.

All this will keep your file in the same format as it was (see Chapter 12 to learn more about the different formats). If you need to make your image file size smaller, JPG will give you great compression, but you will lose some information with each saving. So, let's do a Save As so we keep the original intact and compress the file a lot.

Now, go to **File > Save As…** in the Menu bar.

In the dialog window that appears, you can choose to rename the file or leave it as is. If you don't rename it and you have a Mac or a PC that does not show file extensions, you may have a difficult time telling which is the JPG and which is the original. I recommend renaming it or at least putting it with same name into a different folder. For this tutorial, we will create a new folder that will hold the JPG version of the file.

Click with the LMB click on the New Folder button to the right of the Save In field at the top of the dialog window. A new folder will appear in the search results area, ready to be renamed. Type *JPGs*—you should see the folder being renamed as you type—and press Enter. Now, double-click on the folder to open its location.

Next, click on the **down arrow** to the right of the Format field. You will see the options available in a drop-down menu appear. Choose JPG (*.JPG, *.JPEG, *.JPE). Press **Save**.

Another dialog box will appear, like you see on the top of Figure 4.3, where you can set your compression, which will affect your total file size. But, since I was working in 16 bit and with the ProPhoto Color Space and I want to make this smaller for the web, cancel out of the JPG options and let's save this a different way.

Go to **File > Save for Web…**. A much more robust dialog box appears, as is shown on the bottom of Figure 4.3. You can convert the color space, preview the effects of the compression, and even load your own lookup table (which is beyond this introductory quickie tutorial, but trust me, it's cool). For now, make sure you have changed your file preset to JPG and hit **Save…**. The folder we created previously is still there even though we canceled out of the previous save. So, we can navigate to the JPG folder and save. You have now saved a file with the same name

Figure 4.3

Saving as a JPG two different ways.

into a new folder named JPGs. That's it! You've accomplished both interpretations of the question with the finesse of a pro.

OK, now that you've had a taste, let's do another.

2. I Just Want to Make This Color Photo Black and White—or Maybe with Just a Little Color

There are innumerable ways to go about taking a color photo to black and white or with just a little color (Figure 4.4). The absolute quickest way is to open your file and just hit **Ctrl+Shift+U/⌘+Shift+U**. That will instantly desaturate the image of any color and you can save the file: Done.

Notice, however, the tutorial does not end here. I think I would be doing you a disservice if I left it at that. Even if I show other ways of creating a black-and-white image from a color image in other parts of this book, I think you should have something here with a little more control. So, let me show you another quick, but not as dirty, way.

Open the file that you would like to convert: **File > Open**. On the top menu bar, you could go to **Image > Adjustments > Black & White**, but I will have you go instead to **Layer > New Adjustment Layer > Black & White**. Just click OK in the dialog that pops up to accept the default name for the layer.

Figure 4.4

Color to black and white.

In case you haven't noticed by now, any time a menu selection is followed by an ellipsis (that's the three dots for those who have been out of grammar school for a while), it is an indication that a dialog box will follow.

Figure 4.5

Black and White dialog box.

In the Black & White dialog box that follows (Figure 4.5), adjust the sliders as you feel fit to create the most aesthetically pleasing contrast and tone. You can LMB click and drag the title bar of the dialog box and move it around so you can see the parts of your image that are covered. When you have tweaked the sliders to your heart's content, click **OK**.

You are done! To keep the adjustment layer, save as a PSD. If you like it and know you don't need to keep the exact information on changing the image, you can save out the file by flattening the layers and going to the top menu bar and choosing **File > Save** or by pressing **Ctrl+S/⌘+S** to overwrite your current file. Alternatively, you can choose **File > Save As… Ctrl+Shift+S/⌘+Shift+S** to save your file under a different name.

But, before you do all that, you need to see the method to my madness. I had you apply this adjustment as a separate layer, so now let's take it a little bit further: Let's bring back color to just a section of the photo.

If you look carefully at the Black & White adjustment layer, you will see mask thumbnail, which is the white rectangle linked with a chain symbol to the adjustment. The mask is 100% white, indicating that everything is completely visible. Make sure your mask is selected (see Figure 4.6); a dark outline indicates this.

Choose a soft brush and choose pure black for its color (pressing **D** will set the foreground color to pure black and the background to pure white). Again, making sure you have the mask selected, paint in the areas where you want to bring back the color. In this case, I brought back the color of the flower, but I felt it was too harsh, so I reduced the opacity of my brush to obtain the softer, "tinted" look (Figure 4.7).

Figure 4.6

The dark outline indicates that the mask is selected.

3. I Just Want to Sharpen This Picture a Little

Chapter 5 shows how to sharpen in Adobe Camera Raw (ACR). We will also see how we can apply these sharpening methods to a non-RAW image. But, one of my favorite, if old-school, ways to obtain a strong but controllable sharpening effect is using the High Pass method.

Open a photo that needs some sharpening. You can use Bridge or Mini Bridge or simply **File > Open**. Duplicate the image onto a new layer; you can do this quickly with the shortcut **Ctrl+J/⌘+J** while having the background layer selected.

Go to **Filter > Other > High Pass**. A dialog box should appear, and the image should look like a gray stamped print with bits of color near the edges. Drag the radius slider to about 8.0; you can increase or decrease as you wish, but overdoing it can create a halo effect. The effect of the slider depends on the size of your image (this image was about 3000 pixels wide), so start with something that gives you the effect seen in Figure 4.8 and you can undo if it needs to be adjusted.

Click **OK**. You will now have a layer with a gray. Set that gray layer's mode to Overlay. You can now see your sharpened picture (Figure 4.9). I think the full setting is too much, so I've lowered the opacity until I obtained something that looked more pleasant.

Figure 4.7

Black and white with color flower.

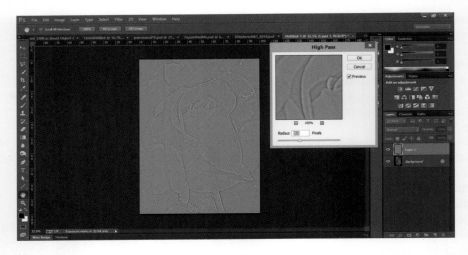

Figure 4.8

High Pass.

Figure 4.9

Our sharpened picture.

4. I Just Need to Get Rid of That (Wire/Timestamp/Other Annoying Inclusion)

Take a look at a beautiful photograph from my trip to Fiji (Figure 4.10). At the time, I time-stamped everything so I would know when it was taken on a trip, which would also tell me which country I was in (by my itinerary). Well, now advances have made it such that even the cheapest camera keeps metadata, so such timestamps aren't necessary. What do I do now with this?

Luckily, Photoshop has also advanced since 2002. What would have been a complicated procedure will now be a simple and quick fix (Figure 4.11).

Open LionRockOriginal by going to **File** > **Open** and navigating to where you have downloaded the file. Create a duplicate of the background layer by pressing **Ctrl+J/⌘+J**. Select the new layer by clicking on the layer.

Choose the Rectangle Marquee Selection Tool . LMB click drag a marquee around the date stamp. Select the Lasso Tool. Holding down the **Shift** key so that the selection is added to your current marquee, drag around the bit of boat that is intruding into our picture on the lower-left corner.

Figure 4.10

Lion Rock in Fiji.

Go to **Edit** > **Fill…** (Figure 4.11). The Fill dialog window will appear. Make sure the Contents indicates Content-Aware. If it does not say so in the Use: field, then LMB click on the menu arrow on the right end of the field to bring out the drop-down menu and choose Content-Aware. Blending mode should be Normal with opacity at 100%. Click **OK**.

Figure 4.11

Timestamp area selected.

Figure 4.12

Detail of content-filled area.

Voila! Magic! Let me now proclaim my undying love for Content-Aware to the Adobe powers that be. Figure 4.12 shows how nicely Content-Aware Fill filled in the time-stamp area. And, just because we have so much time left, let's get rid of the bird flying in the background. With small bits like this, you can use the Healing Brush. Choose the Spot Healing Brush Tool and make sure the Content-Aware option is selected in the toolbar. Adjust the brush size to just fit around the bird (see Figure 4.13). Now, paint over the bird. A single daub/click should do it. Voila! Magic! Have I proclaimed my undying love for Content-Aware yet?

You can just save over the existing image, but you can't have a "before and after" if you do that. So, save the image by going to the top menu bar **File > Save As...** or by using the shortcut **Ctrl+Shift+S/⌘+Shift+S**. Name it LionRockFixed and click **Save** (Figure 4.14).

Figure 4.13

Size the brush to be just larger than the bird and make sure the Content-Aware option is selected in the Options bar.

Figure 4.14

Cleaned up Lion Rock.

5. I Just Want to Crop This Picture for Better Composition

With each of these quickie tutorials, I feel like saying "Oh, I get asked this one a lot," but you already know that. If you just want to crop a picture for better composition, open the file you would like to crop (Figure 4.15), **File > Open**.

Navigate to where you have saved your image and click on **Open**. Your image should come into view, fitted to the screen. Should this not be the case, press **Ctrl+0/⌘+0** (use zeros for this operation). This will fit the image to the screen.

Although the Crop tool will allow you to nondestructively change your composition, this instructional is the simple, straightforward standard crop that deletes the cropped pixels. Choose the Crop tool, then LMB click drag a rectangle to represent the crop you would like. Don't worry if it's a little off; you will be able to adjust it.

Once you release the LMB, you will see a rectangle denoting your current crop, with a 3 × 3 grid representing the rule of thirds that helps you with alignment. The parts that will be "cut" are darkened to help you visualize the crop. To adjust the area of interest, LMB click on one of the corner or edge control handles (see Figure 4.16) and LMB click drag to the desired size.

Figure 4.15

Changing the composition.

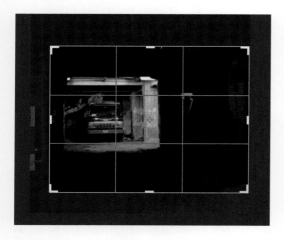

Figure 4.16

Cropping an image.

Figure 4.17

If you didn't want to have separate files, you could have deselected "delete pixels" in the Options bar and have a nondestructive crop.

Now, let's say, in my recomposition I would like to give it a Dutch Tilt for dramatic effect. In yesteryears, we would have had to do separate steps to accomplish this task, but no more. Just LMB click outside the box (you will see your cursor change to a rotate cursor) and click drag until you have the angle you wish to see. After playing with the angles, I decide to forego a Dutch Tilt, but it's nice to be able to visualize it while cropping.

Once you have the composition you like, hit Enter or the check icon in the top menu bar. Save your file **File** > **Save Ctrl+S/⌘+S.** This will overwrite your current file, and cut areas will be permanently lost. To keep your original, **Ctrl+Shift+S/⌘+Shift+S** and **Save As** a different file.

Note that to have the crop be "nondestructive," you need to have set the crop settings so the cropped pixels are not deleted and then save the file as a PSD (Figure 4.17). Other file formats will not remember the crop. But, in a case like this, I would just keep the original and the cropped version as two different files.

6. I Just Want to Replace …

Figure 4.18

Our starting "school picture."

To replace anything, be it a background or a foreground object, you need to create a selection. Photoshop has a variety of effective ways to do this, but we'll do one example here. The tutorial in Chapter 1 uses many different selection methods, so you can see the pros and cons of the different methods all in one tutorial. Let's keep it simple here.

For anyone who has taken a school picture for the yearbook at any time past 1995, you've probably seen that you have a whole variety of backgrounds available—but you only took one picture. How was that done? Let's start with a picture like that in Figure 4.18. This is a striking young girl, but let's try a few different backgrounds.

1. Choose the Magic Wand , then in the Options bar, make sure the Sample Size is set to 3 × 3 Average (if not, then click on the drop-down menu and choose 3 × 3). Set the Tolerance to 20 and make sure the Anti-alias, Contiguous, and Sample All Layers buttons are checked on. You can see the settings in Figure 4.19.

2. Click on the background of the picture, in this case the off-white wall. The selection is indicated by a moving dotted line, often referred to is "crawling ants," around the perimeter.

3. In the Menu bar, select **Select > Inverse**. The crawling ants now show the selection to be around the girl. You could have also selected the inverse by using the shortcut **Ctrl+Shift+I/⌘+Shift+I**.

4. You should notice, however, that the areas near the edge of her hair need refining. Because you still have the Magic Wand selected, click on the **Refine Edge…** button in the Options bar. A dialog will appear. Set the tool options as shown in Figure 4.20.

5. Now, gently paint on the edge of the hair, overlapping both hair and wall. Do this all around the outline of the girl. You can use the Zoom Tool in the dialog box or even the zoom shortcuts (**Ctrl++/⌘++** to zoom in, **Ctrl+-/⌘+-** to zoom out) to zoom in and out for better control. As you paint over the edges, you should see the matte being cleaned up along the flyaway hairs.

6. When you are done, click **OK.**

7. Now, click on the Mask button on the Layers palette.

Figure 4.19

Magic Wand settings.

Figure 4.20

The Refine Edge dialog settings.

Figure 4.21

Putting in a new background.

8. Your subject is masked, and you have a gray-and-white checkerboard denoting transparency behind her. You may have noticed also that the layer name is now Layer 0 instead of Background.

9. Bring in a picture for the background. I chose a picture of a sky. Because I have my windows tiling vertically, I can just click on the sky and drag it to the girl and release the LMB. This will place the image on a layer above the girl. You can also just cut and paste: In the sky photo, **Select > All**. Then, **Ctrl+C/⌘+C** to copy the sky into the clipboard. Select the girl photo and press **Ctrl+V/⌘+V**. The sky is pasted into a new layer above the girl.

10. You should now see *only* sky, even though you are in the girl photo file. Press **Shift+Ctrl+[/Shift+⌘+[** and the sky layer should move down one layer and now be "behind" the girl.

11. Move the sky background until it has the appropriate look and fills the background. That's it! You can use any other photo, and as long as the layer is below the masked layer, you can move and adjust and put in any other background (Figure 4.21). When you have what you want, save it as a PSD so that all your layers and masking information are saved.

Changing the background or replacing something in the foreground is a form of compositing. This particular example was a simple replacement, but this book abounds with tutorials that use this same principle because it is key to many Photoshop creations.

Figure 4.22

An image of gray brick.

7. I Just Want to Make a Seamless Pattern

Maybe you want to create a background for a web page and want some kind of tiling pattern. Or, perhaps you want to make a texture map that can be applied in three dimensions (3D) seamlessly. This is one skill that comes in handy often, and Photoshop has made this easier than before to pull from a photo and create a pattern.

If you want to make a pattern that is hand drawn, you can skip past this photo section. But, often we want to pull from a photo.

Prepping a Photo for a Seamless Pattern

Open the image (see Figure 4.22); in this case, I have a picture of some gray brick that I want to make into a repeating tile that can fill a background. The picture is already pretty flatly lit, so at least I don't have to worry about taking out shadows and light direction too much. But, we won't be able to create a repeating tile with the perspective that is in the picture.

Right click on the Crop Tool 🔲 and find the Perspective Crop 🔲. You will need to define the "square" that you would like to use as your pattern. Click one corner at a time. As you click the third point, you will see a grid start to form by default (see Figure 4.23). You can use this grid to make sure of your alignment as you click the fourth point. If you find your quadrangle to be slightly off from the brick lines, you can simply left click any corner and adjust it to make the grids line up perfectly with the brick. Once you are satisfied with the alignment, hit **Enter**. Photoshop will crop and flatten the perspective all in one step.

Now, if you were to make this into a pattern, it would look odd because the bricks on the edges will show a harsh line where they join to the repeating edge. We will need to paint this to match.

Figure 4.23

Perspective Crop in action.

Making the Seamless Pattern

If you are painting your own repeating pattern, rejoin the discussion here. Go to **Filter > Other > Offset…**. The Offset dialog will appear, and the image will be offset by the pixel number indicated in the sliders. Make sure that Wrap Around is selected in the undefined regions. Adjust the pixels both vertically and horizontally to about half the dimension (Figure 4.24).

So, if you have a 100-pixel square, offset the pixels by 50 in each direction. It's not crucial to do exactly half, but you want to give yourself enough room to paint so that you are not painting too close to an edge. Click **OK**.

You'll notice that the vertical offset is barely visible. We selected well, and the horizontal grout hides the repeat. The horizontal offset is more visible. It looks like we have two little stubby bricks sliced together. So, we need to paint these to

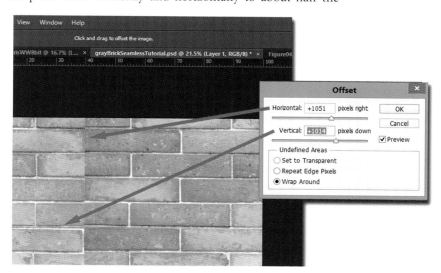

Figure 4.24

Offsetting the pattern.

Figure 4.25

"Healing" the seams.

Figure 4.26

Our pattern in the pattern presets.

look like a single cohesive brick. When I say "paint," I say that in the loosest term, as we'll be using the healing brush to clean up these seams.

Choose the Healing Brush Tool 🖌 and brush along the apparent seams (Figure 4.25). After a few strokes, we can't even find our seams anymore. Just to be sure, offset once more, to a different number, say, a quarter of your dimensions. Go to **Filter** > **Other** > **Offset…** and repeat the offset, but this time with a quarter of your dimensions.

Our pattern still looks seamless. We are good to go. If you are using this for a 3D application or a web application, you have your asset, and you can now leave the room.

But, if you would like to obtain some added value and learn how to make this into a pattern that you can access in Photoshop to fill any canvas or selection, well, read on.

Adding Your Pattern to the Pattern Library

To add your pattern to the pattern library, choose the entire tile by pressing **Ctrl+A/⌘+A** or by going to **Select** > **Select All** in the Menu bar. In the Menu bar, select **Edit** > **Define Pattern…**. Enter a name for the new pattern in the dialog box. Click on the Paint Bucket Tool 🪣, and in the tool options bar, change the fill type to Pattern (Figure 4.26). Does the last one in the palette look familiar?

Now, let's see this pattern in action. Create a new large canvas. You want to be able to see the effects, so you want it to be at least five times as large as your pattern. Select the Paint Bucket Tool 🪣, making sure to switch the fill from Foreground to Pattern in the tool options bar. Apply the pattern by clicking anywhere on the canvas.

Voila! The entire canvas is filled with gray bricks (Figure 4.27). You'll notice that there is a discernible repeating pattern. We can either go back and lighten up the dark bricks that are conveying the pattern or, if we know there will be other layers working with this (such as grunge/dirt, paint, etc.), then we can leave it be—all is good in the world.

8. I Just Want to Get Rid of the Noise in the Photo

Lucky you if you just want to get rid of the noise in the photo. Photoshop has improved its noise-reduction abilities so much so that I almost didn't include this as a tutorial. It sort of feels like cheating. It's just *too easy*.

Open your noisy image. If it is a RAW file, then ACR will automatically open. Stay in ACR, as we'll get rid of the noise using ACR.

If you are opening another file format, you can still do this, but you will need to apply ACR as a filter (Figure 4.28). If your file is already open in Photoshop, select from the **Menu Bar Filter** > **Camera Raw Filter…**. Click on the Detail icon 🔺.

You'll see the Noise Reduction section on the lower half. Click and drag the **Luminance** slider to the right. Don't try to get all the noise out with Luminance, as it

Figure 4.27

Our pattern can fill any vast canvas seamlessly (almost).

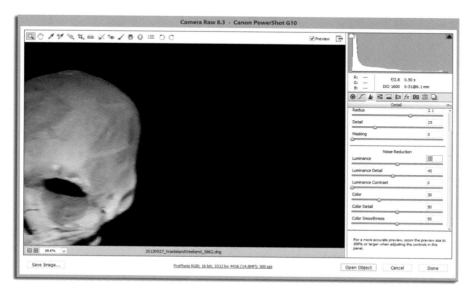

Figure 4.28

ACR noise reduction sliders.

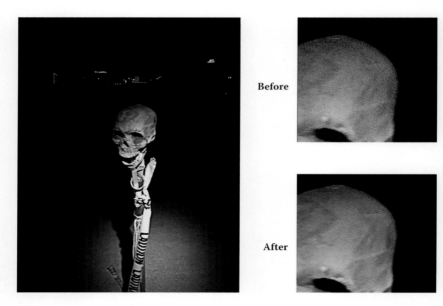

Before

After

Figure 4.29

Before and after noise reduction.

Figure 4.30

Red-eyed and ready for a fix.

can get blurry looking. Switch down to the **Color** slider and slide that to the right also.

If you find that you seem to have found a great setting for reducing noise but things are looking a little flat, you can add in some **Luminance Contrast** and bring back some depth. I rarely use Color Detail and Luminance Detail much more than a smidgen.

Once you have your image looking good (Figure 4.29), just click **OK**.

9. I Just Want to Get Rid of the Red Eye in the Picture

For a long time, lesser packages were offering one-click red-eye reduction, and we of Photoshop loyalty often would sneak into the free Photoshop Elements that was offered with so many printers to just click away the red eye. Now, Photoshop has finally incorporated this one-click wonder into our tools, so no more sneaking around behind Photoshop's back. If you just want to get rid of the red eye in a picture, open your photo of your favorite demon-possessed person or animal. Figure 4.30 shows my favorite demon.

Choose the Red Eye Tool 🔴 found with the healing tools. (Alternatively, press **Shift+J** until the Red Eye Tool cycles up.)

Zoom in to see the eyes clearly. Click drag to cover the area you would like to have affected. A marquee should appear as you are dragging. On release, Photoshop calculates and fixes the red eye (Figure 4.31). That's it! You're done. I told you it would be one click (per eye). Don't forget to save.

10. I Just Want to Make This Picture into Something that Looks More Graphic

OK, so really, this question is more like, "Can I take a picture and make it look like *this* kind of graphic?" Or, "I wish I was artistic enough to create something like *this* [points to some graphic image]." I have to break it to them that it could be done with a photo and a few filters. To which, of course, they ask, "How?"

Here is a tutorial to make a graphic image from a photo. This isn't the easiest of photo-to-graphic conversions, but most people looking at it can't figure out that it was derived from a photo, and I thought it would be better for this section to have a more convincing filter conversion. If you like it, for more of these types of conversion effects, check out Chapters 7, 9, and 11.

For this tutorial, I'll show you how you can get a really nice graphic look with the combination of two filters: Cut Out and Photocopy. Let's apply them to our photo of a Japanese Lantern (Figure 4.32). Press **Ctrl+J/⌘+J** to duplicate the image to another layer, or you could drag the layer to the New Layer icon ⬛ on the layers palette, if you prefer. While we are at it, let's do that one more time so we have two duplicate layers.

Now click on the **first duplicate (layer 1)** to select it. Go to **Filter > Filter Gallery….** The Filter Gallery dialog will open. Choose Cutout from the Artistic category. You will have three sliders to play with. Figure 4.33 shows my settings for this picture, but you can play with your settings until you get something that achieves a similar look. Click **OK** when you are done.

Next, click to the other duplicate layer (layer 2, in my case). We will go to **Filter > Filter Gallery** again, and this time we will choose **Photocopy** under the Sketch category. Figure 4.34 shows my settings for this lantern. There really is no definite recipe to what settings you should use, as it depends on the color and contrast and your own personal taste. When you have it looking the way you want it, click **OK**.

You should have a black-and-white "photocopy" layer over a "cutout" layer. Right now, both are at 100% opacity, so the photocopy is obscuring the cutout layer. With the Photoshop layer containing our photocopy selected, change the layer blend mode to Multiply and reduce the Opacity a bit so it's not so harsh.

Figure 4.31

Better than any eyedrops on the market.

Figure 4.32

Our starting photo of a Japanese lantern.

Figure 4.33

Filter Gallery Cutout settings.

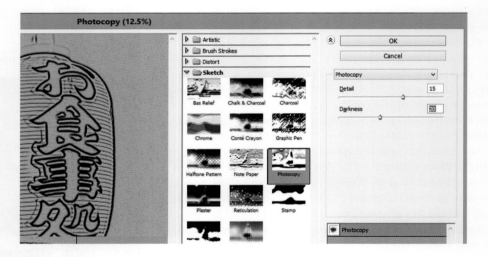

Figure 4.34

Filter Gallery Photocopy settings.

In my case, I have it at 79%. (Really, you could have put it at 80%; it doesn't make that much of a difference, but this is the number it stopped at when I was playing with the slider.)

This is looking like a graphic drawing, but we want to clean the background to have a clean black background. In the Menu bar, go to **Layer > New Adjustment Layer > Levels…** (Figure 4.35). You can name the Level Layer in the ensuing dialog box if you want, or you can accept the default name Levels 1 and click **OK**. Slide the black level indicator to the right just a smidgen so that the background becomes clean. There you go! It now

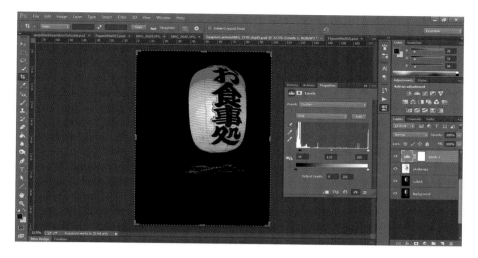

Figure 4.35

Level Adjustment layer.

looks like a perfectly executed graphic image. If you want, you can change the background (see question 6 in this list of top 10 questions to see how to do it) and obtain something that looks like Figure 4.36.

11. I Just Want to Print These All on One Page

Surprisingly, the desire to print on one page involves one of the most common questions I am asked. It is also the most misunderstood question. There are several different aspects to this. Size and resolution are basic concepts, but I meet experienced professionals who still are confused because of messy semantics.

The first and the easiest to solve is when a person is confused about size and resolution. The fastest and easiest way to resolve this is to make sure you are working on a canvas that is the same size as your paper. So, if you are in North America and using your home printer, you probably need "letter size", which is 8.5 × 11 inches.

1. In the Menu bar, choose **New...**.
2. In the ensuing dialog box, change your Preset to U.S. Paper as seen in Figure 4.37.
3. A new drop-down menu will appear that will give you common paper sizes. In my case, I chose Letter. This will automatically set the dimensions to 8.5 × 11 inches.

Figure 4.36

Final Graphic Look image.

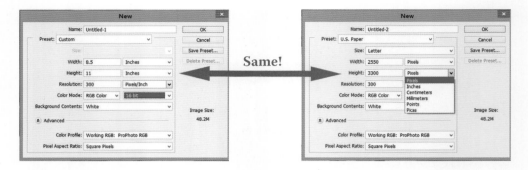

Figure 4.37

Setting paper.

4. Make sure that your Resolution is set to 300 pixels/inch, as that is the standard printing resolution. This means that the document will be 3300 pixels high. For some reason I cannot fathom, many people get stuck on entering the dimensions in anything other than pixels and then are confused when things are resized.

5. Click OK. Now, you should have a document that will print similar to what you see on the screen. Just paste in anything that you want to be on the page, and you are good to go.

6. Once you have everything set up to look the way you would like it to on paper, then just go to the Menu bar and choose **File** > **Print**.

7. When you choose to print, different printers will have differing abilities to print to the edge, so keep that in mind when you plan your page. Many people like to set their page to 8 × 10 inches with 300 dpi so they avoid cutting off or shrinking to fit.

Oops! So you've done all that, and you forgot that this needs to be printed at 300 dpi. Perhaps you were at 150 dpi—oh, what to do? No worries, mate! Photoshop's ability to upsize is so good that you can upsize to 300% of your original and still look pretty good.

Go to **Image** > **Image Size…**. The Image Size dialog will appear. The first fields are Pixel Dimension Width and Height. You can choose to increase by percent or pixels. If you change the value in the field, you will see the other value change to maintain proportions. The image is constrained by default. Let's keep it at percent for now and increase our resolution to 300 dpi, the generally accepted resolution for most printers.

Generally, however, this is not the question the person is really asking. What they *really* want to know is if there is an easier way to print a group of photos onto one sheet without having to resize them, line them up one by one, and so on. In other words, they want a contact sheet.

Well, ask and I shall deliver.

How to Create a Contact Sheet

Let's say you have some hypothetical situation, like you have a book that you are writing, and throughout the book, there are little icons that are printed into the text. You need a way to quickly reference these icons to input the correct icon number into the manuscript.

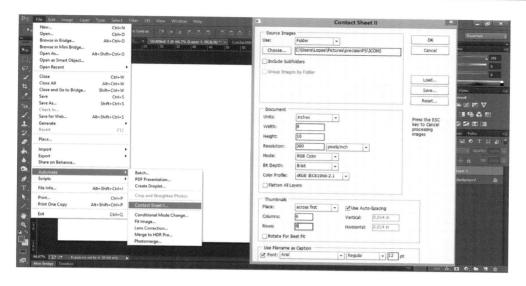

Figure 4.38

Contact Sheet dialog.

You happen to have all the icons numbered and in one folder but would like to have them on a printed page because, well, you're just a little old school in that sense. Of course, this is purely hypothetical, but the answer is not.

1. Go to the Menu bar and choose **File** > **Automate** > **Contact Sheet II**.
2. A dialog box like that in Figure 4.38 will pop up. At the top, you can specify the files you would like to have on the contact sheet either by folder or by choosing specific folders.

You can create the contact sheet (Figure 4.39) from Bridge also. Select the images in Bridge, then go to **Tools** > **Photoshop** > **Contact Sheet II**. The same dialog box that you see in Photoshop will appear, but with the images already selected. If you do not select any images when you launch the Contact Sheet Tool, then Bridge will automatically select all the images in the current folder (excluding subfolders).

---

3. Make sure your document is the proper size, as discussed in the previous part of this section, 8 × 10 inches with 300 dpi. I use Adobe Pro Photo for my Color Profile, as most current printers can handle the profile and it has a much wider gamut than Standard RGB (sRGB), the color profile most used for web graphics. You can also choose in this section to flatten all layers, but I like to have the images and text all on separate layers so I can adjust or tweak it a little before printing.
4. Once you have the images you want to put on your sheet and you know what size your sheet is, you will want to decide how many you would like to place and whether they should be arranged in rows or columns. In the Thumbnails area,

---

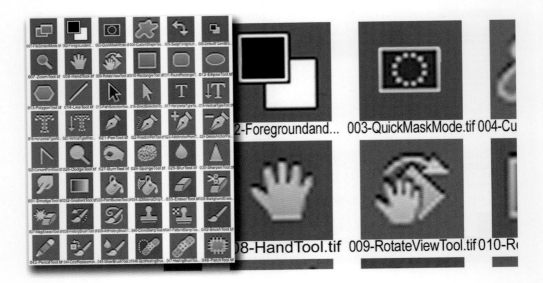

Figure 4.39

Contact Sheets.

if you choose "across first," your images will read like rows: from left to right, one row at a time all the way down. If you choose "down first," then your images will read like columns, from top to bottom, then left to right.

5. Enter the number of columns and rows you want on a sheet. Photoshop will automatically size and space the images for us (that's what the **Use Auto-Spacing** check box is for—keep that checked).

6. The last detail is to have Caption as the file name. If you would like to use the file names as labels, make sure that is checked and select your choice of font and size.

7. Click **OK** when done.

Voila! You now have a well-organized and professional-looking contact sheet of your images.

Wait—there are 11 questions here, and I said these were the top 10 questions. Well, remember, I also said the first one was free. But, since we have 11, let's just make it an even dozen.

12. Aw, These Shadows Ruined My Pictures

"Aw, my pictures are all backlit and ruined." Or, "These shadows ruined my picture" Have no fear. This is an easy problem, especially if you shot in your camera's RAW format.

Open your image in ACR. If you are opening a RAW format image, Photoshop will automatically open it in ACR. If your image is something other than a RAW format, then you can apply ACR as a filter by going to **Filter > Camera Raw Filter**.

Figure 4.40

Not a perfect solution, but who knew we could bring back so much from a "ruined" picture?

Now, go to the Shadows slider in the Exposure section. Drag the Shadows slider way over to the right, and the shadowed areas come back. Of course, this can only be taken so far, but I was amazed at how much this can bring back without flattening and washing out everything (Figure 4.40). Playing with the whites and blacks afterward can help even out the areas.

Click **OK**, and you're done.

5

Going RAW

The RAW "Format"
Working in the RAW: Adobe Camera Raw Workflow/Controls
Merge to HDR Pro

The RAW "Format"

What RAW Is Not

It is a common mistake to think of RAW files as if there were one standardized format. Every camera model saves RAW images in a unique format, but Adobe Camera Raw (ACR) can process many RAW file formats with default image settings based on built-in camera profiles for supported cameras and the EXIF (Exchangeable Image File) data. These RAW files are often referred to as "digital negatives." (This should not be confused with Adobe's RAW format DNG, which stands for Digital Negative and is therefore often called that). Like a negative, the digital negative cannot be used directly as an image but has all the information needed to create an image. It preserves the data captured by the sensor, along with other environmental information of the capture called *metadata*. These metadata can include exposure settings, date, whether a flash was used, camera lens, color profile, and so on. In the case of motion picture film scans, the time code, key code, and frame number in file sequence also can be included.

Figure 5.1

Some RAW files have an XMP sidecar.

Some RAW files need an XMP (eXtensible Metadata Platform) sidecar that stores all the metadata and RAW settings, but Adobe's RAW format, DNG, the file format used in ACR, stores it in the file itself (Figure 5.1).

So What's the Big Deal about RAW?

The benefit of working with RAW files is that you have the maximum data you can obtain from the sensor, and you are able to determine how these data should be interpreted instead of having some automatic conversion making those calls for you. What's more, whenever you make adjustments to an image in ACR, such as sharpening, adjusting exposure, applying a filter, or even using the spot removal, it is nondestructive. So, you can edit to your heart's content, export the edited image, and keep the original intact for future use or other adjustments.

RAW files in general will also have higher image quality. Because of the wider gamut of information contained in the image file, there will be more information in the shadows and highlights, for example, allowing for more precise and specific manipulations. Most RAW conversion software such as ACR allows for finer control and has more parameters because of this and works with better algorithms to calculate these changes out, resulting in fewer artifacts.

Photoshop now has the ability to open other files, such as JPGs and TIFFs with ACR. But, unlike RAW files, if you edit a JPG or TIFF in ACR, you still affect the actual pixels of the original image. You would be better off applying the ACR filter as a smart filter if you wish to make an ACR adjustment to a non-RAW image. But, that still does not beat shooting and adjusting in an actual RAW file itself. Remember that any time you have anything that is *not* a RAW file format, you are dealing with something that has already been interpreted by some process. Ergo, it is possible information has already been obliterated. Manipulating with ACR afterward cannot bring back that information.

Why Not Always Keep Everything in RAW?

So, why not always work in RAW? Essentially, you have to weigh practical considerations and situational considerations (Figure 5.2). Camera RAW file sizes are typically two to six times larger than JPG files. And, in the world of electronics, size matters—a lot. Really, you don't need this kind of quality for your Twitterfeeds or Facebook posts, right? Also, beyond storage or sending, you have to consider how it affects memory while working on the image.

Speaking of working on an image, you are reading this book because in the end you want to work on your image in Photoshop and access all the wonderful tools and capabilities that Photoshop has to offer. ACR can only work to a certain level in the RAW format.

Once you are working in Photoshop, you will probably save files as PSD files, and then when you save out a copy of your final image for your client, you will probably use a widely accepted standardized format such as TIFF or JPG.

Figure 5.2

Which images do you really want in RAW format?

Why Should I Use RAW Again?

Why should you use RAW? It's like going to university or having money: It gives you more options. And, the better start you can have, the easier it will be for you in the future.

With that in mind, let me show you some of the main adjustments of ACR.

Adobe recommends that you adjust settings in ACR from top to bottom: White Balance to Saturation. In general, that's a good workflow, so let's start there.

Working in the RAW: Adobe Camera Raw Workflow/Controls

White Balance

Even with a studio shot, or with your camera set to Auto White Balance (AWB), sometimes there is an unwanted colorcast that you need to adjust. A colorcast may be induced

Figure 5.3

Adobe Camera Raw dialog.

by the misinterpretation of the subject matter where a neutral average isn't apparent for adjustment of the camera's algorithm.

ACR has some built-in White Balance presets; you can get rid of the blue tint of outdoor shade, or the green tinge of fluorescence, for example. By default, ACR will set your White Balance to "As Shot." If you click on the White Balance field, a pull-down menu will appear with all of your options (Figure 5.3). Your options are As Shot, Auto, Daylight, Cloudy, Shade, Tungsten, Fluorescent, Flash, and Custom. But, if you are opening ACR on a non-RAW image, you will find that you only have a limited selection: As Shot or Auto.

Click through to quickly check the effects of each option and choose one of the presets that works best. Then, continue fine-tuning it by adjusting and tweaking Temperature and Tint. You'll notice that as soon as you make a change to any of the sliders, the White Balance field changes to Custom.

Another way to quickly adjust the white balance is to use the White Balance Tool ✐. It's the third button from the left in the top tool panel of ACR. Click on the tool and then click in your picture on something that should be a neutral light but not white color. The ideal would be to click on something you know is 18% gray, but unless you have a card in the picture, you just have to eye it. The good news is that you are not receiving a grade for this, and you can click in different areas and try repeatedly as often as you would like until you feel it's good. Then, you can still adjust the Tint and Temperature to tweak it even more (Figure 5.4).

Remember, this wasn't to send a perfect picture out the door (although that can happen); this was just the first step.

(Indecent) Exposure

There is a reason why White Balance is the first control in ACR and Exposure is the second. These two controls alone can make a picture go from "meh" to "OMG." The Exposure slider will adjust your midtones so you obtain an overall feel of lightness and darkness, emulating increasing and decreasing the exposure settings on a camera. Just as Tint and Temperature were part of the White Balance, Contrast, Highlight, Shadows, Whites, and Blacks all help with perceived exposure (Figure 5.5).

Usually when we want to adjust the exposure, it is because the image is either too washed out or too dark. So, it seems elementary to slide the exposure to the right to brighten and to the left to darken. Often, this results in a somewhat flat-looking image. Adjusting the Contrast here in exposure will help with that and bring back some depth by making the bright areas brighter and the dark areas darker. Do not confuse this Contrast with Photoshop's Contrast in **Image > Adjust > Brightness/Contrast**; I have to think these two use different algorithms as they seem to behave quite differently.

Now, if you have played enough video games to have developed exceptional peripheral vision, you may have noticed these little lights going off on the histogram—specifically those little poo symbols up in the corner. Yes, you read that right. I said *poo*. In every reference I have read, they refer to those little clipping warning symbols as "triangles." You can take a closer look for yourself, but I distinctly see something that is not a smooth sharp triangle. But, let's put the shape discussion aside and take a look at the clipping warning (Figure 5.6).

Before

After

Figure 5.4

Corrected color cast before and after.

If your warning triangle is black, then nothing is being clipped. But, if it changes to any other color, then that means that one of those color values is being clipped. Each color indicates a particular channel being clipped, and if it is white, then all channels are being clipped.

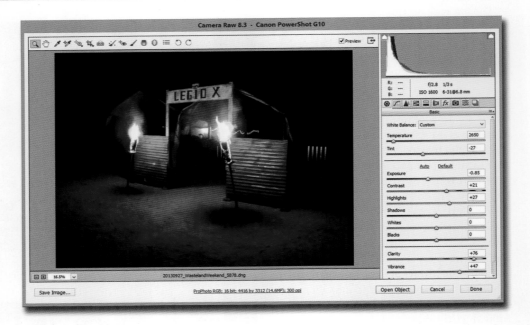

Figure 5.5

The exposure settings in ACR.

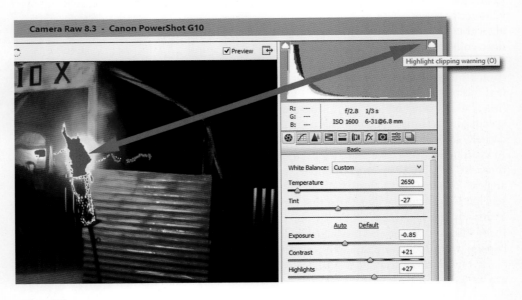

Figure 5.6

Do you see the warning "triangle"?

Clicking on the triangle symbol will highlight the clipped areas, and you can see if there is something you need to worry about. If there is, you can adjust highlight, shadows, whites, and blacks to bring it back down a bit.

When You Do Not Really Need to Adjust Exposure

Sometimes, you might think you need to really crank the exposure to bring out the details in the shadows, but Adobe's shadows control in ACR are pretty good on their own. Check out tutorial 12 ("Aw, These Shadows Ruined My Pictures") in Chapter 4 to see it in action.

A Moment of Clarity

It's amazing what a moment of clarity can give you. In this case, just upping the Clarity slider in ACR can do wonders. What exactly is it? How does it work? The simplest answer is that it adjusts the contrast in the midtones. Some call this "local contrast." So, you can really pop textures without blowing out the image and obtain that really hi-definition gritty look that is the look du jour. In most cases, photographs will benefit from touching in about 10 points of clarity on the slider.

Going the other way also can be of great benefit. I find that if I am working with beauty shots, I like to bring down the clarity by quite a bit. This softens the skin and will reduce the contrast without coming across as blurry (Figure 5.7).

Vibrance versus Saturation

I am often asked what the difference between vibrance and saturation is. I like to think of vibrance as a smarter saturation (Figure 5.8). Whereas saturation pushes up the intensity of colors uniformly, vibrance increases the vividness of the muted colors more than saturated colors and works to avoid saturating skin tones (orange tones). I once heard someone call it a "fill light" for saturation, and I think that's a nice way to think of it.

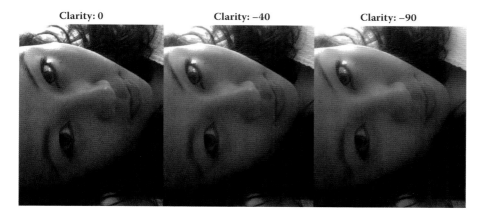

Figure 5.7

Lowering clarity gives a softness perfect for beautiful skin.

Figure 5.8

Vibrance versus saturation.

Figure 5.9

Landscapes come alive with saturation.

Vibrance is great for increasing the vividness of photos with people, as it does not increase the skin tones to that strange 1980s tan orange color that happens with saturation. In fact, I rarely like to increase saturation because I feel it often ruins a picture more than improves it. The exceptions are landscape photos; the overall boost, especially in the greens and blues, really helps many landscape photos (Figure 5.9).

You can make a tremendous difference with just the basic panel of ACR. Of course, the other nine tabs all have value of their own, but let me go over some of the main ones I use the most.

Detail/Sharpening

When your camera shoots a JPG, it is actually still capturing in RAW and converting it to JPG. No sheep, Sherlock, right? But, what most people seem to forget or don't know is that the conversion includes quite a bit of sharpening. So, if we are working from an ACR file, we want to make sure we add at least a little sharpening to the image. ACR already adds in a little by default (continuing the ignorance of users to the existence of sharpening to their image).

Click on the Details tab ▲ to access the Detail panel. The Detail panel will look something like Figure 5.10. The first section is *Sharpening*. The Amount slider determines how much sharpening is applied, but often cranking this up will result in "halos"—a light outline along the edges. This is because sharpening is the end effect of edge contrast being enhanced. If the edge area being considered is too wide, then halos are created.

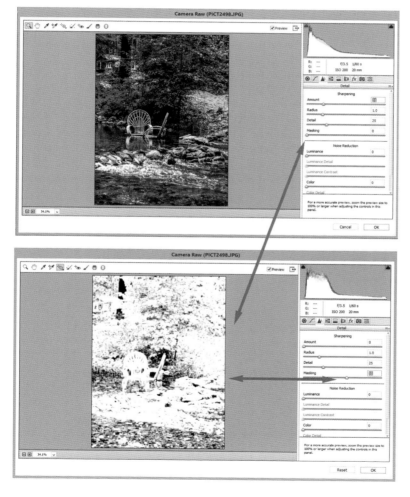

Figure 5.10

Alt+Drag/Option+Drag on the Masking slider to see mask.

Hence, the next slider is used: *Radius*. The default of 1 pixel will work for most consumer images, but with more people bringing in photos from their phones, you still might find the sharpening "sensitive." On the other hand, with current professional digital single-lens reflex (SLR) cameras shooting at over 24 megapixels (MP), you might need to increase the radius.

I thought it was odd to have a *Details* slider in the Details tab—it makes it seem like this would be the slider of increasing the amount of sharpening, you know, bringing out the details. What the Detail slider is used for is to determine the level of sharpening: lower will sharpen only larger clearer edges, and higher settings will bring out finer edges.

Masking acts like suppression or a limit to what is sharpened. Often, there are particular sections of the photo that need sharpening and you don't want to have to apply the sharpening to the entire image. **Alt+Drag**/**Option+Drag** on the slider and you can see the mask change; white represents where the sharpening is being applied.

Let's Not Be Noisy

Noise changes depending on exposure, camera, tonal weights within the composition, and whether you are shooting digital or film. Noise is composed of two types: color (or chroma) and luminance. ACR addresses both color and luminance noise. The effects of these sliders are best seen when you are at more than 100%, so make sure you zoom in while adjusting these sliders (Figure 5.11). Clearing some of the noise will distinguish your images as more professional—the trick is not to overdo it and lose the details in an image.

By default, ACR applies a reduction of color noise (25) but leaves the luminance slider at 0. This is because reduction of the color noise doesn't generally cause the kind of loss of detail that the reduction of luminance noise does, and most images can benefit from

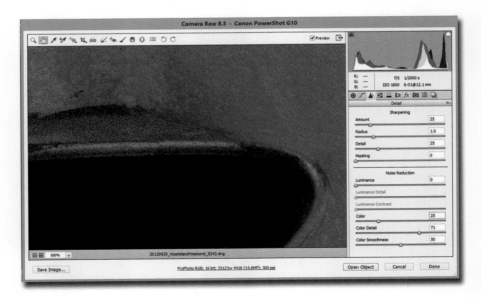

Figure 5.11

Noise reduction is best seen zoomed in.

a slight reduction in color noise anyway. Under both Luminance and Color, there are detail sliders. These control the noise threshold. Increasing the Color Detail may remove color speckles but may result in color bleeding. Increasing Luminance Detail will preserve more detail, but noise may still be visible, and lower values produce cleaner results but you may lose detail.

Noise has been the bane of my existence for a long while. And, as good as the noise reduction tools are, it takes a bit of know-how and finesse to get rid of noise nicely. Check out the tutorials in Chapter 10 to see some of the methods gleaned from years of experience.

Lens Correction

All cameras have some type of imperfection that the lens introduces to the captured image. In most cases, applying the proper lens correction will benefit the photograph. Doing so could get rid of vignetting (darkening near the corners of the frame), barrel or pincushion distortion (curving of otherwise-straight lines), or chromatic aberration and color fringing ("rainbows" near edges of objects in photos).

ACR can detect what type of camera was used and apply the proper lens correction (Figure 5.12). Click on the Lens Corrections tab 🖿 to see the panel dialog. Once you click the Enable Lens Profile Corrections, ACR will automatically access the metadata to find what lens correction to apply, display these data in the Lens Profile section, and reflect the changes in the preview. This will work for most cameras, but occasionally either the metadata have been deleted or the profile is not recognized for some other reason. If so, you can manually choose your camera by choosing your make and model in the Lens Profile drop-down menus. You can override the default settings with the sliders in the Correction Amount section. If you are experiencing chromatic aberrations, you can

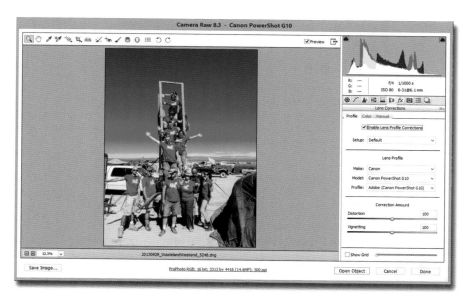

Figure 5.12

Lens correction.

Figure 5.13

Fixing chromatic aberrations.

reduce them in the Color Tab. Remember that Chromatic Aberrations are like noise—it is best to see the results if you are zoomed in to about 200% or so. Luckily, in most cases just clicking the Remove Chromatic Aberrations check box will do the trick (Figure 5.13). In addition, you can use the Manual tab to create manual transforms. This can be useful if you find you need some additional warping or perspective adjustments

---

Some cameras have the ability to apply lens correction before exporting. If your images seem "off" after lens correction, you might want to look into it to see if lens correction was already applied.

Merge to HDR Pro

What is an HDRI? And, does it need to be 32 bit? What does this have to do with RAW? HDRI stands for high-dynamic-range imaging or image. The dynamic range of an image is the ratio of luminosity between minimum values of the darkest regions and maximum values of the lightest regions. Our eyes can see detail in shadows and highlights and adapt to different brightness levels that are difficult to fully reproduce using digital equipment. Photoshop, via HDR Pro, can merge several standard photos (LDRI, low-dynamic-range images) into a single 32-bit HDRI that more accurately represents the extended luminosity tonal range of the scene (Figure 5.14). This in turn can be tone mapped to a LDRI with specific control for greater detail. You can consult Chapter 12 to see which file formats support HDRI.

When starting this type of operation, I generally like to start from Bridge so I can see and select the images I want to merge before selecting **Tools > Photoshop > Merge**

to HDR Pro…. You can also go from within Photoshop by going to **File** > **Automate** > **Merge to HDR Pro….** in the menu bar, but you'll have to browse to find the images you want to use once the dialog box opens. If you already have them in one folder, then you might as well launch them from Bridge, as shown in Figure 5.15.

Regardless of how you got there, once you have your files you want to make sure the **Attempt To Automatically Align Source**

Figure 5.14

Several LDRIs can be merged to create a single HDRI.

Images is checked. This will help reduce ghosting that might appear because of the imprecise lining up of the images. HDR Pro will not allow pictures of different sizes to be used, so make sure they are the same size. For optimal results, use a tripod and bracket them every one or two stops. Obviously, the more images you have, the better it will be, but the minimum should be three. Remember that Merge to HDR Pro only works with differently exposed images of the identical scene. Click **OK** when you are ready.

The Merge to HDR Pro dialog will appear with the default settings applied. At the bottom of the dialog, there are thumbnails of all the images you selected along with their Exposure Value (EV). To the right of the main image, you will see the dialog with a wide range of adjustment sliders.

Right under presets, you'll see a check box, **Remove Ghosts**. If something moved between exposures, it can appear as a ghost image. If you see some ghosting, checking

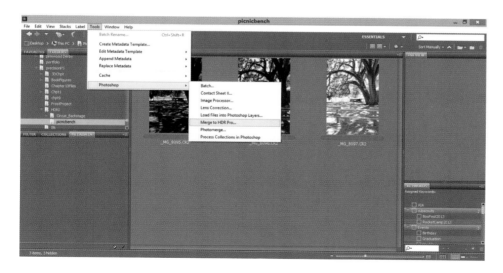

Figure 5.15

Selecting images and merging to HDR Pro from Bridge.

this box can help, but it may introduce some unwanted noise; so depending on what is ghosting, you might want to leave it and retouch it later.

So, then the question is, do you *have* to have it be 32 bit? Frankly, yes. Only a 32-bit floating-point numeric can hold all the information that is needed for a true HDRI. However, not all features are supported at 32 bits. You can save out the 32-bit image first, then work on a copy in 16 bit to access some of the functionality. But, your 32-bit image should always be your master. Let's say you know you are going to work in 16 bit. Then, you would obtain the best results by adjusting the image in the HDR Pro dialog. Change your mode to 16 bit and you obtain a plethora of tools in the HDR Pro dialog to balance out your image for your needs. Figure 5.16 shows the HDR Pro dialog for 32 bit, and Figure 5.17 shows the HDR Pro dialog for 16 bit.

Keep **Local Adaptation** for the conversion method. The gurus at Photoshop have tried to make sure that the sliders appear in the order they should be used, and I generally find that, at least for the first few sliders, they are spot on.

Edge Glow sliders: The key here is to find the right balance between the two sliders. Think of defining tonal regions in an image. If the light and dark areas are large and distinct, start with the radius rather high so Photoshop will calculate contrast within each region more pleasingly. If the lighter and darker areas are more entangled, a lower radius would serve better. The Radius slider defines the size of the tonal calculations, and the Strength slider controls the contrast or the intensity of the edge. Ignore the **Edge Smoothness** toggle box right now. We'll come back after adjusting the other parameters.

Gamma: Gamma defines the relationship between a pixel's numerical value and its actual luminance. Therefore, technically, any HDRI would have a gamma of 1. But, the Gamma slider here is more about setting the balance. Knowing that, adjust the Gamma to set the contrast of your midtones. You may not have to touch this at all.

Exposure: The Exposure slider controls the overall exposure, much in the same way as ACR. Dragging to the right brightens and dragging to the left darkens.

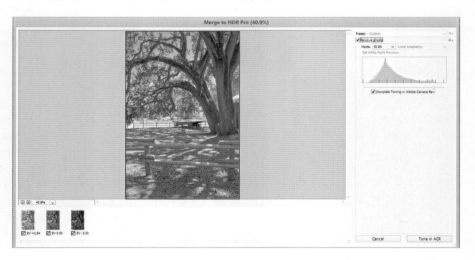

Figure 5.16

Merge to HDR Pro dialog for true HDRI 32 bit.

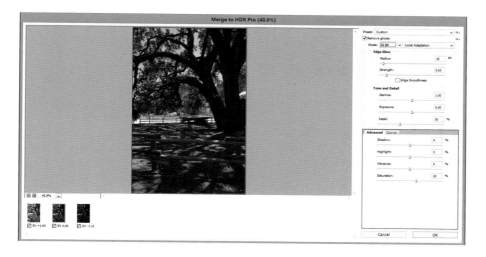

Figure 5.17

Merge to HDR Pro dialog for 16-bit conversion.

Details: This slider works similarly to ACR's Clarity slider. You can really exaggerate this for that "HDR look."

Once you have it where you think you would like it, you can tweak more sliders under the Advanced tab. The Shadow and Highlight, Saturation, and Vibrance are there for additional tweaks, and they work much like the ACR sliders.

Let's go back to the **Edge Smoothness** box we skipped previously. Click on the **Edge Smoothness** check box. You'll see a nice overall change with smoothness and details. You might have to readjust and retweak some of the sliders, but changes should be minor.

Choose **Save As** from the File menu and name your file. Make sure you are saving it in an HDR-compatible format. You are done! This doesn't mean that you can't adjust more in ACR or even in Photoshop. But, now you have a master HDRI. What does this have to do with RAW? I have seen loads of tutorials on how to create an HDRI from a single RAW file. These fall into one of two categories: the ones that are trying to develop the HDRI look or the ones that try to fake multiple exposures and more information.

Because a single RAW file only contains data captured by the sensors for *one* exposure, that means the dynamic range you can reconstruct can never really be more than what your camera can capture. This is in effect an exercise in tone mapping, and your single RAW file is your HDRI. The single image may not have the range that you obtain from a multiple-exposure true HDRI, but the RAW file has more information than a printer or monitor can display. So, it comes down to why you need the HDRI. If you need it for a source in visual effects for a movie, the "trick" mentioned wouldn't work. VFX will need to access the layers of data. If you are just trying to get out a single picture, then you could "develop" your single RAW photo into what would look like an HDRI.

Painting on HDRIs

HDRIs are often used for image-based lighting in three dimensions (3D), and high-end productions such as feature films will sometimes need HDRIs painted. This is a tricky

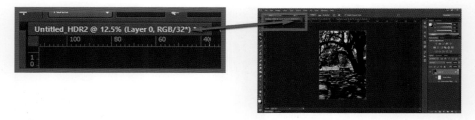

Figure 5.18

Your bit depth is displayed in your Picture tab.

endeavor because you can't just paint on it the way you would paint on a standard painting in Photoshop.

When painting on an HDRI, you need to paint at different exposure settings and keep track of how it looks at the same time. You are also somewhat limited as to what you can use to paint because the tools to paint on 32-bit images are limited.

Here is a list of tools you can use on 32-bit images: Blur, Brush, Eraser, Gradient, History Brush, Stamp tools, Smudge, and Sharpen.

To start, you would open your HDRI as you would any other file: **File > Open...**. Your image name should show that it is a 32-bit image (see Figure 5.18). If it does not show 32 bit, then check your file; it probably is not a true HDRI. Changing the mode to 32 will not make it suddenly HDR, so don't do it. (This should be obvious, but you'd be surprised how many artists I have had to reprimand who thought they could get away with that.)

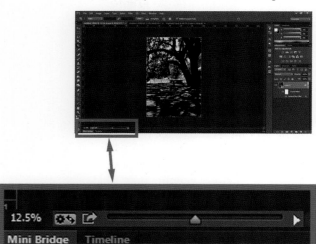

At the bottom of your workspace, change your status bar to show 32-bit Exposure (see Figure 5.19). This is a pre-view adjustment so you can see how your painting is affecting the different exposures. Any time you want to see the default exposure, just **double-click** on the slider.

Often when I need to paint an HDRI, it is because something is coming through at a certain exposure that the director does not want to see or wants to see more of at another exposure level. So, you may want to see the image under a specific setting. In that case, go to **View > 32-Bit Preview Options...**. In the dialog box, you can use the sliders or input a specific number in your gamma or exposure settings (see Figure 5.20).

I want to show you a case for which we want to have some of these highlights be a little more readable in the lower exposures. Normally, I would just sample the color of

Figure 5.19

Status bar set to show 32-bit Exposure slider at bottom of workspace.

the highlights, slide across to a lighter color, and paint in the extra highlights. But, to do this properly so it reads in the different exposures, you want to use the **HDR Color Picker**

Figure 5.20

A 32-bit Preview Options dialog box.

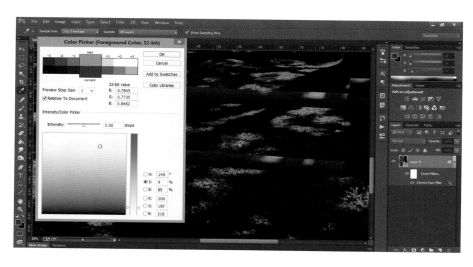

Figure 5.21

HDR Color Picker dialog.

and use the intensity slider to adjust the brightness. Click on the foreground color and you will see the HDR Color Picker dialog (see Figure 5.21).

When you choose a color, the Preview area lets you see how the selected color will display at different exposures. If you adjust the intensity with the intensity slider, Photoshop will calculate the proper 32-bit value. Take a look at Figure 5.22. On the left, I have chosen a color the traditional way, by just choosing a lighter color for painting. On the right, I have chosen a lighter color by increasing the intensity. You can see how

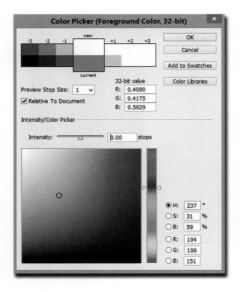
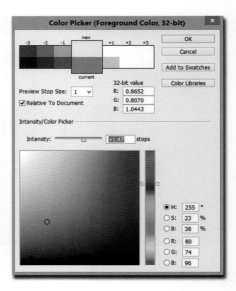

Figure 5.22

Comparison of painting with color chosen from standard color picker.

Figure 5.23

RAW and HDR go hand in hand.

the preview shows different stops—and how the colors differ from my original pick. If I were to paint with the first method, the paint would be apparent at different exposure levels.

The bottom line with painting HDRIs for high-end use (Figure 5.23) is to keep tracking the different exposures. Slide around often and make sure the changes you make work for other exposures.

Another trick you can use to keep track of all the exposures is to open the document in several windows and have them at different exposures and magnifications. To do so, go to **Window > Arrange > New Window for filename** to open simultaneous views. Set the exposure preview slider for each window to a different setting and, if applicable, change the magnification. Changes done on one will be updated to all the others.

6

One-Night Stands

Introduction

The tutorials in this chapter are a different kind of quickie; they involve higher concepts, require specific source images, or require a bit more artistic finesse. None of these tutorials will take more than one night, so they're perfect for some fun after work.

Spacescape

I think our first one-night stand should indulge in a little fantasy—space fantasy, that is. We'll do it from scratch, with no photography and no real painting skills required. What? How do we make a painting with almost no painting and no photos? This is what makes Photoshop so fantastic my young Padawan.

   Make a new file of the size of your choice. You don't want it too small, so say it should be larger than 1K (1024 pixels) wide. Once it opens, create a new layer by clicking on the New Layer Icon  in the Layers palette.

Select the Elliptical Marquee ⬭, and while holding down **Alt+Shift**/**Option+Shift**, click and drag out a perfect circle selection. Before we go to the next action, hit **D** so that you have the default foreground and background colors (Pure Black and Pure White).

While the selection is still active, go to **Filter** > **Render** > **Clouds**. You should obtain something that looks like Figure 6.1.

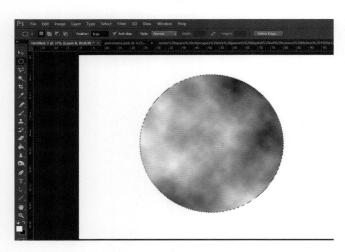

Figure 6.1

And just like that, you have a moon.

Notice that the selection is still active. Create another new empty layer by clicking on the New Layer icon ⬚ in the Layers palette, and this time go to the Gradient Tool ▣. Your colors should still be black and white. Choose the Radial Gradient in the Option bar and click drag to obtain something like Figure 6.2.

Go to **Image** > **Adjustments** > **Levels…** and adjust the levels to obtain something similar to Figure 6.3. We want to save this as a channel for selection further in the process. Finally, you can deselect the circle by pressing **Ctrl+D**/**⌘+D**. Change the background to pure black so your sphere looks like it is slightly backlit. Click over to the Channels palette behind the Layers palette and click on one of the channels (it doesn't matter which one because this begins as a black-and-white image). In the pull-down menu, choose

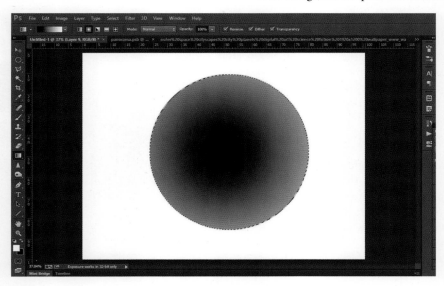

Figure 6.2

Using a gradient to shade the planet.

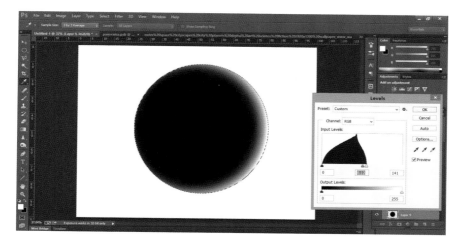

Figure 6.3

Refining the gradient with Levels.

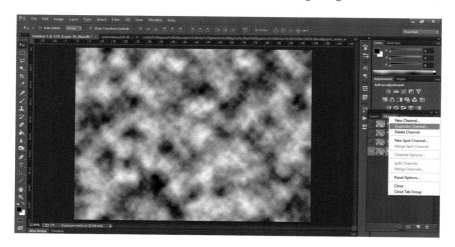

Figure 6.4

Clouds created and saved as Bump alpha.

Duplicate Channel…. Save it as "Planet Glow." Click back onto the RGB (red-green-blue) channel, then return to your Layers palette.

Make another new layer (that's right, that little New Layer button ▣ in the Layers palette again). This time, we will fill our canvas with the clouds. Go to **Filter** > **Render** > **Clouds**. Your layer should fill with black-and-white clouds such as those in Figure 6.4. Click over to the Channels palette behind the Layers palette and click on one of the channels, such as Blue. In the Channels pull-down menu ▦, choose **Duplicate Channel….** You can name it anything you want, but I'll foreshadow a bit and call it Bump. Once Photoshop has created the alpha channel, click on RGB and go back to the Layers palette.

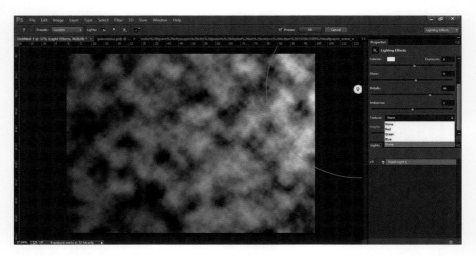

Figure 6.5

Applying the Bump alpha in lighting effects.

You should still be on the Cloud layer. Go to **Filter > Render > Lighting Effects…**. Make sure you are on Point Light and click to move the light just off to the right of the canvas. Scroll down the Properties tab until you get to the Texture section. From the pull-down menu, you should be able to choose your new alpha (Figure 6.5).

Was Lighting Effects grayed out? It could be that you are not in 8 bit; check your mode and make sure you are in 8-bit RGB (**Image > Mode**). Still grayed out? If you have Photoshop CC, there are some known issues with the graphics card. Go to **Edit > Preferences > Performance** and make sure your Graphics Processor Settings show that your card is being recognized, and that you have Use Graphics Processor on.

Figure 6.6

Looks like a moonscape, doesn't it?

You should notice your clouds now suddenly look like a moonscape. Play with the Texture Height, Light position, and characteristics and you should have something like Figure 6.6. For us to use this, we need to make it look less like a head-on flat shot; with the moonscape layer still selected, go to **Edit > Transform > Perspective** and adjust the perspective until it looks like Figure 6.7.

Next, use the Liquify filter (**Filter > Liquify…**) to bulge and pinch and move it around until you can squint and see mountains (Figure 6.8). Click **OK**.

Are you ready to start assembling our spacescape? Select the cloudy round sphere and go to **Select > Load Selection…** and load in the Planet Glow alpha you saved previously. Once you see the crawling ants, click on the Layer Mask ▣ in the Layers palette to apply it as a layer

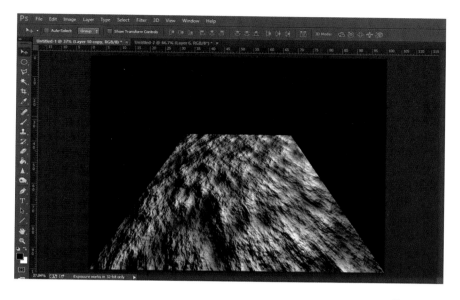

Figure 6.7

Distorting the moonscape.

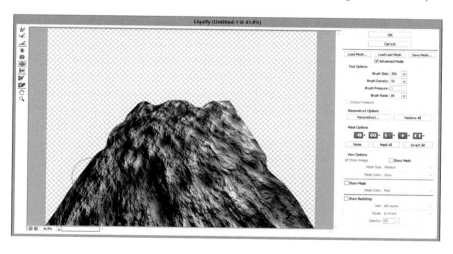

Figure 6.8

Liquify dialog.

mask to your sphere. Press **Ctrl+J/⌘+J** twice to duplicate your "planet"; you can transform them so that they are three different sizes. Use **Edit > Transform > Scale** or the shortcut **Ctrl+T/⌘+T**. Hold **Shift** while scaling to make sure your planets stay perfectly circular. Compose the three planets together. Remember to reduce the opacity of the farther one so that it gives the effect of atmospheric distance. You can see how my three planets look in Figure 6.9.

Figure 6.9

The start of our planets.

Figure 6.10

Gradient overlay options for the sky.

Make a new layer above all the planets (**Ctrl+Shift+N**/⌘**+Shift+N**) and select the Gradient Tool 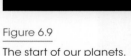. Make sure it is reset to linear gradient between foreground and background and make a sky color of your choice. Test how it will look by changing the gradient's layer mode to Linear Dodge. Figure 6.10 shows how two different gradients look with my planets. I decided to go for the evening look over the dawn look.

Next, either cut out a section of your moonscape or duplicate the whole layer and place it over the planets. Reduce the opacity to half and change the layer mode to Overlay. Use your method of choice to erase most of the texture so that just a hint of planetary atmosphere or geography is visible. You can use a layer mask or just erase it, whichever way comes easier to you. Depending on how you laid out your planets, you may need to paint in a shadow or darken the dark side to be more in shadow. Take a look at mine to this point in Figure 6.11.

Figure 6.11

Overlaying texture on planets.

We could at this point add in a flying ship and some stars and call it a day. But, just to show how easily you can paint in scenery, we'll add in a tree line and reflective water. Choose an almost black color and a rough brush. You can see in Figure 6.12 that I squashed an existing brush and just scrubbed it up and down in a zigzagging motion across the horizon. My brush was at 30%, so with a few swipes it looks like I have water beneath the trees.

Figure 6.12

Creating shadowy landscape.

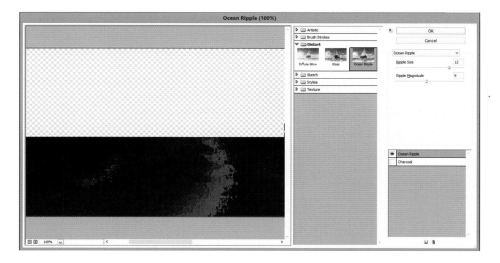

Figure 6.13

Filter Gallery.

Using the Rectangular Marquee ▦, I have selected a section of the sky to reflect into the water. **Ctrl+Shift+C/⌘+Shift+C** will copy it to the clipboard, and **Ctrl+V/⌘+V** will paste it into a new layer on top. I have reduced the opacity to 70% and used Free Transform to give a little perspective and to flip it to a mirror image. To give a ripple effect, first let's apply the Ocean Ripple filter. Go to **Filter > Filter Gallery...** and apply the Ocean Ripple filter as you see in Figure 6.13. Click **OK**.

Figure 6.14

Our finished spacescape.

Figure 6.15

So many pictures and so many planes of focus.

Next, go to **Filter > Distort > ZigZag** and give it a good amount of pond ripples. That's about all you need. Behold! You have created worlds (Figure 6.14).

Auto-Blend to Sharpen

There are times when we do not want an entire image sharpened. Many people would then use a mask to sharpen just the parts they wanted to sharpen, but sometimes the project just isn't that simple. If you have had experience with macrophotography, which involves many close-up shots, you may obtain something in which the shallow depth of field has caused some part of the picture to be blurry that you really wanted to be sharp. Then, you have a bunch of photos with each having one thing or another out of focus and none of them quite right. This is not exclusive to macrophotography, although it is definitely more prevalent in this case. It could have been that your contacts were dry and you had a hard time focusing the lens. Or, perhaps you relied on the autofocus; when you arrived home, you found a bunch of photos with none perfectly clear. We will use a method of merging multiple images focused on different planes to create a single image that appears to have a wider depth of field.

Load the images in Photoshop as layers. You can use your own series of photos or download the series that you see in Figure 6.15 from our website. When dealing with multiple photos that you know you are going to want to have as one Photoshop file, you can load them as such automatically through Bridge.

In Bridge, select your images, then go to **Tools > Photoshop > Load Files into Photoshop Layers…**. A file will be created in Photoshop with each photo in its own layer and its file name as the layer name (Figure 6.16). Nifty, eh?

If you take a look at these images, they are not perfectly aligned. There is just a bit of offset, and we will need to correct this before we sharpen.

Select all the layers, **Ctrl+Alt+A/⌘+Option+A**. Then, choose **Edit > Auto-Align Layers…**. In the ensuing dialog box (Figure 6.17), make sure that you have Automatic selected and click OK.

Figure 6.16

Loading multiple files into one Photoshop file from Bridge.

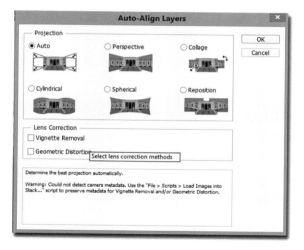

Figure 6.17

Auto-Align Layers dialog.

It might take some time for Photoshop to compute and get all the layers aligned. Your result should look something like Figure 6.18.

Let's continue to sharpen the image. Make sure you still have all your layers selected or just press layers **Ctrl+Alt+A**/⌘**+Option+A** to select them all again. Now, go to **Edit > Auto-Blend Layers…**. Make sure you have Stack Images chosen (Figure 6.19). Check the box for Seamless Tones and Colors, then click **OK**.

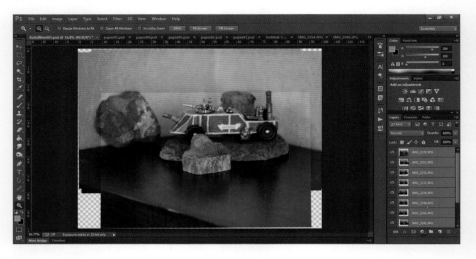

Figure 6.18

The result of Auto-Aligning.

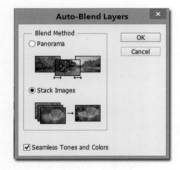

Figure 6.19

The Auto-Blend dialog; make sure you have Stack Images selected.

Photoshop beautifully sharpens based on the layers you brought in, making it seem like there is a wider depth of field than was originally shot. At this point, what you want to do with it is up to you. Because this is a separate file, you can flatten and save, or you can save a copy and keep this PSD file with the generated mattes for tweaking further. You will probably have to crop in to get rid of the excess "flaps" and either heal or bring in specific parts to clean up the final image (Figure 6.20). But, considering the complexity of the original task, this system will get you to a good point much faster than hand painting in the different layers and give better results than just sharpening one image.

Figure 6.20

One clearer image.

Create a Panorama

In the previous tutorial, we loaded images into a single Photoshop document, then aligned the photos, then blended them together—a three-step process. And, maybe during that time you noticed a few panorama options. Well, before you start exploring that road, let me show you a shortcut. Photoshop's Photomerge does all three in one step.

Go to **File** > **Automate** > **Photomerge…**. A dialog will appear that looks strangely familiar, right? Figure 6.21 shows the dialog. Along the left edge of the dialog box, you'll see choices for the layout of the images. Auto is always a great place to start. Usually, Auto can figure it out, but you can always try one of the other options if it comes out wonky.

A couple of other choices are at the bottom. Blend Images Together creates intricate Layer Masks. The edges of these masks are intelligently along edges that have similar tone and color and thus usually help line up images. If you do not choose to blend the images, it is in effect just an Auto-Align with overlapping edges.

If your images have darkened corners and you haven't removed these vignettes in Lightroom or Adobe Camera Raw (ACR) (lens correction), check the box for Vignette Removal. If there is a lens profile for the lens you used, the vignette will be cured.

Likewise, Geometric Distortion Correction will compensate for fish eye, barrel, or pincushion distortions in the individual images.

For your source files, you can choose an entire folder or selectively choose your files by browsing to their location (Figure 6.22). I chose three images and pressed **OK**. The files are imported, placed, warped, corrected, toned, and masked—all in one go. Notice, however, that the horizon is curved. There are several ways to correct this, as there always are several ways to do things in Photoshop. Let me show you two.

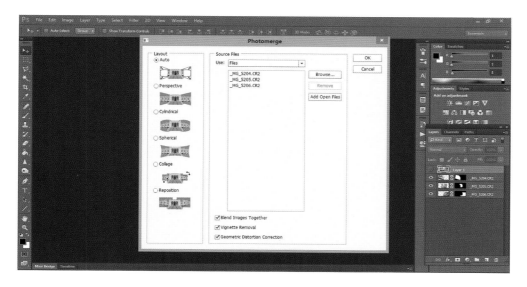

Figure 6.21

Photomerge dialog.

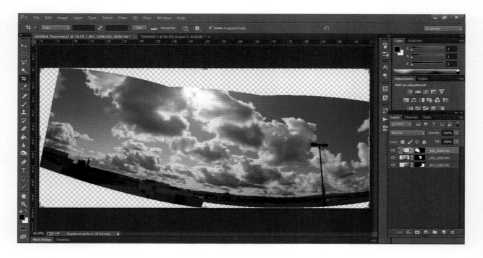

Figure 6.22

The resulting photomerge.

Figure 6.23

Adaptive Wide Angle dialog.

First, make a merged copy on a new layer, **Ctrl+Alt+Shift+E**/⌘+**Option+ Shift+E**. With this small panorama, we can use **Filter > Adaptive Wide Angle…**. Figure 6.23 shows the dialog for Adaptive Wide Angle. Select the Line Constraint Tool in the upper-left-hand corner and draw a line along what should be straight and move the controls until you have everything lined up. If you don't like where your control is, you can hit the backspace button while it is selected and it will be taken off. You can have multiple constraints. When you have it straight, hit OK.

Sometimes, we have a much wider panorama; as you can see in Figure 6.24, this stitch is more than a little curved. Personally, I find the Adaptive Wide Angle not as helpful in these types of situations, so I use Puppet Warp.

Go to **Edit > Puppet Warp**. Make sure Show Mesh is on, and increase the expansion a bit. Think of the waviness as an animation and put a pin where the "joint" would have to be. Then, click and move the pins to straighten the panorama (Figure 6.25).

In both cases, there was extra room around the panoramas. You *could* just crop the entire thing in so that there is no empty space. But, being the sneaky little professionals that we are, we can crop it a bit and fill in the rest.

Use the Crop Tool ⬚ and crop in. Next, using the Magic Wand Tool 🖎, select the areas you need to fill. Make sure you are on the merged copy as the context-aware fill needs to be able to "see" what it's trying to match. Go to **Edit > Fill…** and make sure you have Context-Aware selected. Hit OK and watch the magic.

There is a little cleanup, but overall this is a satisfactory experience in panorama creation (Figure 6.26).

Figure 6.24

A much bigger, wavier panorama.

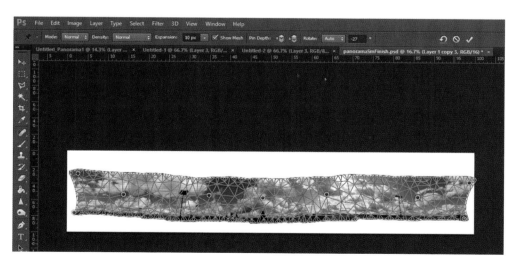

Figure 6.25

Using Puppet Warp to straighten panorama.

Figure 6.26

The fill isn't perfect, but it does a great job. Nothing a little healing brush can't fix.

Photomerge to Get Rid of People in a Scene

Don't you ever wish you could just get rid of all the people? Not in the creepy serial killer way—more like the uber-rich, "This national landmark is closed to the public for a private viewing"-type of way. Because we just did a couple of photomerging tricks, I'll let you in on a little secret: Photomerge can examine multiple images and average them, so the static background and consistent landmarks remain, but anything moving from frame to frame disappears. Obviously, the more images you take of a scene, the better this feature works. Place your camera on a tripod in a busy area and just *try* to get a clean shot with no people—when you get a bunch of shots, come home and try this:

Go to **File > Scripts > Statistics…**. Choose Median as the Stack Mode and Browse to the files you wish to average. After some processing, Photoshop will return a nice clean image. As a benefit of averaging, you receive a reduction in grain and noise and all the people vanish! That's it.

Old Photograph

There is something about an old, worn-out photograph that is so appealing. It's ironic that while so many people are trying to save and restore their old photographs, we work on techniques to make a good picture look old.

First, we are going to start with the photo and lower the saturation and specifically bring out more of the ochre tint of old photos. Note that we are not going for the sepia tones here, just that old faded color photo look (Figure 6.27). Go to **Image > Adjustments > Hue/Saturation** to lower the saturation a bit, then use the Color Balance function to bring a bit of an ochre tint (**Image > Adjustments > Color Balance**). Alternatively, you could use the ACR filter and also increase the Clarity while you are at it.

Now, we bring in our scan of an old piece of textured paper (Figure 6.28). I suggest either getting an old book from a thrift store and tearing out the plain cover page; unless it's really decrepit, use tea and coffee to create an old look that you can use over and over.

Figure 6.27

We want to fade this picture to help give an older feel to the photo.

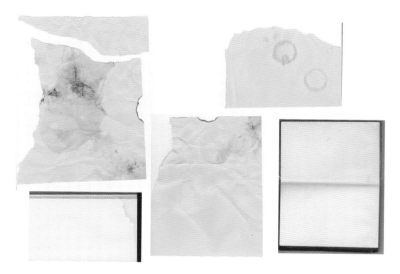

Figure 6.28

My worn-paper scan.

Or, crumple a yellowish sheet of construction paper. Rub some coffee grinds into it and tear off some edges. Whatever you decide to do, having a practical sheet of paper to work from gives a better end product.

Choose a paper background and put it on a layer below your picture layer. Switch your picture layer's Layer mode to Multiply. Notice how the picture already is becoming a yellowed tone from the color of the paper. Now, we need to "wear out" some parts; create an Exposure adjustment layer above by going to **Layer > New Adjustment layer > Exposure…**. Drag the sliders to the right to obtain an almost-white, washed-out look. Click on the Mask thumbnail ▣ so it is selected and go to **Filter > Render > Clouds**. The mask will fill with some random patterns. Go to **Image > Adjustments > Curves** and set the curves to some extreme setting, like Figure 6.29, that will give high contrast to your matte.

Now, using a mottled shape brush, brush in some wear to the mask with white. You should obtain some spots of wear. Alternatively, you can import an image of concrete and adjust the contrast and use it as a mask, which will give a very natural wear look to it.

Create a new layer by clicking on the New Layer button ▣ in the Layers palette. Change the mode to multiply and paint in some drip or coffee stains (see Chapter 7 for making custom brushes, such as coffee rings).

To finish, we just need a couple more finishing details. Group all your layers together by selecting all your layers except the background layer and pressing **Ctrl+G/⌘+G**. With the Group selected, click on the Mask button ▣ in the Layers palette. The mask is attached to the group and will affect the entire group's visibility. Paint judiciously with black using the brush of your choice along the edges of the matte to give the edges a worn look.

Did you know you can layer effects to a group? Well you can. With the group selected, click on the Layer Effects button ▣ in the Layers palette and choose **Drop Shadow…**. You should see a bit of a shadow; adjust it until you have just enough to add a little dimension and weight to the old photo (Figure 6.30).

Figure 6.29

Using clouds as a mask for an exposure layer.

Figure 6.30

Our "vintage" photo.

Pencil-Drawing Effect

This is a really short and easy tutorial that could be called more of a quickie than a one-night stand. But, when well done, the pencil-drawing effect gives the look of more effort than it actually takes. Open up the picture you want to use to make a drawing. In this case, I have a picture of my friend Suze talking and looking out at the Sydney Harbor in Australia (Figure 6.31). Duplicate to a new layer by pressing **Ctrl+J/⌘+J.**

Set the Layer mode of your new layer to Color Dodge, then invert the layer by pressing **Ctrl+I/⌘+I**. Your canvas should look blank or white.

Go to **Filter > Blur > Gaussian Blur…**. Start with just a couple of pixels of blur and move the slider until your image has some nice tonalities, but still has a lot of negative or white space, like you see in Figure 6.32. Click **OK**.

Next, go to **Layer > New Adjustment Layer > Levels…**. Don't worry about setting any kind of setting yet. Just accept the default name and default settings and click **OK**. Then, go to **Layer > New Adjustment Layer > Black & White**. Again, don't worry about the settings. For now, just leave the sliders in their default settings.

You will notice that your image is already starting to look like a pencil drawing. Click back down to the Levels adjustment layer and click on the Adjustment Layer icon ⬛. In the Properties tab, you will see the controls for the Levels. Click and drag the midgray

Figure 6.31

Suze at Sydney Harbor picture.

Figure 6.32

The blur reveals a tonal image.

triangle to adjust the look until you get some nice darks and shading happening like you see in Figure 6.33.

Next, click on the Black and White adjustment layer; in the Properties tab, adjust the colors to obtain a better tone for specific color ranges. For example, in my case, I liked the darkness that was being brought in with my Levels adjustment, but it made

Figure 6.33

Our pencil drawing is starting to come together.

the skin too darkly drawn, so I increased the red slider to lighten the skin areas. Depending on what your original photo is, the different sliders will behave differently, but it would be impossible for *none* of them to have an effect.

You can go back and forth until you get most of it where you want it. In more complex pictures, you may want to mask different areas to customize the adjustments.

Now, notice that there appears to be a bald spot on her head. I'll form a new

Figure 6.34

A copy of our merged image converted for smart filters.

layer on top of everything else by clicking on the New Layer icon 🔲 in the Layers palette and just hand paint the area.

To quickly add some "sketch lines," let's make a merged copy of our almost complete "drawing." Press **Ctrl+A**/⌘+**A** to select all and then **Ctrl+Shift+C**/⌘+**Shift+C** to copy merged; then, with the top layer selected, press **Ctrl+V**/⌘+**V** to paste in the image. You should obtain a single layer like you see in Figure 6.34. Convert this layer to a Smart Object by going to **Filter > Convert for Smart Filters**. This will allow you to adjust and change things even after you have applied the filter.

Figure 6.35

Close-up of masking and using filters to emulate "hand-drawn" look.

Now, apply a small bit of Cross Hatching—or your favorite sketch filter of choice (some like Angled Strokes better, for example). Go to **Filter** > **Filter Gallery** > **Brush Strokes** > **Cross Hatch** and adjust the settings until you achieve a natural stroke length and weight, then click **OK**.

The secret to making a filter like this look more "natural" or "real" is not to apply it all over. Click on the Mask thumbnail next to Smart Filters in the Layers palette. With the mask selected, press **Ctrl+I/⌘+I** to invert the Mask so that the cross-hatching is not visible; the Mask thumbnail should look black in the Layers palette. With a medium-hard brush, brush with white onto the mask in the areas that would make sense to have some strokes visible (Figure 6.35).

Personally, I like to go in again and smudge and blur and hand paint more details, but that's all up to you. In the end, you have a pretty convincing "pencil drawing" (Figure 6.36).

Figure 6.36

Our finished pencil drawing.

Tilt-Shift Miniaturization

The tilt-shift miniaturization effect has been popular for a few years. It is based on our visual perception that a short depth of field must mean we are looking at a miniature. Depth of field shortens as magnification increases, so this acts as a visual cue for distance to our eyes. To really make this effect work, however, you need not only the blurring of the depth of field but also other visual cues, such as increased saturation and contrast, to make us think that this is a miniature. Take a look at the image in Figure 6.37.

This photo is a good candidate. It has clearly defined lateral planes of depth. As a bonus, it has out-of-focus foreground elements that will help sell the blur. Had these foreground elements been in focus, it would have ruined the effect, and we would have to have blurred the foreground elements by hand separately. This is already a cheat, as it is not using Zdepth, so the fewer "exceptions" there are to paint around, the better.

Before we apply the Tilt-Shift Blur, we want to sharpen and saturate our image. Go to **Filter > Camera Raw Filter**.

Increase the Clarity, Vibrance, and Saturation. Being a little heavy-handed here will make the illusion more convincing in the end. Now, we are ready to apply the Tilt-Shift Filter. Go to **Filter > Blur > Tilt-Shift**. The Tilt-Shift Blur tool overlays the image (Figure 6.38).

A round pin is at the center of your image, with two solid lines designating your focused area, and the fade-off designated by the dotted lines. The wider the distance between the solid and dotted lines, the slower the fade-off will be.

The gray ring around the pin controls the amount of blur to be applied. It is an on-screen equivalent to the Blur slider in the Tilt-Shift panel. Click and drag around the ring and you will see the Blur slider move in sync.

Figure 6.37

Our starting image.

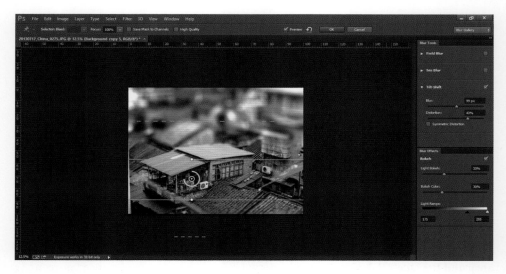

Figure 6.38

Applying the Tilt-Shift Blur.

If you are adjusting the settings and not seeing any reaction, first check to make sure the Preview check box is checked in the Options bar. Pressing **P** should also toggle the Preview Mode.

Let's move the pin to the center of the part of the picture we want to keep in focus. We can adjust the area of focus and the blur fade-off by click dragging the solid or dashed lines up or down. We can also adjust the tilt by moving the cursor over the white dot on the solid line above the pin until we obtain the curved arrow, then click dragging left or right. As you are adjusting the settings, you may find that the tool controls interfere with your visualization of the blur. Simply hold **H** to temporarily hide the Tilt-Shift Blur controls. Occasionally, I have a picture for which the blurred areas have a particular shape that is distracting, usually because of the combination of color and contrast. Instead of blurring it more, I will adjust the Distortion slider under the Blur slider until the details are less distracting. Also, under Blur Effects, there are some additional sliders that you can tweak to obtain the look you want. I like having a little Light Bokeh to bloom out some of the highlights. If I am going for a "magical" look, I'll add more Bokeh and crank up the Bokeh Color. I'll also increase the Light Range so more things sparkle. This is probably not what you may want on a photo, but it is great for adding some mood to artwork. How these sliders will react strongly depends on your starting image, so play with it to get a feel for it.

If in the process of adjusting, you happen to accidentally create another pin, just click on it and hit the **Backspace/Delete** key on your keyboard. The additional Tilt-Shift will be deleted, and it does not affect your other existing one.

Figure 6.39

Before and after miniaturization.

Before we finalize this blur, check out the Options bar and make sure your focus is 100%. Changing this will add blur to your center section. The only time I use this is when I have multiple planes of depth in my focal area and I need to run the filter twice—once to obtain the miniaturization blur and a second time with the Focus blurred so I can use it for the background blur of the focused area. This keeps the blur natural and blends easier.

Also in the **Options bar**, you can check Save Mask to Channels. This will save the mask for future use. If you are curious about what the mask looks like, you can hold **M** to see the black-and-white matte.

When everything looks good, simply click the **OK** button in the **Options bar** or hit **Enter/Return**.

Check out Figure 6.39 for the before and after effect.

7

Brushes

Introduction

The Photoshop Brushes tools have to be some of the most powerful tools on the planet. Yet, there are plenty of artists who will never touch this tool, relying on the photo-manipulation tools, filters, and effects for their creations. Some will even say that they are not "artistic enough" to really work with the brushes. Poopennanny! The Brushes are powerful and can be overwhelming at first, but no one said you have to study everything at once. I like to think of the Brushes as like your favorite restaurant. You don't have to eat every dish in one sitting, and you can be fine ordering the same couple of dishes whenever you go, but why not at least give some of the other dishes a try? You never know what may be your next favorite thing.

Photoshop's brushes are so powerful, they can unlock artistic potential that was confined to your imagination. And, for those who are transitioning from traditional painting, you can bring that knowledge to Photoshop; you just have to adjust your brushes to behave a bit more like traditional painting.

Most other books just tell you what each function on the Brush palette does, but I find it more useful to know how it will be used by the user—by the painters and the nonpainters. You and I both know that it is a necessary evil to have to do an overview in a book like this. Nonetheless, if the idea of spending an entire chapter going through each brush's options makes your eyes glaze and sends you into a coma, skip over to the Custom Brushes section to create a couple of custom brushes and see some of the functionality in action. Then, watch yourself skip back to this point to read through the other options. You can't say I didn't tell you so.

Finding Brush Controls

As is common in Photoshop, there are several ways to access brush controls. When you have the brush tool selected, the Options bar at the top of the screen will show the tip shape and size (see Figure 7.1). Click on it to access the pull-down menu. This condensed option window has brush roundness and angle controller, size, and hardness sliders and a brush tip shape selector. You can also access this same menu by **right-clicking**/**option-clicking** while hovering over the canvas.

By default, the moment you click on the Brush Panel icon  in the Options bar, the Brush panel will open up attached to the collapsed panels docked on the screen right (see Figure 7.2). Notice that the Brush Panel icon on the right palette dock does not have the folder around the brush pot. I'm sure there is some story about why the two icons are different—but that doesn't affect the functionality, so let's continue. As I was saying, this is where most of your magic is going to happen. Just about every option under the sun is nicely organized into this small palette.

But wait! There's more. You can open the **Brushes palette** by either choosing **Window > Brushes** or pressing **F5**. The latter is a toggle function, so if the Brushes palette is open and you want to close it quickly, you can simply press **F5** again to close it.

Figure 7.1

Options bar for Brush Tool.

7. Brushes

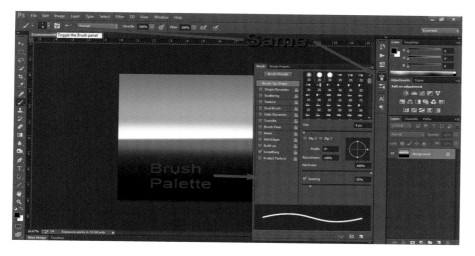

Figure 7.2

Two different icons for the same palette.

Speed Tip

The keyboard shortcut to access the Brush palette is **F5** for both Windows and Mac. If you are on a Mac laptop or other integrated system that has a function assigned to this key (such as volume or keyboard lights), hold down the fn key on the lower-left corner of your keyboard as you press **F5**.

The Brushes Palette

Open your Brushes palette (**F5**). The palette is divided into three sections or frames (Figure 7.3). The left frame holds the many adjustable options, and the right frame holds the controls for the selected option. Then, there is a handy-dandy brush preview window on the bottom. The preview window instantly reflects the attributes you assign to the brush, so you can ensure that the brush behaves the way you intend. It is only a black-and-white preview, so no color information is reflected. Think of it as a thumbnail of a single example stroke of the brush at its current settings.

Brush Presets

The first setting on the Brush palette's left frame is the **Brush Tip Shape**, and it is automatically highlighted when you open the palette. However, there is a **Brush Presets** button right

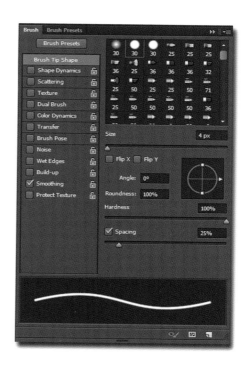

Figure 7.3

Brush palette.

above the Brush Tip Shape selection. Clicking **Brush Presets** automatically moves you to the **Brush Preset** tab in the **Brush palette** and reveals the available brushes in a scrolling visual list of tip shape followed by stroke thumbnail. This is the same list that is accessible in the Brushes submenu in the **Options bar**. Clicking on **any preset** will set your brush with all the options of that particular preset. You can still further adjust the settings to your liking by clicking back to the **Brush tab**. But, to access those same adjusted settings in the future, you will need to save your new presets in this tab by clicking on the New Preset Brush icon ⬚ on the bottom of the screen. You can see step-by-step details on how to do this in this chapter's discussion of custom brushes. For now, stay on the Brush palette.

Brush Tip Shape

The first setting on the Brush palette's left frame is the **Brush Tip Shape**, and it is automatically highlighted when you open the palette. Do you want to duplicate the look of a traditional airbrush? Or, do you want to paint a flurry of leaves? The shape of your brush will be a major contributing factor.

Select the **Brush Tip Shape** control options if it is not highlighted already. It should be highlighted in blue if you have it selected. You should also see the options for changing the fundamentals of the brush in the right frame. What is displayed depends on the type of brush you have selected.

Custom or Old-School Standard Brushes

The old-school standard brush tips display the diameter, angle, roundness, hardness, and spacing of the brush. The first option is the diameter. Your brush tip can have a pixel width of 1 to 5000 pixels. The Use Sample Size button appears if you modify a custom brush, allowing you to revert to your originally created size. (You'll learn how to make your own custom brush later in this chapter.)

Speed Tip

Want to nudge your brush size up or down? Use the left bracket [to decrease and the right bracket] to increase the size of your brush. Maximum brush size is 5000 pixels.

You can adjust angle and roundness interactively or numerically. Note that if you have a symmetrical brush, you don't see the angle change. The allowable angles are −180 to +180 degrees, equaling an entire 360 degrees. The hardness slider controls the falloff of the edge of the brush tip. The falloff is the rate at which the "ink" decreases from the center of the brush. A 100 percent falloff makes the edges very sharp; 0 percent gives the softest edge. This option is not available on custom brushes.

Spacing controls the amount of overlap that falls between the brush shape as it is stroked across the canvas and can be anywhere between 1 and 1000 percent. A spacing of 100 percent lines up the shapes edge to edge, a spacing of 200 percent leaves the brush shapes exactly one shape width apart, and a spacing of 50 percent puts each shape overlap halfway through the last one. Of course, instead of thinking numerically, you can just play around with the slider until you get the look you want.

Take a look at the settings in Figure 7.4. With just these settings, you can create a variety of brushes. Changes in one setting may give the illusion of a different adjustment.

Erodible Brushes

The Erodible brushes emulate real-world pastels and pencils in that they wear down as you draw. This is controlled by the **Softness** slider. Setting the Softness to 0% will cause no erosion and 100% wears down quickly. So, a point will become duller and thicker, and these "imperfections" are the features that add a sense of realism to the brush. You will need to have a stylus to really take advantage of this because different angles will show as different strokes.

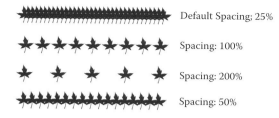

Default Spacing; 25%

Spacing: 100%

Spacing: 200%

Spacing: 50%

Figure 7.4

Play with the settings and note the behavior.

You can return the tip to the original sharpness by clicking on the **Sharpen Tip** button in the Brush panel (Figure 7.5). Unfortunately, if you want a shortcut for sharpening the tip, you'll have to assign one yourself because there is no default keyboard shortcut. Check out Chapter 11 for instructions on how to make your own shortcuts.

Airbrush

The Airbrush has come into its own, with its own brush tip to emulate more closely a virtual airbrush. Whereas previously there was an "airbrush option" in the **Options bar** that let any brush you were using simulate the kind of buildup an airbrush left on, now the brush head responds with a little more complexity, including to the pressure and tilt of your stylus. You can control Spatter Amount and Spatter Size, along with how grainy the paint spatter will look, via the **Granularity** slider. Pressing harder brings the "airbrush" closer to the "paper," giving you a tighter spray, and tilting sideways will give you spatter like a real airbrush.

Figure 7.5

Erodible tip example.

Bristle Brushes

The **Bristle Tips** come in a variety of real-world brush types: round fan, flat angle, round point, and others. They have controls to determine density, individual bristle thickness, and bristle stiffness. Like Erodible and Airbrush, Bristle brushes will respond to pressure and tilt and change accordingly.

You probably noticed that the Bristle, Airbrush, and Erodible tip brushes have a Brush preview that pops up in the upper-left corner. I find it more annoying than anything, so I click on the Brush Preview button at the bottom of the Brush palette to toggle it off. If you like it and want to keep it up, you have the option of clicking on it to see the brush from different sides, moving it around to a different area of the workspace, or making it larger or smaller by pressing the collapse/open triangles in the window.

Shape Dynamics

The **Shape Dynamics** setting enables you to specify randomness and variation in a stroke. Some of its options are only available if you are using a pressure-sensitive digital tablet. What?! You say you don't have a tablet? Using Photoshop without a tablet is sort of like going snorkeling without a mask. As long as you have the snorkel, you technically are snorkeling, and yeah, you can see … sort of … mostly … but you really miss out on a lot. So, get a tablet!

What Is a Tablet?

When I mention tablet, I'm not talking about your iPad. A tablet is another form of input interface with your computer, as your mouse and keyboard are. A tablet acts like a map of your screen, and you use a digital pen to interact—like painting on paper with a pen. There are many options available to purchase, with Wacom Tablets the most popular and predominant brand in the industry. Among some of the most popular tablets are the Wacom Intuos Touch Sensitive Screens that some of my fellow artists swear by. I still prefer the "old-fashioned" tablet with stylus as I find my hand gets in the way when I try to paint on screen. But, hey—to each his or her own.

Click to highlight the Shape Dynamics option on the left frame of the Brush palette. You can see your options for the shape dynamics on the right.

Angle Jitter lets you control or randomize the brush tip angle, which is great in a couple of instances:

- You are creating a texture that has to follow some logical change in angle. An example is arrows pointing along a path (0 percent jitter, but using direction).
- You want to give a more natural look to a shape (leaves blowing in the wind, 100 percent jitter).

Roundness Jitter controls the roundness that you have set for Brush Tip Shape. Minimum roundness sets a limit on how flat the brush can go.

Scattering

Click on **Scattering** on the left frame of the Brush palette to see the options available on the right side (Figure 7.6). Scattering distributes the amount and position of brush marks on a stroke. The higher the scatter percentage, the further the brush mark may be from the line of the stroke. Selecting Both Axis scatters the marks radially, while deselecting the option scatters only on the perpendicular of the stroke.

Count specifies the number of brush marks at each spacing point, and Jitter randomly varies that number along the stroke by the percentage you set. Setting the Count and Variation to 0 percent uses your Brush Tip Shape settings. Setting Jitter to 100 percent gives the maximum randomness.

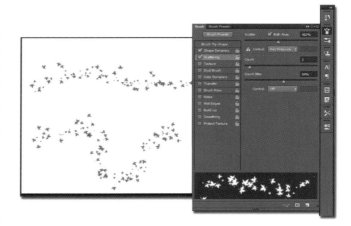

Figure 7.6

Scattering example.

Texture

The **Texture** control applies either a preset or user-defined texture pattern to a brush stroke. It makes the strokes look like they were done on a textured canvas. To see the texture options, click on the Texture option on the left frame of the Brush palette. The texture controls will be listed on the right frame.

Invert reverses the light and dark pixels in the pattern. **Scale** sizes the pattern in each stroke.

The **Texture Each Tip** option activates the Minimum Depth and the Depth Jitter controls. This option adds the randomization to the Texture application over the stroke as it is applied to the canvas. Texture Each Tip renders each tip as it is stroked, giving a more saturated effect. **Depth** controls the amount of the pattern integrated with the stroke, specifying how deep the paint penetrates the texture. The lower the number, the more covered the pattern is; at 0 percent, the pattern is completely obscured. Specifying a minimum depth will limit how low this percentage can dip when you are using Depth Jitter. Depth Jitter will randomize the depth. At 0 percent, there is no change over the course of the stroke. The higher the percentage, the more randomized the depth will be. Mode lets you choose one of Photoshop's blending modes, which determine how the texture and paint interact. These modes are the same as the brush blending modes that are covered later on in the chapter.

Dual Brush

Dual Brush uses a second brush tip, blended in, in a single stroke. This is great once you're familiar with all the brushes. You can even specify and control the mode with which the second brush is applied to the first brush.

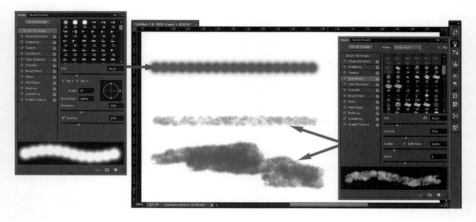

Figure 7.7

Dual Brush visual.

To display these settings, click on the Dual Brush option on the left side of the palette, and you will see the settings on the right side of the palette (Figure 7.7). (You *do* see the trend here, don't you?)

Color Dynamics and Other Dynamics

Next are the **Color Dynamics**. By now, you should have figured out you need to click on the left side to see the options on the right side.

Color Dynamics allows color variation in a stroke, which gives a natural, organic feel. **Foreground/Background Jitter** determines how paint varies between the two colors. To the left (0 percent) is all foreground color, but to the right (100 percent) is *not* all background color: It is a full mix. Think of it as a 0 percent mix and a 100 percent mix.

FYI

Unfortunately, you can't see the Color Dynamics settings you're creating in the preview window. Kind of defeats the purpose of a preview window, doesn't it? One day, I know it will happen—color thumbnails. Until then, I continue to pine away.

The **Hue, Saturation,** and **Brightness Jitter** choices introduce variation to their respective aspects. The higher the percentage, the more the variations deviate from the numerical setting. The best way to understand this is to think of painting in HSB (hue, saturation, and brightness). Looking at an HSB slider, you can see how the variance affects you. Painter had this option long ago, and I'm glad to see Photoshop has finally included it.

Purity is simply the saturation level. At 100 percent, it is fully saturated, and at −100 percent, it is fully desaturated (*grayscale*).

Transfer

Transfer introduces jitter to the opacity and the flow aspects. The settings do not override the main brush opacity setting, but give variation from the point at which they were set. For instance, an opacity jitter of 50 percent does not jitter around 50 percent, but jitters 50 percent of the opacity set. In other words, if you have a brush set at 50 percent opacity, a 50 percent jitter randomizes between 25 and 75 percent opacity, a 100 percent jitter randomizes between 0 and 100 percent opacity, and a 10 percent jitter gives you an opacity between 45 and 55 percent. The Flow Jitter works on the same concept.

Brush Pose

You can achieve stylus-like effects without a stylus or override your stylus information and set tilt, rotation, and pressure here.

Other Brush Tip Characteristics

These other brush tip characteristics are toggles: They either are on or off. Clicking on these options on the left frame of the palette will not bring up anything on the right frame; hence, you will notice that there is a line that separates these characteristics from the options above.

- **Noise.** Applies more randomness to the brush tips but does not fade the noise to match the edges of a soft brush. Brush tips that contain gray values (fading areas) see the effect more prominently.
- **Wet Edges.** Lightens the central portion of the stroke, giving a watercolor brush look because of paint buildup at the outer edges.
- **Buildup.** Represented on the Options bar as well as the Brush palette, it emulates a traditional airbrush. It produces a soft buildup that increases the paint saturation and gives the wider buildup airbrush effect if you hold your brush down in one spot.
- **Smoothing.** Smoothes freehand strokes to eliminate any hard edges.
- **Protect Texture.** Overrides any brush texture preset so that if you're painting with several brushes, the texture remains consistent over the entire image. Use this to simulate a consistent canvas texture, for example.

Putting the Brush Palette to Use

You will put most of the Brush palette options into effect throughout this book, but here's an example of how the brush controls have made life so much easier. The graphic in Figure 7.8 was created with only four strokes of custom brushes.

FYI

You will need to save your new Scattered Maple Leaves brush settings as a New Brush Preset if you want to keep the brush. Otherwise, you will lose all your settings with the next brush you use. Go to the 'Save Save Save' section in the Custom Brush section of this chapter to see how to save the preset.

Figure 7.8

A painting in four strokes.

Background color is almost overwhelming, isn't it? Well, hold on to that *almost* because all of the brushes can be applied with different blending modes, which are much like layer modes.

Brush Blending Modes

Beyond adjusting the brush's behavior via shape and color, you can affect how the paint interacts with the canvas. Photoshop has 29 blend modes that you can select for a brush, and these blend modes determine how the colors interact with the base image. You can find these modes in the Options bar when you've selected a painting tool.

For the most part, the blend modes for the brush and for the layers react identically (Figure 7.9). A couple of brush blend modes don't exist as a layer blend mode, and a few brush blend modes react a bit differently from their layer counterpart. Although these are addressed here, the best way to understand the modes is to experiment and play with them.

Normal

Normal is the default mode, which appears as Threshold in a bitmap or an indexed color image mode (Figure 7.10). At 100 percent opacity, your application colors are unaffected by the base layer. In other words, whatever color you choose appears the same—there's no blending or influence from the base layer.

Dissolve

Dissolve only comes into effect when the opacity is less than 100 percent. It allows randomized pixels to show through.

Behind

Behind affects only transparent parts of a layer, giving the illusion that the strokes are behind the layer. Obviously, there is no "behind" layer blend mode. You would just put the layer, well, *behind* another.

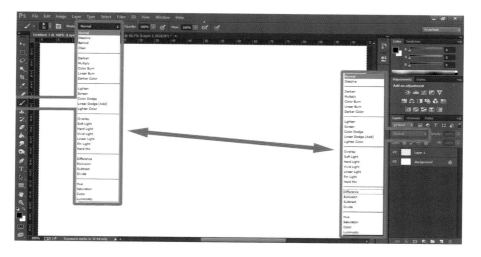

Figure 7.9

Brush Blending modes versus Layer Blending modes: Sometimes they are the same and sometimes different.

Caution

The Behind and Clear modes will not be available options on any locked layers. So, by default, you will not be able to use these modes on the background layer.

Clear

Pixels are made transparent, like the eraser. There is no such effect for the layers; you can't have a layer on top negate a layer on the bottom to transparency, although it is an interesting concept.

Darken

Darken compares each color at the channel level; those colors that are lighter than the applied color are replaced, and the darker colors are left alone. The replaced colors are not just darkened but color the result by the application color.

Multiply

Multiply darkens all colors until they reach black. It looks at the color information in each channel and multiplies the base color by the application color. Using a light color

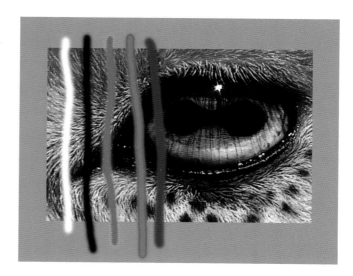

Figure 7.10

Normal blending mode.

allows more control over the effect, and painting repeatedly over the same area produces progressively darker colors, much like coloring with a marker. Coloring with black is like multiplying by 0: You'll get black. Coloring with white is like multiplying with 1: You'll get the same color in return.

Color Burn

A darker color darkens and saturates the base layer when you use Color Burn mode. It darkens by increasing contrast. Blending with white on either the base or application produces no effect.

Linear Burn

If you want to darken your work, use Linear Burn. It does its thing by decreasing the brightness of the base layer, which tints and affects white. Even light colors subtract from the base layer.

Lighten

The opposite of Darken, the base colors that are darker than the applied color are lightened. However, colors that are lighter than the applied color stay the same when you use Lighten mode.

Screen

Screen is the opposite of Multiply; the end result is always lighter with Screen mode. It looks at each channel's color information and multiplies the inverse of the application and base colors. Painting with black gives no effect, but even an almost-black color lightens the base.

Color Dodge

Another lightening effect, Color Dodge infuses the base with the applied colors and brightens the base. The opposite effect of Color Burn, this lightens by decreasing contrast. As you can see in Figure 7.11, the effects of Color Dodge as a brush and applied as a Layer Mode are quite different.

Linear Dodge

Similar to Screen mode, Linear Dodge brightens the base to reflect the application color. It is a bit harsher than Screen, and it tends to go to white faster.

Overlay

Overlay is like a combination of multiply and screen: It *multiplies* (darkens) dark areas and *screens* (lightens) light areas. The base color is tinged with the application color.

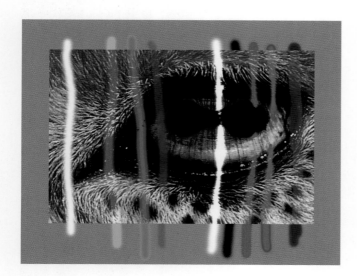

Figure 7.11

Color Dodge. The left lines are 100% opacity normal brush lines on a separate **layer** set to Color Dodge mode. The right lines are drawn directly on the image with the **brush** set to Color Dodge.

Soft Light

Similar to Overlay, but softer, Soft Light applies a color lighter than 50 percent gray lightens, and an application of a color darker than 50 percent gray darkens. Luminosity values in the base are preserved.

Hard Light

Harsher than Soft Light, Hard Light works similarly but tends to emphasize contrast and exaggerate highlights. Painting with pure black or pure white will obliterate all information to black or white.

Vivid Light

Vivid Light is like the Soft Light and Hard Light modes, but instead of multiplying and screening, it uses a combination of Color Burn and Color Dodge (Figure 7.12). If the blend color (light source) is lighter than 50 percent gray, the image is lightened by decreasing the contrast. If the blend color is darker than 50 percent gray, the image is darkened by increasing the contrast. The left lines are drawn with normal brush on a separate layer with layer mode set to Vivid Light. The right lines are drawn with Light Mode directly on the image.

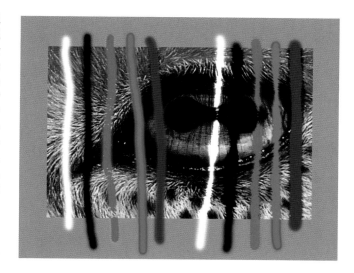

Figure 7.12

Vivid Light.

Linear Light

Linear Light is the same concept as Vivid Light, but Linear Light uses Linear Burn and Linear Dodge. If the blend color (light source) is lighter than 50 percent gray, the image is lightened by increasing the brightness. If the blend color is darker than 50 percent gray, the image is darkened by decreasing the brightness.

Pin Light

Like Overlay, Pin Light divides and affects those pixels that have a brightness greater than 50 percent one way and pixels that have a brightness of less than 50 percent another way. If the color applied has a brightness greater than 50 percent, then it replaces any affected pixels that are darker than 50 percent brightness. If the color applied has a brightness lower than 50 percent, then pixels lighter than it in the underlying image are replaced by the color applied.

Hard Mix

Hard Mix creates a posterized, graphic effect by reducing all colors to the primary additive colors (red, green, blue) and white and black. For CMYK (cyan, magenta, yellow, key) images, the colors are reduced to the primary subtractive colors (cyan, yellow, magenta) and black and white.

Difference

Difference creates a *negative,* or inverted, effect by subtracting the applied color from the base color or the base color from the applied color, depending on which has the larger brightness value. A white application inverts the base colors, and black produces no change.

Exclusion

A lower-contrast version of Difference, Exclusion also has less saturation. A dark application color tends to convert the base colors to shades of gray.

Hue

The color, or *hue,* of the applied color is applied to the *luminance* (brightness) and *saturation* (intensity) values of the base color.

Saturation

Uses the applied color's saturation to blend with the hue and luminance of the base color.

Color

Color uses both the saturation and hue of the applied color to colorize the base's luminance.

Luminosity

Opposite of Color, Luminosity uses the applied color's luminance to blend with the saturation and hue of the base color.

Pencil

Figure 7.13

Pencil versus hard brush.

The Brush tool shares its space with the Pencil tool. Some have asked why you'd even use the Pencil. Isn't it the same as setting the brush to a hard edge? Actually, they exhibit a few differences not only in their hardness, but also in their function. With the Pencil, there is an autoerase option available in the Options bar that automatically switches your pencil to the background color when you try to draw on a color that matches your foreground color. The brush does not have such an option.

In addition to the functional differences, take a look at the image in Figure 7.13. A hard brush is still antialiased, so on close inspection it's quite different from the hard stroke of a pencil. The main difference between a brush with a hard edge and a pencil is the antialiasing, which is less visible if you use a large brush.

Color Replacement Tool

The Color Replacement Tool is used to colorize an image with your choice of color. You can paint onto a grayscale image, or you can replace a specific color with your application color while completely preserving the tonality of the image. The benefit of this over just painting on a Color Layer mode is that you can choose to have only a specific color replaced.

Figure 7.14

Using the color replacement tool to "ripen" green grapes.

Figure 7.14 shows an example of this brush in action. Using the Color mode, I replaced the green grapes to be more along the purple hues of the other grapes. The brush is set to replace the sampled color in the Background Swatch with the Foreground Swatch color.

Mixer Brush

The Mixer Brush is supposed to be for simulating realistic painting where colors mix and streak, but this brush has so much more to offer. You load paint onto the brush by clicking **Alt+Click**/**Option+Click** on the canvas (much like the Stamp tool or other reference sourcing tools) and specify how much to load up. Lower amounts "dry out" more quickly. How wet you set it to be will determine how much paint the brush picks up from the canvas; you also can set the ratio of mix.

These properties were originally developed to make painting-like creations (Figure 7.15). But, you can use them to act like "smart brushes" that can paint almost like a clone stamp. It is hard to explain, so I would recommend flipping to Chapter 10 to see how you can make the Mixer Brush into a smart brush.

Custom Brushes

Now you will learn how to save your favorite brushes and create some specific custom brushes that will exemplify the range of possibilities that the brushes can offer.

Figure 7.15

The common usage for the mixer brush is to blend and simulate realistic paintings.

Getting Dirty

You know how just about everyone had acne as a teenager or how just about every baby eats dirt at some point? The same kind of idea holds true here: Just about every digital painter creates a dirt brush. One of the most common brushes you use as both a matte painter and a texture painter is a dirt brush. A dirt brush is an organically shaped brush that makes it easier to paint on any type of grime, wear, or dirt—much like the way do-it-yourselfers use a sponge to give a textured or aged look to walls and furniture.

Creating the Brushes

The following steps show you how to make a couple of custom dirt brushes:

1. Create a 200 × 200 blank white canvas by going to **File > New** in the Menu bar.
2. Click the New Layer button at the bottom of the Layers palette to form a new transparent layer.
3. Using black, create a smudgy, dirty blob like the one I have created in Figure 7.16.

   Don't worry about going to the edges; you clean this up later. Because this is going to be a brush, it needs to have an organic shape. Any part that goes to the edges will end up giving a tiled, hard-edge look. You may not even notice or see the edge, but even 10 percent opacity shows up when you try to use your brush.
4. Use the Lasso tool to cut away at the edges, making sure not to have any minute smudges going to the edge. After you have cut away to clean edges, you can soften the edges by running an eraser over the edges at 40% opacity, blurring the edges, or use whatever other means is most comfortable.

Figure 7.16

Dirty blob. I like him. I think I'll call him George.

Although it may seem that a 200 × 200 image is pretty small, that is a pretty large brush. In the old days of Photoshop custom brushes, you had to make different sizes of the same brush manually and save each one separately. Because this is no longer the case, you can jump into making this map into a brush.

5. Select the entire layer by way of one of these methods:
   • Marquee tool
   • **Ctrl+A/Option+A** shortcut

   Go to **Edit > Define Brush Preset**. A dialog box asks you to name your brush; give your brush a descriptive name. The brush is now saved to the Brush Presets and by default is all the way at the bottom. You can see it in Figure 7.17.

Photoshop will use the entire active canvas to determine the Brush Preset, but it's safer to make a selection to ensure that the proper image is used to create your brush. Also, if you should want to use just part of the image to create a brush, you only have to make the selection around the area that you want to use, and Photoshop will create the brush preset from your selection.

Figure 7.17

You can see George at the bottom of the presets.

6. Hide the layer on which you created your first brush map and create a new transparent layer.
7. Do the same steps you just did and make another dirt brush.

Adjusting the Settings

You're going to go to the brush options to give these two brushes the proper dirty variations characteristics. That way it won't look like a bad sponge-on type of dirt. I had you make two brushes so you can blend the two for more variation.

1. Choose the first brush you made in your brush presets.
2. Open the Brush palette in the palette well.
3. Start with the Brush Tip Shape options, increasing the spacing so the brush details can be seen more.

   Don't let it become so far apart it looks like a stamp. Figure 7.18 has an example of good spacing.

Figure 7.18

Example of the kind of spacing you want.

4. Turn on **Shape Dynamics**. Go to the options and jitter everything to break up any repeating patterns. Don't be afraid to go wild with the controls. You can always change them later if they don't work.

5. Go to **Scattering** and play with the settings.

    These settings change the number and placement of brush tips to a stroke. Everything in this dialog box is as intuitive as the previous dialog box, except for that little Both Axes check box at the very top. As you select and deselect the check box, you are witnessing the difference of scattering the brush tips in a radial direction from each spacing point or in a perpendicular direction to the tangent of the path. Again, there is no right answer: Slide the sliders, select the check boxes, and find a combination that you like.

6. Go to the Dual Brush options and find your Other Brush Tip in the thumbnails.

    Now comes the play of your two brushes. Unlike the Brush pull-down menu, the tips may not necessarily be at the very bottom. In my case, they were in the middle.

7. Choose a blend mode (at the top of the dialog box). This determines how this second brush interacts with your main brush.

8. Play with the sliders at the bottom of the dialog box until you find a good setting (see Figure 7.19).

9. Continue onto Color Dynamics and Other Dynamics, playing with the sliders.

I also like turning on Smoothing and Airbrush, but that is not necessary for a good dirt brush. This is a pretty forgiving brush; I mean, how can you mess up dirt smudges, right? If the worst happens, you just come back and tweak some sliders some more.

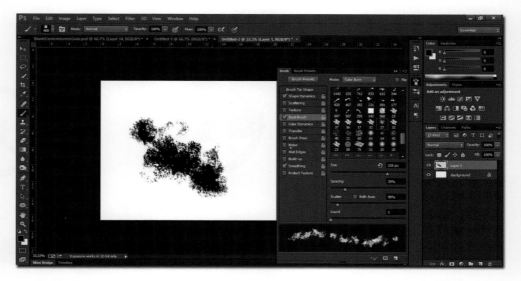

Figure 7.19

Blending the two brushes in Dual Brush.

Save! Save! Save!

Great! You have a wonderful dirt brush. Before anything happens, save the brush.

1. Go to the Brush palette's pull-down menu ⚙ and choose New Brush Preset. This saves the brush as a separate and different brush than the two you used to create this brush. If you want to access the brush with these specific settings in the Tool Presets palette, make any adjustments you wish to the settings, then go to the Tool Presets palette in the upper-left corner of the Options bar. Press the New Tool Preset button 🔲; a dialog box appears in which you should name your brush.

2. Because the tool preset name is listed in the palette, give it a descriptive name (such as dirt scattered 75% opac color) that gives some details to remind you of your settings.

   The New Tool Preset is placed above the preset you have highlighted at the time of your save (see Figure 7.20).

3. Last but not least, save your brush and tool preset libraries. Under each palette's pull-down menu, you will find a Save Brushes or Save Tool Presets option.

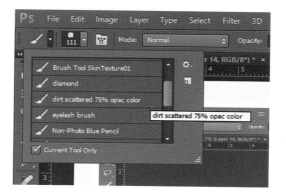

Figure 7.20

My New Brush Preset.

Natural Color

When I paint textures, I like to use my special custom brushes that have a certain amount of HSB variations built in. This gives a more natural look, especially to solid-color objects. Without these variations, the objects tend to look flat, computer generated, or fake. The following steps create one of the brushes I use often.

1. Grab a soft brush as I've done in Figure 7.21. I chose a 15-pixel-wide soft brush with 0 percent hardness.

2. At the Brush Tip Shape options, increase the spacing a bit. Aim for a slightly spaced-apart look like you see in Figure 7.22.

3. Select **Shape Dynamics** and give a bit of size jitter to your brush. This ensures that the variations you add don't look as mechanical because the brush stroke's size variation masks any color pattern.

Figure 7.21

Soft brush to start.

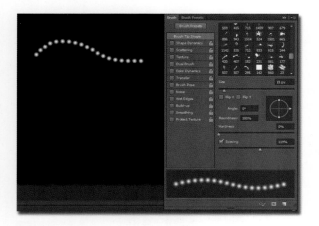

Figure 7.22

Set your spacing similar to what you see here.

4. Go to the Scattering options and give the brush a bit of scatter. You can see my settings in Figure 7.23

This allows the different colors and sizes to show up more because the brush stroke isn't confined to a single vector. Now comes the really nice stuff. This is a function I used to love Painter for and always complained about Photoshop lacking.

5. Select the Color Dynamics options and play with the Hue, Saturation, and Brightness Jitter settings you see in Figure 7.24.

The goal is to have a setting that doesn't create a calico (bright and multicolored) effect but subtly varies the color enough that it doesn't seem flat. I used a brighter, more saturated blue than I would have chosen for the two-color combination, but felt that I needed to exaggerate the second color to show the effect. When using this brush for snow, choose two colors that are bit closer in range.

6. Now that you have a setting that is nice, save it the same way you saved the dirt brush.
7. Go to your tool presets and click the **New Tool Preset** button ▣.
8. Give your brush a descriptive name and click **OK**.

This is my snow speckle brush. Take a look at how this particular brush makes a difference in a finished painting. In Figure 7.25, see how flat the solid colors look in the left image? See how much more natural the right image looks? I used the same foreground and background colors, but I used a standard brush on the left and our newly created speckle brush on the right.

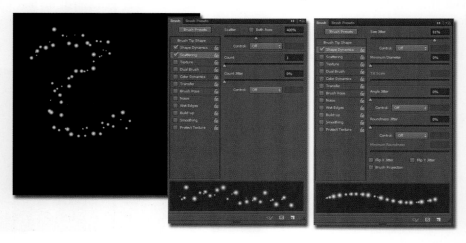

Figure 7.23

Settings for shape dynamics and scattering.

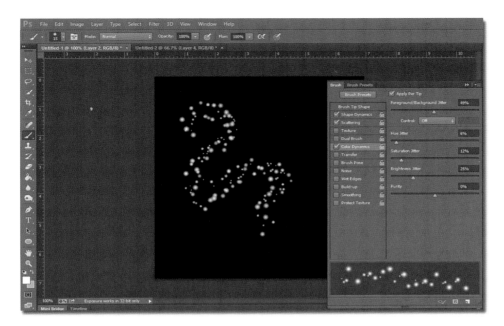

Figure 7.24

Match your color dynamics settings to those here.

Figure 7.25

Comparison of snow brush and airbrush.

You'll be amazed at the variety of uses you can find for this brush—and this is just the tip of the iceberg! You can create a fish brush and create a school of fish, or you can produce a brush that paints trees or bushes. Your only limitation is your imagination.

Brush Libraries

Now for the part you've been waiting for: how to make sure you don't lose all your beautiful brushes. You will create brush libraries.

Caution

Even though the brushes appear in the Brush Preset pull-down menu, if anyone resets the brushes to factory settings (as you did at the beginning of this book), you are out of luck—brushes are lost. It's best to save a brush library that can be loaded when you wish.

---

1. Choose **Save Brushes** from the Brush Presets pull-down menu ⚙.
   Photoshop should automatically take you to your preset brushes folder.
2. Enter a name for your brush library and click **Save**.

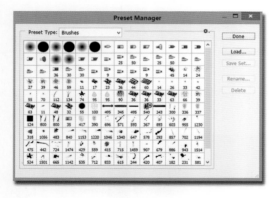

Figure 7.26

Preset Manager; Brushes.

This saves *all* the brushes currently in the Brush palette. Your new brush library name appears at the bottom of the Brush Preset pull-down menu ⚙, accessible by either right-clicking on the canvas while using the Brush tool on the Brush Preset drop-down menu in the Options bar. Now you know the general way to save a library. But, how do you save just the newly created dirt brushes in their own library?

As you create more brushes, you may find yourself getting more particular about the brushes that are available in the palette. Unused brush tips become a hassle that clutters your workspace. You can manage this library or any other saved preset with the **Preset Manager**:

1. Go to **Edit** > **Presets** > **Preset Manager** to bring up the dialog box.
2. Make sure your preset type is set to Brushes, as in Figure 7.26.
3. Click one of your dirt brushes.
4. Hold **Ctrl**/⌘ and click any other brush you wish to include in the library.
5. Press the **Save Set** button and give your library a name in the ensuing dialog box.

So begins your journey to your own personal library of brushes. Part of being a professional is having the right tools for the situation. To help you on your journey toward building this fine library of tools, I have a few libraries for you to have and to use; these are available on this book's website.

8

Second Date

Introduction

There comes a time when you get tired of the quickies and one-nighters and look for something a little more involved. Our senior generations might consider us as having an attention deficit—blaming our short attention span on rock videos or electronic gadgets. I have no idea how all that relates to these tutorials, but I feel a lot better now.

Chemical and Cross Processing

The chemical and cross-processing look originated from the deliberate processing of photographic film in the wrong chemical solutions meant for another process. This created interesting color shifts and increased contrast and became a popular method for fashion photography in the 1980s. With the purveyance of Instagram, this look came back into vogue. Instagram offers different filters to emulate a variety of looks, many of which are cross-processing looks. Instagram also offers chemical fade looks, such as photos from the 1970s would experience, and film borders

emulating the film rebate of film processing. This is all fine and dandy when you are using your phone, but what if you wanted to make a large-scale print with this same kind of look? Then, it's Photoshop to the rescue!

The best way to break this down is to figure out the kind of look you want to achieve. In my case, I want the type that has a high contrast, blown-out look with bluish shadows and yellow tones. There are a few ways to go about this, so I'll show you those.

One of the first and quickest ways is to use Split Toning in Adobe Camera Raw (ACR). If you are working with a RAW file, then ACR will open automatically when you open your file. If you are not working with a RAW file, then open ACR by going to **Filter > Camera Raw Filter...** or use the keyboard shortcut **Ctrl+Shft+A/⌘+Shift+A**.

In the ACR dialog, click on the Split Toning ▬ tab to access the Split Toning controls (Figure 8.1). As would be expected from something called Split Toning, the controls are divided into a Highlight sections and a Shadow section with a balance slider in between. Let's start by adding that warm golden tone to the picture. Move the Highlights slider to an orangey color and increase the saturation. Next, target the shadows by moving the Shadow slider to a blue color and increasing the saturation (Figure 8.2). Tada! Done. You may need to fiddle with the balance if you feel that one color is dominating the other and needs a little spreading out, but otherwise you can call it a day.

That was sort of a cheap date, so let me make it up to you and show you another way to go about getting that cross-processing look. Open your image again and again go to ACR (**Ctrl+Shift+A/⌘+Shift+A**). This time, we will work with curves. Click on the Tone Curve ◤ tab to access the curve controls. Click on the Point tab, and you'll see

Figure 8.1

ACR Split Toning controls.

Figure 8.2

Cross processed.

Figure 8.3

Tone Curve controls look familiar.

controls that look very similar to the image adjustment curves we use in Photoshop (Figure 8.3).

In the Channel drop-down menu, change from RGB (red-green-blue) to Blue and drag the bottom-left point of the curve upward and the top-right corner down. Notice how that affects the shadows and highlights (Figure 8.4).

Figure 8.4

Effects of adjusting the tone curve.

Figure 8.5

Create an *S*-shape curve like this.

Next, go to the Green channel. If you click on the curve, a control point will be added. Click and add two points so you can create a wavy *S* shape as seen in Figure 8.5.

Create a similar, if slightly shallower, version in the Red Channel. If you accidentally add a point when you didn't mean to, just click and drag the point off the control window, and the point will be taken off. Figure 8.6 shows where we are so far.

Figure 8.6

The curve so far.

Figure 8.7

Another successful cross-processing effect.

This looks pretty good, but I'm going to tweak it a bit. Click over to the Parametric tab and balance out the image—or in this case, "balancing" would mean blowing out some of the highlights and bringing up the darks to create a slightly washed-out look. Tada (again)! Yet another successful cross processing is accomplished (Figure 8.7).

Now, to add to the effect, I think this needs some vignetting. The photo already has some, but I want to add more. You'll see people painting black and fading it around

Figure 8.8

Create film rebate.

the edges, which is fine. But, you also can do this in ACR. Open ACR; you can do this as a filter in **Filter > Camera Raw Filter…**. Click on the Lens Correction ⊞ tab and click on the Manual tab. Look at the bottom two sliders that control vignetting. Most people are trying to get rid of vignetting, not adding it, so our choice is to drag the Amount slider all the way down to the left, then drag the Midpoint slider toward the left and see how the vignetting is soft and pleasant. When you have something you like, click **OK**.

The finishing touch I want to do is to add a messy black frame around the edges. I could look for a film rebate (Figure 8.8) that would make it seem like a film clip, but this is just a second date, so I'm going for the simple brush tool in black around the edges.

Create a new layer by clicking on the New Layer icon ⊞ at the bottom of the Layers palette. Choose a rough-edge brush or a chalky brush and just sketch around the borders.

Figure 8.9

Our starting picture.

Eye Cream

Have you seen those advertisements that show some miracle cream that gets rid of wrinkles? There are before and after pictures that show that the cream takes off what looks like 120 years. OK, I may be exaggerating; it looks like maybe 60 years. Isn't that fantastic? It never ceases to amaze me how bad some of those photos are; some are so badly Photoshopped that I cringe (which does not help my eye wrinkles one bit).

The best way to do this is to take some average middle-aged eyes and make them older, then make them younger. Let's start with the typical photo shown in Figure 8.9. Her eyes just aren't "old enough"; they are too pretty for our miracle cream before photo. At the same time, these eyes do not radiate the youth that would be the selling point for an eye cream. So, let's start with the easy part; we'll make the after picture be the epitome of youth and vitality. We'll have to fake some translucent hydration, some subsurface.

But first, let's get rid of all of her wrinkles. We'll need different copies of these eyes, so press **Ctrl+J/⌘+J** twice to create two duplicate layers of the eyes. Make sure you are on the topmost layer and go to **Filter > Camera Raw Filter…**.

A quick trick to get the skin looking smooth and flawless is to bring down the Clarity slider. You can adjust some of the other sliders to obtain a more vibrant feeling of youth if you want, but for my image, I think clarity alone did enough for now. Click **OK**.

You can see the results of just decreasing clarity in Figure 8.10.

Next, select the Spot Healing Brush and brush away some of the leftover wrinkles (Figure 8.11). Be careful not to get too close to the edges of the eyes or other points of high contrast because the healing brush will bleed them out. And, don't forget those faint wrinkles on the bridge of the nose.

Now, as any informed eye cream consumer would know, a good eye cream also lifts the eyes. So, we will use Liquify to nudge the eyes just a bit to appear more youthful. Go to **Filter > Liquify....** The Liquify dialog will appear. Set your brush size to slightly larger than the area you want to move and adjust the strength so that it moves the skin without distorting it. You may have to test a corner of the eye and undo a couple of times to get it right for your image. My settings can be seen in Figure 8.12.

Figure 8.10

ACR Clarity: instant eye cream.

Figure 8.11

Using the Spot Healing Brush to eradicate the last lines.

Don't overdo it. You want a youthful lift, but not necessarily notice it right off the bat—like facelift surgery. Also, remember to push up the bottom lid just a tad so that it looks thinner. One of effects of gravity is the drooping not only of the upper lid but also of the lower lid. Once you are happy, click **OK**.

Younger skin has a bit more of a glow and some rosy subsurface, so we'll use a soft brush with the opacity set to 20 percent and brush in some pink "youthful glow." That will do for the youthful eyes for now (Figure 8.13). Name this layer "After" and hide it by closing the Eye icon .

Now, click on the next layer down, which should be a duplicate of our original eyes. Let's start by emphasizing the existing wrinkles. Go to **Filter > Camera Raw Filter....** This time, we'll bring up the **Contrast** and the **Clarity** sliders to emphasize the wrinkles; while we are at it, let's take down some of the rosiness and saturation to make the skin look a little thin and dry. You can see my settings in Figure 8.14. Click **OK**.

This is going to be a base for us to add more wrinkles. The easiest way to do this is to find some eyes with a good amount of wrinkles and cut out sections to overlay. I have some eyes that have a similar skin tone. Use the Lasso Tool and lasso a section that you want to overlay; don't take too much at a time, just try to use regions.

You can go to **Edit > Copy**, but it's much easier to use the keyboard shortcuts; press **Ctrl+C/⌘+C** to copy the wrinkles, then go to your layer in the working set of eyes and press **Ctrl+V/⌘+V** to paste them onto a new layer above the working set. Set the layer blend

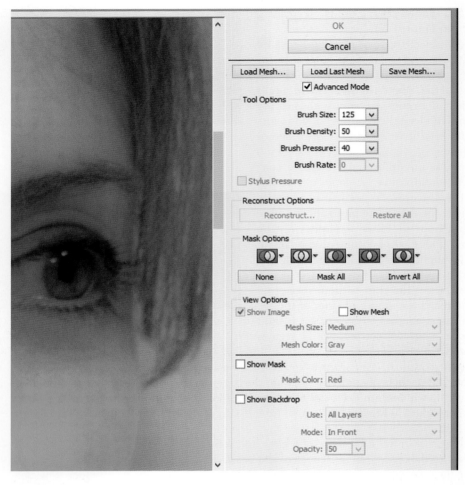

Figure 8.12

Liquify settings for eye lift.

Figure 8.13

Our younger eyes so far.

Figure 8.14

Using pieces from other eyes.

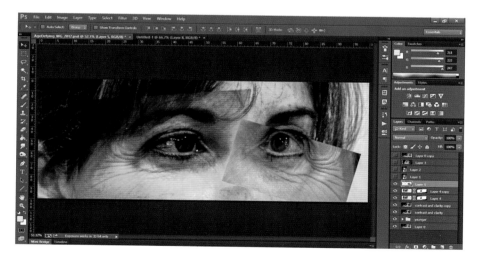

Figure 8.15

Wrinkles taken from another person and a different angle can still be warped to work.

mode to Soft Light and set the wrinkles to fit as best you can. In this case, the wrinkles need a little bit of shaping to fit the face, so let's use **Edit > Transform > Warp**. You can now click in the area you want to move and nudge it around similarly to Liquify and with more control than just the Free Transform (shortcut **Ctrl+T**/⌘+**T**). Move the wrinkles until they fall in the right places (Figure 8.15).

Do this with the rest of the eyes. You can erase or mask overlapping areas that don't work well together and adjust the blending mode and opacity to work. Because we desaturated the face a bit, the multiple overlays and soft lights aren't oversaturating the face too much. I came up with what you see in Figure 8.16.

If you are happy with the wrinkles, make sure you have the original background eyes hidden, and from the Layers palette pull-down menu ▭, choose **Merge Visible**.

You should now have three layers: our original starting eyes, the youthful after eyes, and now our older before eyes. But, looking at them, they really don't look like the same person. Part of the problem is the difference in eyebrows and coloring that shouldn't have changed. So, we are going to use the original eyes and bring back the eyebrows and eyes, things that our miracle cream wouldn't really affect. There are many ways you can do this, but I prefer to use two layers and a mask—and using a mask on this project seems apropos for the subject matter, don't you think? First, the colors are too far apart. Make a copy of each of our before and after images by dragging the layer to the New Layer button ▭ in the Layers palette. You should now have the background original

Figure 8.16

Our older eyes so far.

eyes, a before layer, a before copy layer, an after layer, and an after copy layer.. With the after copy layer selected, go to **Image > Adjustments > Match Color....**

The Match Color dialog window will appear (Figure 8.17). In the Image Statistics section, set the source to be your current Photoshop file and the layer to Background. This should make your painted layer have the same coloring as the original. You can adjust the Fade slider if you think that it is a bit too much but try not to adjust the other

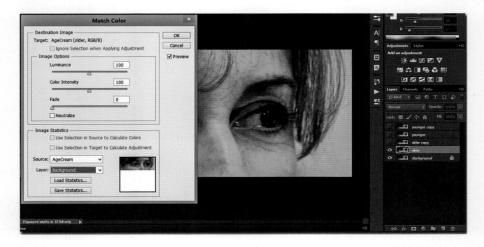

Figure 8.17

Match Color dialog.

sliders for this project because we want all three to have a similar feel. Click **OK** when you are done and do the same steps for the other copied layer.

Hide the first before and after photos and let's work on the eyebrows and eyes. Make a copy of the original eyes and move that layer above the before copy layer. Click on the Layer Mask button ▣ in the Layers panel. A Mask thumbnail will appear on that layer. Make sure you have the Mask selected (the thumbnail is outlined) and press **Ctrl+I/⌘+I** to invert it to black. The thumbnail should turn black and render the original eye copy invisible. With a small, white, smooth brush, brush back in the eyebrows and eyes. Then, do the same for the after copy.

Now, we *could* end here, but consumers are a bit more astute about Photoshopping than previously. So, we are going to adjust the perspective just a tad and hand draw a couple of eyebrows and eyelashes in so that it seems more like the client came in on another day to take the picture.

Voila! Before and after (Figure 8.18)—well, technically, it would be after and before, but that will be our little secret, right?

Adding Depth of Field

Sometimes, you have a great photo of a subject but the environment is so distracting you really want to just blur it all out, which is what a lot of people do. But, such a sudden flat blur can be a distraction itself. If you can create a Z-depth-fed blur, that would be optimal, but not all subjects need that kind of precision. In this case, we'll layer in different blurs to obtain the effect we want in a nondistracting manner.

Take a look at my starting photo in Figure 8.19. The adorable knight on his mighty steed is somewhat hard to find amidst the clutter. Often, people use an Iris Blur to focus on the subject. Let's start with that.

Make a copy of your image by pressing **Ctrl+J/⌘+J**. Do that once more so you have two copies of your original. Let's apply the iris filter as a smart filter, so first select your topmost layer and go to **Filter > Convert for Smart Filters**. (We're kind of jumping ahead, as

Figure 8.18

Before and after shots.

Figure 8.19

Starting photo.

Figure 8.20

Iris Blur.

we cover Smart Objects in Chapter 9; you can read more about Smart Objects there.) Now apply our iris filter: **Filter > Blur > Iris Blur....**

The controls appear as a center and an adjustable circle around the center that determines the area of focus (Figure 8.20). Move the center of control to the center of the boy and click drag on the outer circle to rotate and squeeze so that it fits just around him. The four white dots within the circle determine the rate of falloff for the blur from the center focus. You also can move those to your liking. Use the slider on the right and adjust the amount of blur to be applied; click **OK**.

As you can see, although it does indeed focus on the boy, it is odd that the background directly behind him is in focus, yet it is out of focus to the left and right of him. Let's hide this layer and try another blur. Click on the Eye icon 👁 to hide it and click on the other copy layer.

Do the same **Filter > Convert for Smart Filters**, but this time follow it by **Filter > Blur > Tilt-Shift Blur....** This time the controls are in the form of lines. Normally, this is to focus on a very specific plane of focus, and we want to focus on the boy. Move the center control to the center of the boy's feet near the floor. The first lines indicate the area of focus. So, click and drag those two solid lines to be near the front of the rocking horse and the back of the rocking horse's legs. Slide the Blur setting on the slider on the right until you obtain just enough blur to smooth out the background (Figure 8.21). The dotted lines are for the rate of falloff; set that to a pleasing setting. Obviously, the boy is completely blurred out, but don't worry about that right now. Click **OK** when the floor looks like it has the right amount of blur.

Notice that both of our blurred layers have a mask and have retained the blurs as a sort of adjustable layer. Take a black brush, and making sure you have the Mask selected, paint out the boy so he is not included in the tilt-shift blur (Figure 8.22).

Figure 8.21

Blur the background.

Figure 8.22

Painting in the mask.

Now, unhide the iris blur and reduce the opacity just a bit so that you can see the lower layer; paint in the mask a soft gradation that will soften the tilt-shift blur a bit and make it more of a lens focus blur. You can readjust the blurs and repaint the mask until you obtain a more natural blur effect. If you would like to add bokeh, you apply the same method we used but use the Lens Blur. Blend and adjust until it is *precisely* what you want (Figure 8.23).

Figure 8.23

Final result.

Figure 8.24

Starting image.

Gritty Photo Koala

I still like this grungy, gritty photo effect—and so do a lot of other people, judging by how popular the demand for this process is. Usually, you see this with an old man looking directly at the camera, taking an average soft old grandpa looking vacant to a hardened coal miner giving you the eye. You can apply this technique to just about any photo; take the soft fuzzy koala in Figure 8.24, for instance.

First, let's sharpen him up a bit; go to **Filter > Camera Raw Filter…**. Increase the clarity and contrast. Then, crush the highlights way down. The image becomes a little too dark, so increase the blacks. For the koala's nose, I want that to have a nice grungy gradient going across it. When you have something like what I have in Figure 8.25, click **OK**. Now, make a duplicate of that image by pressing **Ctrl+J/⌘+J**.

We still need to sharpen it, so we're going to run the high-pass filter over this copy and use it to sharpen the image and give it a slight metallic feel (Figure 8.26). Go to **Filter > Other > High Pass**. Adjust the slider until you obtain a good amount of detail, but not so much that you have a halo around the nose and eyes. Click **OK** to accept.

Change the mode of the high-passed layer to overlay; you can adjust the opacity if you think it is a little too much, but at this stage, if it is looking too strong, it is more likely that

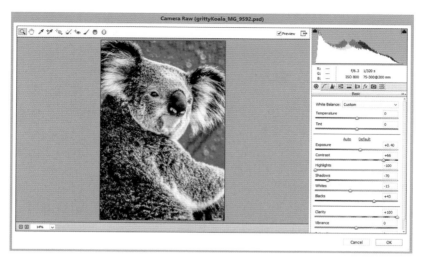

Figure 8.25

Koala with increased clarity and contrast.

you overdid it with the high pass. Now, make a duplicate of the merged result by pressing **Ctrl+A/⌘+A** to select all, then **Ctrl+Shift+C/⌘+Shift+C** to copy the merged image; last, use **Ctrl+V/⌘+V** to paste it into a new layer. Make this layer mode Hard Light. Paste the image again and make the new layer mode Saturation. This should reduce the color saturation greatly. I felt at this point that the contrast was a little too hard, so I reduced the Hard Light layer's opacity to 87 percent. Are you with me so far? Check your progress in relation to Figure 8.27.

The nose is also a little too harsh, so I need to create a rounder-feeling nose. Paste in another merged copy (**Ctrl+V/⌘+V**), and this time run **Image > Adjustments > Black&White**. Adjust the sliders until the black-and-white image has a nice range of tones on the nose. Don't worry about the other parts of the bear; this layer is just for the nose. Once you are satisfied with the nose, click **OK**.

Click on the Mask button ◻ in the Layers palette and, with the Mask thumbnail selected in the layer, press **Ctrl+I/⌘+I** to invert the mask. Now, with the white brush, bring back the nose in the areas to make your koala's nose attractive.

One of the key components in this look is the startling eyes. Amidst the grime and grunge, the surprising glint of sapphire or topaz gleams out at you. To do this, create a new transparent layer above everything else by pressing on

Figure 8.26

High-pass filter.

Figure 8.27

Compare your progress and your layers.

Figure 8.28

Drop bear (final Koala).

the New Layer button ◰ in the Layers palette. Choose a nice golden color and color in the eyes and paint it. Set the layer blend mode to Color Dodge and lower the opacity until the eyes read more as "gleaming" and less like "possessed."

There you go: gone is the soft, dopey koala, and in its stead is the steely glint of a deadly drop bear (Figure 8.28). (You'd have to have been to Australia to get that one.)

What Is Your Type?

My type is hot. Really hot. So hot, it's on fire! Take a look at Figure 8.29.

Open a new blank document. I made mine 2048×1550. First, let's set up a background. Choose the Gradient Tool ◱ and choose the Radial Gradient option in the Options bar. Setting your colors to a brown and black, create a smooth gradient like you see in Figure 8.30. Notice that the "center" of the gradient is not in the center of the canvas. This is because we know that our text will be off to the lower right, so we are putting the hottest spot where the fire will be.

Now, open an image of stone or concrete and bring it in on top. You can do this with one click using Mini Bridge. Click and drag to your canvas, and the image is placed as a smart layer. Set the layer blend mode to overlay and adjust the opacity (Figure 8.31).

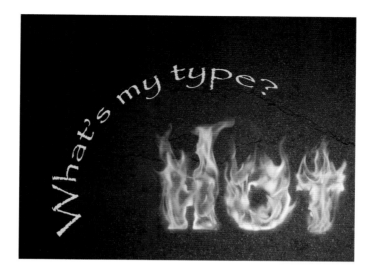

Figure 8.29

Hot text.

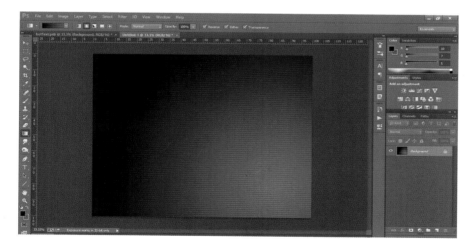

Figure 8.30

Create a smooth gradient.

Now, select the Type Tool ![T]. In the Options bar, you can choose the font—in my case Papyrus—and the other characteristics, such as size and color. Click on the top-left corner and type in your phrase or question (Figure 8.32), in this case, "What's your type?"

Hold **Shift** and click on the center of the canvas. A new text layer will form, and you can choose the font and size and color again for the next word. In this case, just type the letter *H*. Hold **Shift** and click next to the *H* to create another text layer and type *O*. Again, hold **Shift** and click to form a new text layer and type *T* (Figure 8.33).

Figure 8.31

Concrete set to overlay at 100 percent.

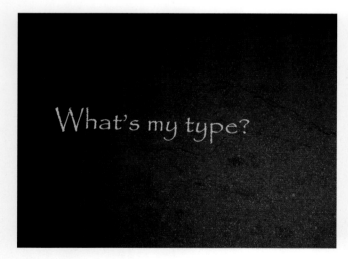

Figure 8.32

Type in a phrase.

Now that we know where the letters *HOT* are, let's curve the question so it curves around the corner; click on the question layer and make sure you have the Text Tool selected (Figure 8.34). In the Options bar, there is a Warp Text button that will bring up a dialog. Right now, there is no warp attached to the text, so the style says None. Click on the pull-down menu and choose Arc. Increase the bend to 80 percent and click **OK**.

The text is bent, but we want to position it a bit more into the corner and possibly reduce the size, so press **Ctrl+T/⌘+T** and use the transform controls to rotate and resize the text to fit.

Now, we can go back to the fiery letters. You can stay on T, but I'm going to click on the H layer and apply my layer effects to the letter *H*. Click on the Layer Effects button on the bottom of the Layers palette and choose **inner glow**. In the Layer Style dialog, increase the size of the glow and increase the opacity so you see a nice inner glow. Don't click on OK yet; go down and click on **Drop Shadow**. The parameters pop up on the right, and the check box automatically checks. Change the blend mode to Normal and click on the color swatch next to it to change the color to a bright red. Increase Opacity to 100 percent, but change the distance to 0, and increase the Spread until a red glow shows around the outside of the letter. For me, that was 24%. I also set the Size to 40.

We will also add a **color overlay**, choosing a color so that it feels almost like we are looking through the letter to the background. Check out my settings for **Satin** and all the mentioned styles in Figure 8.35, along with the look of the letter. Click **OK** to move on.

We want to apply the same combination of effects to the other letters. To do so, simply hold **Alt**/**Option** and click drag the fx from the H layer to the O layer. Then, repeat for T.

Now, we need to give some wavy fire-like movement to the type. To do that, we will need to rasterize the layer style. **Right-Click**/**Ctrl-Click** on the layer and choose **Rasterize the Layer Style**. Next, we will go to **Filter > Liquify…**.

In the Liquify dialog, use the forward warp and brush along the edges, breaking up the outline, giving it some heat waves, and pulling up to create some small flames (Figure 8.36).

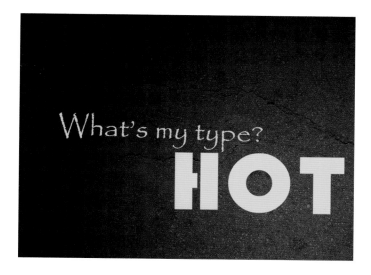

Figure 8.33

Placing the HOT.

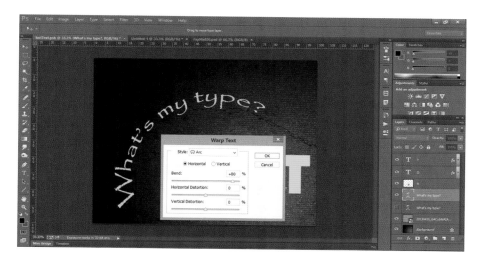

Figure 8.34

Curving the question.

The main thing to keep in mind is that flames go upward, and the edges should not be equal thickness. Pulling the brush from different areas will bring more yellow or more red or orange into the mix. Once you are done, do the same to the other letters, rasterizing the layer style first, then breaking up the edges to look fiery.

Before we start adding flames, we need to get rid of the top lines of our text (Figure 8.37). Click on the Layer Mask button ▣ and paint on the layer mask with black to break up the top

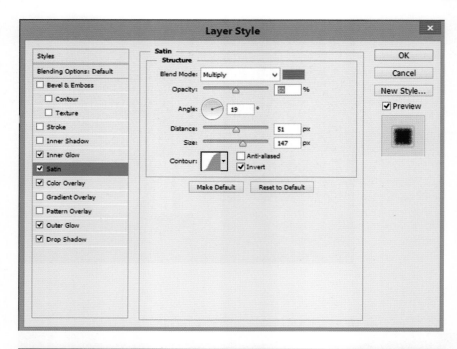

Figure 8.35

Layer fx settings.

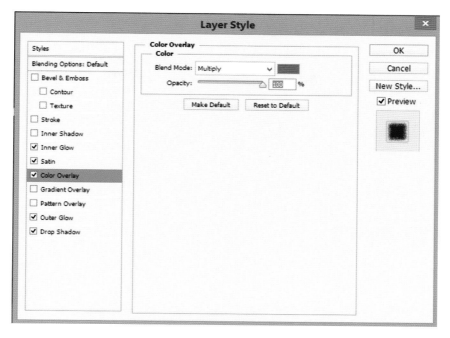

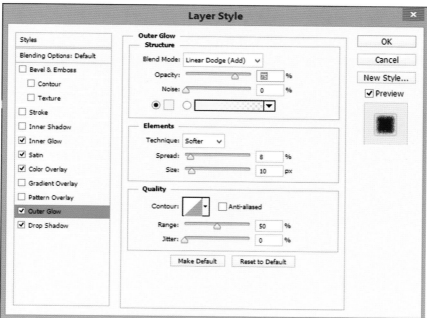

Figure 8.35 (*Continued*)

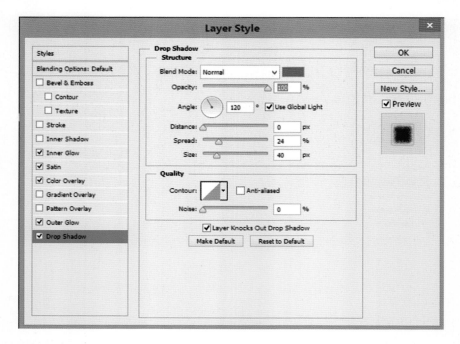

Figure 8.35 (*Continued*)

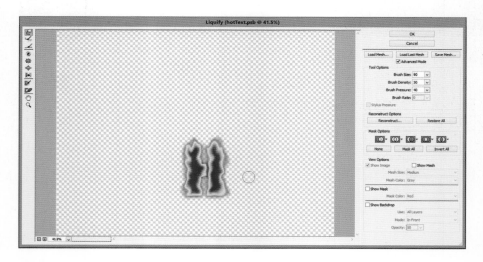

Figure 8.36

Fiery letters liquify.

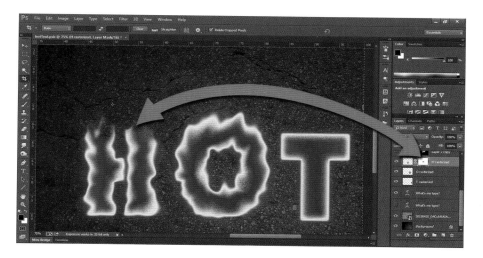

Figure 8.37

Getting rid of top lines.

Figure 8.38

I just took some pictures in my backyard for fire reference. It would have been better if I had dropped a black background behind the chimera.

edges of the letters. We do this because flames flow upward, and the horizontal lines of the letters will interfere with the read of the flames. Once you have done this for each letter, we can add flames.

Now, we need to add some flames. I took pictures of flames (Figure 8.38), but you can easily find pictures of flames on the Internet. Open the file and go to the Channels palette.

Figure 8.39

Final HOT text.

Hold **Ctrl**/⌘ and click on the Green channel to obtain a natural-looking selection. Click back to the Layers palette and hit **Ctrl+C**/⌘**+C** to copy the selection out of the flames. Click back to your canvas and press **Ctrl+V**/⌘**+V** to paste the flames onto a new transparent layer on top of the type.

Find an area that looks good on the letter. Use the Eraser Tool ✎ to get rid of sections you do not want or use the Lasso Tool ◎ to select and delete sections. You can also press **Ctrl+T**/⌘**+T** to transform the shape of the fire. Work on one letter at a time. Once you are done with one letter, move on to the next, using the same steps. When all three letters are done, you can add a few overall flames to the bunch to unify them (Figure 8.39).

9

Smarter in So Many Ways

Introduction

Why use three dimensions (3D) if I'm not a 3D artist? Or, why do I care about video? These methods that are "outside the box" are the stuff creative juice is squeezed from. Many purists may feel like using these "tools of other professions" is like using a spade for a spatula, but I disagree. I think it's like bringing indoor furniture outside or vice- versa; done the right way, it's called "inspired design." These features add flexibility to your workflow. Smart Objects will give you nondestructive transformations and one-click template content replacement. 3D can bolster your painting skills and opens a whole other world for play. Video can also expand your horizons into dimensions you didn't even realize you were already in partially.

You might be familiar with one of these categories in Photoshop, but rarely have I met anyone fluent in all of them. That will change, though. More and more people are starting to realize how valuable diversification can be.

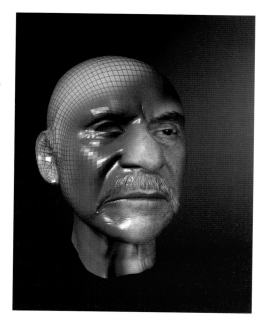

Smart Objects

Smart Object Features

If you had a good memory and could bring back anything at will, you would probably be considered smart. Think of Smart Objects as things that have memory and won't forget: Smart Objects preserve the original image data so that you can edit nondestructively. You can bring in Illustrator vector files as Smart Objects and have changes made in Illustrator update automatically in your Photoshop file. You can link and instance multiple layers and use Smart Objects as placeholders for templates.

An easy example of the difference of Smart Objects would be that if we scaled an image *way* down, then scaled it back up, it would lose resolution. But, if we make it a Smart Object first, then it remembers the original information and scales up well. You can't do pixel-based editing for it to remember, but you can run filters nondestructively, and Smart Objects now support Liquify and Blur gallery.

Photo Sheet Introduction to Smart Objects

Smart Objects are the smart thing to use. The easiest way to show you is for you to make a photo sheet. Open a new document (**Ctrl+N**/⌘**+N**) and choose the US Paper Preset, Letter size.

Now, open Mini Bridge at the bottom of your screen and select an image, any image. Double-click to open it. Copy the image by selecting all (**Ctrl+A**/⌘**+A**) then copying (**Ctrl+C**/⌘**+C**). Then paste (**Ctrl+V**/⌘**+V**) into the new letter-size document (*do not* drag and drop). Next, drag that same image to your document. When you drag, Photoshop automatically assumes it is a Smart Object. To accept the sizing, just hit **Enter/Return**. Now, you have two layers with the same image. Use the Free Transform (**Ctrl+T**/⌘**+T**) and make both of them very small—almost a pinprick. Then, use Free Transform again to resize them back up (Figure 9.1). Notice a difference? The standard layer lost information and cannot be reconstituted. But, the Smart Object is still as clear because it remembers the original information.

Delete the standard layer by selecting it and dragging it to the Trash icon 🗑 in the Layers palette. Now, duplicate the Smart Object layer the way you would normally duplicate a layer, by pressing **Ctrl+J**/⌘**+J**. Create a layout as if you were printing school pictures (remember those? wallet size, 3 × 5, all on a page). You can see my simple layout in Figure 9.2.

Go to one of the layers and **Right-Click**/**Ctrl+Click** and choose from the pop-up menu **Replace Contents…**. Choose another image and click **Place**. *All* the images are replaced with the newly selected image (Figure 9.3). That's because the copies we placed are instances of the original, and as a Smart Object, it remembers all the transformations and applies the same transformations to the incoming image. But, you'll notice that if you try to paint on the layer, you won't be able to do that. To do pixel-based editing such as painting, you need to affect the original file. You can do this by going to **Layer > Smart Objects > Edit Contents**. You can make whatever changes you want, flatten it, and save. Your other document with the Smart Objects will update automatically. Now, *that's* smart!

There may be a time when you don't want one copy to change. Then, use **Layer > Smart Object > New Smart Object via copy**. Then, the changes to this copy will not be propagated to the others.

Figure 9.1

Reenlarging shows the difference between a Smart Object and a non-Smart Object.

Figure 9.2

A simple photosheet layout.

Figure 9.3

The images are replaced.

Throughout this book you will see that many of the tutorials use Smart Objects to give you the flexibility of nondestructive editing.

3D

The ability to integrate and use 3D is a great boon to Photoshop users, bridging that great divide that has long separated 2D and 3D artists. For those of us who have used 3D in helping to set up paintings—this is a godsend. For those who have never used it, let me help you realize it. 3D can give us the flexibility of changing lighting, composition, or angle of view quickly, interactively even, where other setups would take a longer time to repaint or sketch.

And, for those who already use 3D packages and have dismissed Photoshop's 3D after being frustrated by the initial clumsy foray in previous versions, it may be time to take another look. Photoshop has had some great 3D updates. The default IBL (image-based lighting) is better, the ray tracing is better, and there is support for normal mapping in addition to the the standard bump, color, specular, and reflections. The 3D tools are easier to use. I still find myself wanting Maya hot key movements, but since ZBrush went its own path and is still doing well, I guess once we get used to whatever Photoshop settles on, we may also be fine with their tools.

Although far from a stand-alone 3D package, Photoshop has plenty for us to use and work with. You can create geometry from paths, text, images, and shapes. You can import your own model, or you can use one of the presets that comes with Photoshop CC.

Now, for those who are completely unfamiliar with 3D, the fear factor and foreignness of it all may seem overwhelming. But, fear not, for I have faith in you, Great Warrior of Photoshop. This is a path still not taken by most, but with a little guidance, you will find a great reward at the end of the trail, limited only by your imagination (cue inspiring soundtrack).

3D Workspace

Because we will be working in 3D, let's change the workspace to the 3D workspace. Click on the Workspace pull-down menu on the far upper-right corner of the interface. One of the options should be 3D. Choose 3D, then click again and choose reset 3D (Figure 9.4). This will ensure that we are working from the default settings.

There doesn't seem to be much of a difference, right? If you look at the panels on the right, you will see that there is a 3D palette open, but the standard layers and channels are tabbed right next to it. Click on the Layers tab and you'll see your standard layers like you normally use for work. Click back on the 3D tab, and you'll see the palette shows options for creating a new 3D object.

Terminology

Before we can move into creation in 3D, you'll have to have a rudimentary understanding of 3D at the beginning. First, let us review the different components of 3D fundamentals in the language that Photoshop uses for its 3D arena.

Meshes: These are generally referred to as "models," "objects," and more recently (because of ZBrush's increasing popularity) "tools" (which I find annoyingly confusing but have come to accept). These 3D objects are often visualized as wireframe meshes and are called such.

Lights: There are several types in Photoshop: infinite, spot, and point lights, as well as IBL options. You can change the position, orientation, color, or intensity of any of the lights in the scene.

Environment: Think of the environment as the stage in which your object is being shot. If you use an IBL setup, the image you use will light and reflect into your object. You can, however use a different image for your environment than your IBL.

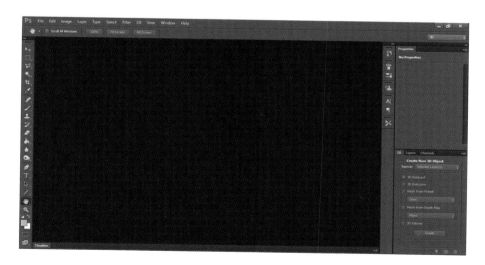

Figure 9.4

A 3D workspace.

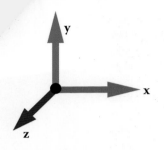

Figure 9.5

Axes.

Axis: There are three axes in the standard Cartesian coordinate system in 3D: *x*, *y*, and *z* (Figure 9.5). It is standard practice to color the axes red, green, and blue, respectively, to coordinate and easily identify each axis. Don't worry, there will be no math test at the end of this chapter.

Materials: A material is what gives a mesh its visual properties. A material has settings for components such as color/diffuse, specular/shininess, illumination, ambient, reflection, opacity, or bumpiness. Photoshop has a slider for roughness and for bump, which can be a little confusing. Think of roughness as the small-scale diffusion of shine and reflection. So, having roughness is an overall textural property, whereas bump is a fake displacement. The 2D image files called *texture maps* can be assigned to some of these qualities.

Diffuse Map: Your diffuse map is your color map, what most people see and think of as 'THE' texture map.

Bump Map: Bump maps can have any color, but only the tonal information is used; hence, for human clarity we use grayscale images. Pure white would make it look like the surface is pushing out, and pure black would make it look like the surface is pushing in. This is not actually displacing the surface, just giving the illusion of it. So, a view from a glancing angle would reveal a still-flat surface.

Displacement Map: The displacement map actually displaces the surface according to the tonal information along the normal of the surface. The quality of the displacement is reliant on the polycount, so detailed displacement would need a dense mesh and would therefore use a lot of memory.

Specular Map and Matte: A specular map can set the color of shine or the amount of shine. Think of a rusted pipe: The areas of rust would need to have less specularity (so matted out with black), and the shiny areas would maintain shininess (designated with various shades of gray or white, depending on shininess).

Opacity: The opacity map uses the tonal information (read: black or white) to determine how transparent the material would be. So, if you wanted a hole in a wall, you would have a white map with a black hole.

Normal Map: Similar to a bump map in that it seems to displace the surface, but instead of a single value indicating movement along the normal, the normal map stores *x*, *y*, and *z* translations to provide fine, high detail on a low-poly model.

Learning Your Way Around 3D

To learn 3D, let's start with something familiar: Create a new document, not too large, as the larger it is, the more intensive the 3D calculations can become. I made mine 1000 × 800 pixels.

Now, in the Layers palette, create a new fill layer by clicking the New Fill or Adjustment Layer button ⬤ on the bottom of the Layers palette. You can choose any color, but I'll keep mine simple with a medium gray. Name this layer Groundplane.

Choose the Text Tool ⬚ and write your name in a large font that takes up most of the canvas (Figure 9.6). This should automatically make a new layer above the fill layer with text.

Bring in an image. Open Mini Bridge and drag in any image of your choice. If Mini Bridge is not visible as a tab on the bottom frame of your workspace, you can bring it back by going to **File > Browse in Mini Bridge**. You can see that I brought in a seashore image. Holding **Ctrl**/⌘, I click on the thumbnail of the text layer with my name on it, and it

Figure 9.6

Feel free to choose a font that appeals to you.

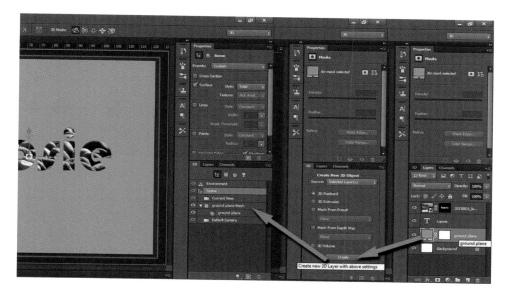

Figure 9.7

Making the ground plane into 3D geometry.

creates a selection. Now, select the layer with your imported image and click on the Layer Mask button ▣. Your name is constructed of the image. To avoid confusion with the tutorial, hide the text layer by clicking on the Visibility icon/Eye ▣ on the layer.

We move now to the 3D aspect of this. Select the Ground Plane layer, then switch to the 3D tab. The 3D tab has the Create New 3D Object selections. Select 3D Postcard and click **Create**. You should see a change in your canvas and in the 3D tab as shown in Figure 9.7.

Next, click back to the Layers palette; select the layer with your name cut out of the photo. Click back to the 3D tab, and you will see the same Create New 3D Objection selections as you had with the Ground Plane. This time, select **3D Extrusion** and click **Create**. Again, you will see the change on the canvas as your text now has dimension (Figure 9.8).

What we have now are two sets of geometry existing in two different worlds. So, we are going to merge the two geometry layers by holding **Shift** while selecting the two layers, then going to the Menu bar and selecting **3D > Merge 3D Layers** (Figure 9.9). The two layers are now in the same environment, but each mesh still is its own individual object. Click over to the 3D palette and select your ground plane mesh. The Properties palette will show Mesh Properties. Click on the Coordinates button 🔘 to obtain the ground plane coordinate controls as you see in Figure 9.10.

Change the x angle to 90 degrees, then click on the button **Move to Ground** to snap the object to the 3D ground plane. Next, select your name and click on the **Move to Ground** button. You should see both move down to the 3D default ground plane.

Now, adjust the view; this is a little awkward at first, as it is a little more complicated than moving in a 2D layer. You can't use the pan hand 🖐 in 3D; select the Move Tool ⊹, and you will see additional options in the Options bar for navigating in 3D at the far right of the bar. If they are grayed out, go back to Layers and make sure you have the 3D layer selected. In the 3D palette, select the Current View. Select the Slide Tool 🔘 in the Options bar, then click drag to see the camera view move. Dragging up pushes the camera back (dolly out); dragging down brings us in closer (dolly in). Click dragging left or right slides us to the left or right (truck left, truck right, respectively). Experiment with the other 3D tools until you have a composition that you like, such as mine in Figure 9.11.

Figure 9.8

Extruding the text.

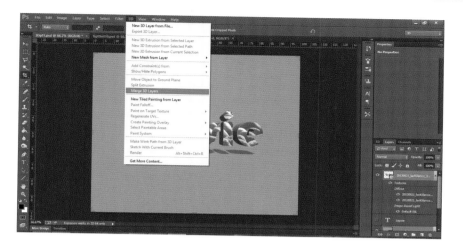

Figure 9.9

Merge the two 3D layers so that they exist in the same world.

Figure 9.10

Moving the ground plane via coordinate input.

Now that we have the basic composition, let's work on lighting and materials. Click on Environment in the 3D palette and look at the Properties. Photoshop now automatically includes an IBL. You can download various IBLs from Adobe, or you can make your own. With the Environment still selected in the 3D palette, click on the 3D Rotate Tool and click drag to see how the IBL affects how your scene is lit. Don't worry about getting it back to where it was originally; this is more about understanding how Photoshop's 3D system interprets information, and we'll be changing out the IBL anyway.

Now, click on the Materials button in the 3D palette so that only the materials are listed. You can see that there is a ground plane material and a material for every face

Figure 9.11

Create your 3D composition.

of the text (Figure 9.12). When you click on one, say, the ground plane, the Properties palette will show you what kind of material is assigned. You have quite a few preset materials available with Photoshop. Let's choose one for the ground plane first. With the ground plane material selected, go to the Properties panel and click on the image of the sphere. A bunch of thumbnails of different materials will appear. Click on the settings ⚙ and from the pull-down menu choose **Large List**. The thumbnails change to a list form so you can see the name and the material thumbnail. Choose a metal one like Iron or Gold. Use the same method to choose a material for the letters. You can add lights, adjust any of the properties of the metals, and move around to change the composition of your piece. All this can be much more flexible than resketching ideas (Figure 9.13).

The best way to familiarize yourself with all these controls is to play with the settings. But, do not rely on the image before you; you will need to render your image to see the full extent of the settings. To render, go to **3D > Render**. You can see that the image information is retained on your name, and the shadows and metallic look is a bit better than the preview. This is just an introductory tutorial (see Chapter 10 for some more complex 3D fun), but it would be a disservice if we didn't adjust and play with the settings.

First, go to the 3D palette and choose Environment as we did previously. Select your IBL image and choose **Replace Texture…**. Choose the same image that you used for your name.

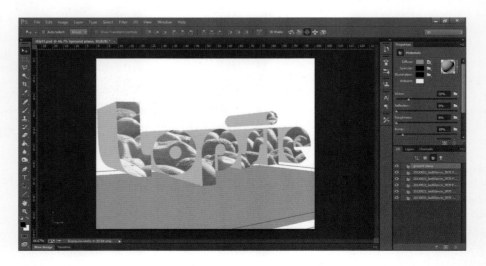

Figure 9.12

Notice the materials. The letters have a different material for each side.

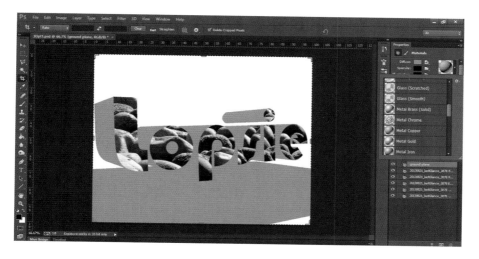

Figure 9.13

The Large List of materials shows a sample sphere alongside the name.

Next, click on the Material View button to see just the materials in the scene. Find the material that is on the extrusion of your name. You can toggle the visibility to find which one it is. Once you have it selected, go to the material sphere in the Properties palette and select the Metal Iron material. Increase the shine to 25 percent and the reflection to 90 percent. Before we render, we'll also add a bump map to the front of our name. Select the front material in the 3D palette, and in the Properties palette, go down to where it says Bump. By default, it has 10 percent assigned to the material, but because there is no map assigned to it, no bump is visible. Click on the Folder icon to assign a bump map. Assign the same map that you have for your diffuse: the image of your name with the image within the text. Now, do a render, **3D > Render**, and see how it looks. This is a good time to get up and get your cup of

Figure 9.14

With just a couple of tweaks, the material renders quite differently.

coffee, stretch, maybe learn a word or two of another language. Although I like the 3D capabilities, the rendering times leave much to be desired. Figure 9.14 shows how different your image can look with just a few adjustments.

Chapter 10 covers some of the more complex ways that the 3D capabilities can be used, including painting on the objects, creating volumes, and using other tricks, but

I hope this little introductory tutorial has piqued your interest and alerted you to the potential possibilities.

Video—Another Kind of 2D

Let's face it: You probably are not going to use Photoshop as a video editor for a TV show or movie, so the real question is, what *would* you use it for? If you ever had to make an asset that was to be used in motion graphics or video/film composition, you would know how handy it is to be able to check your work in something like Final Cut or After Effects. But, of course, that means that you need to learn additional software, *and* you have to export it to the other software. Or, perhaps you just need to do something simple: create a title, some lower-thirds name straps, or some simple sample motion graphics. Photoshop's video capabilities will allow you to do a variety of motion-related tasks.

Chapter 10 has some fun things that you can do with video, but before you can go through those tutorials, you should make sure you understand and can do the basics.

Setting Your Workspace

Before we begin working on a project, let's set up our workspace and familiarize ourselves with the layout. You can set the space to video mode by going to the Menu bar and choosing **Window > Workspace > Motion**. Or you can use the Workspace pull-down menu located at the top right of the interface and choose **Motion** (see Figure 9.15).

The main component of the Motion Workspace is the timeline located at the bottom of the workspace. Here is where you can see and edit a chronological display of your sequence. If for any reason your timeline is not visible, you can reset your workspace

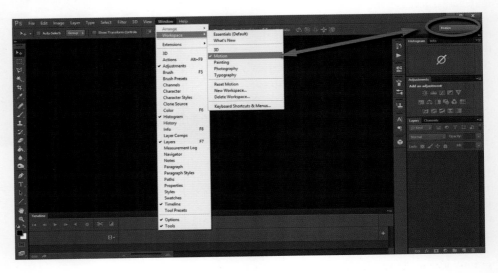

Figure 9.15

The motion workspace.

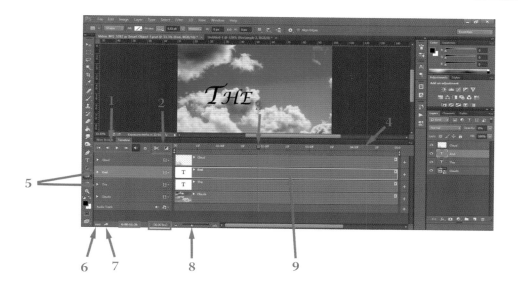

Figure 9.16

Components of the Timeline. 1, transport controls; 2, editing tools; 3, playhead; 4, time indicator; 5, video tracks; 6, frame animation/video toggle; 7, Render button; 8, timeline zoom; 9, footage.

either via the pull-down menu or through the Menu bar **Window > Workspace > Reset Motion**. Or, you could bring up the timeline by going to **Window > Timeline**.

Now, let's look at the components of the Timeline. Figure 9.16 shows the basic components.

- *Transport Controls:* Even if you haven't edited video before, these symbols should be familiar. In order, they are first frame, previous frame, play/stop, next frame. Mute audio playback and set playback options are also located here.
- *Editing Tools:* A splitter and transition tool are here for easy access.
- *Playhead:* This is an indicator to show where the video is in time. It will move across the timeline with a red hairline so you can track what you are looking at, or you can click drag it to scrub across the timeline.
- *Time Indicator:* This is your timeline expressed in seconds and frames. By default, Photoshop works with 30 frames per second (fps). So, 2:00 is 2 seconds. 2:15 is 2 seconds and 15 frames.
- *Video Tracks:* Think of these as the "layers" of video.
- *Frame Animation/Video toggle.*
- *Render button:* With video, you'll need to render to obtain the final composited footage.
- *Current Time:* This is the current time readout of where your playhead is located.
- *Frame Rate:* Your current frame rate is found here.
- *Timeline Zoom:* Scrub to the left to zoom out and to the right to zoom in.
- *Footage:* Blue indicates video, and purple indicates a still frame or image.

Here are a few things to note because we're working with video:

Frame Rate: You'll notice that we are working with 30 fps. That is the typical shorthand rate for video and television in the United States. I say shorthand because it's actually 29.97 fps, but we generally just refer to it as 30 fps or NTSC (National Television System Committee). Motion pictures generally use 24 fps (actually, 23.97 fps), although some movies are shooting at 48 frames per second (We can thank Peter Jackson for leading the way on that!). Most of Europe, Asia, and the South Pacific use a standard called PAL (Phase Alternating Line) for television that is 25 fps.

Artifacts: Because video deals with many codecs and compression, video can sometimes have strange stray pixels that we refer to as artifacts.

Nonsquare Pixels: When you think of a pixel, you probably think of a small square because Photoshop and its images always deal with square pixels by default. When dealing with video or assets derived from video (a still image captured from video, for example), you have to take into consideration that video can have nonsquare pixels. If you bring in an asset that looks squished, you probably have a nonsquare pixel image. To correct it properly, go to **View** > **Pixel Aspect ratio** and change to the proper pixel aspect ratio.

Interlaced: You'll hear of interlaced a lot; it was the traditional way of compressing video for broadcast over the airwaves to our television. Each alternating horizontal line was transmitted separately and played back quickly so our eyes did not see the absence. Now, this is being phased out as it is based on old technology.

Aspect Ratios and Common Sizes for Video: Check out Chapter 12 for sizes and ratios.

Crash Course

Now that you've seen the interface, let's make a movie. Well, actually, we'll start with the end. I think it's pretty cool the way Photoshop can understand our layers and files.

Open a file that has multiple layers; take a look at mine in Figure 9.17. (This is my standard Photoshop file in the Motion workspace; you're just itching to press the Create Video Timeline button, aren't you?) You can either download this one from our companion website or create your own.

I have an unlocked background layer of a picture with clouds. On top, I have two text layers. One that says "The" and another that says "End." Last but not least, I have a single floating cloud on top of it all. It's just a cutout cloud pasted on to a new transparent layer.

Notice that in the timeline, there is a Create Video Timeline button. Do it! Click it. You know you want to—Bam! A timeline is created for each layered image, and the track is named according to the layer name (Figure 9.18). You have just brought your painting into the fourth dimension.

Don't let the factor of time confuse you. Let's say that having the cloud layer called Layer 1 bothered me. I can go into my Layers palette and rename my layer Cloud, and the video track will be updated to reflect my changes.

Now, let's give that cloud some animation. If you click on the little triangle to the left of the track's name, you will see some keyable options. Make sure you are still on the starting frame by clicking the Starting Frame button ◄. Then, click on the Stop Watch icon ⏱ next

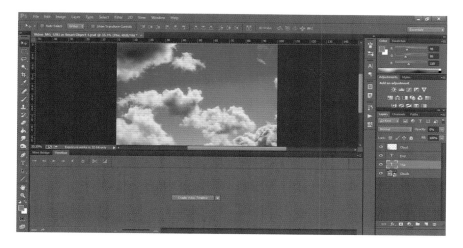

Figure 9.17

A regular Photoshop file with layers.

Figure 9.18

The timeline created from layers.

to the Position attribute. A yellow diamond should appear at the hairline on the track and next to the Stop Watch icon next to the Position attribute declaring that a keyframe has been set. This is our point A, the starting point for the cloud's animation path (Figure 9.19).

Next, slide the playhead to the end and move the cloud about halfway through the frame. The yellow diamond should automatically appear to denote that another keyframe has been set. This is our point B.

Hit Play ▶. You will see the cloud move across the screen from point A to point B.

Now, we'll go down to our text layers.

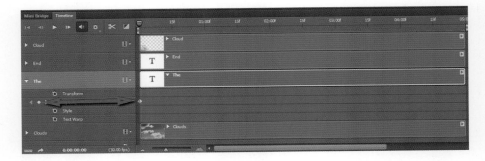

Figure 9.19

Setting our first keyframe.

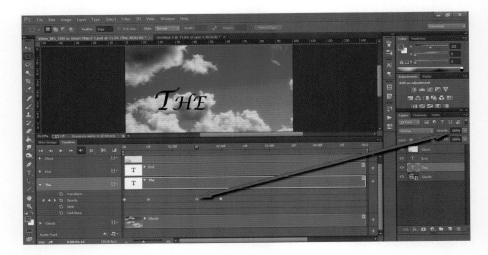

Figure 9.20

Bringing down the opacity.

If you are having a hard time seeing all the track layers, you can drag the frame of the timeline up by clicking and dragging at the separation bar between the canvas and the timeline. You can also use the slider at the bottom to see more or less frames in the timeline.

Open the keyable attributes by clicking on the drop-down menu triangle ▶ next to the track name. Make sure you are on the first frame again by clicking on the Starting Frame button ◄. Click on the Opacity attribute to highlight it, then click on the Stop Watch icon ⏱ to set a keyframe. Make sure the yellow diamond is visible. Now, go to your Layers palette and bring the opacity of the layer down to zero.

Do the same thing for The so the opacity is zero at the starting frame (Figure 9.20). Now, your starting frame has no text and has the individual cloud in the lower-right corner.

Move your playhead to 15 frames and click on the diamond next to the Opacity attribute track so that both text layers have zero opacity at frame 15. Move the playhead to 1:15 (1 second, 15 frames) and change the opacity of The to 100 percent. A yellow keyframe diamond should automatically appear both on the track and next to the Opacity attribute name. Click on the diamond next to the name for End so that End remains invisible (Figure 9.21).

Next, move the playhead to 2:00 and hit the yellow diamonds to set another keyframe. At 3:00, bring the opacity of End up to 100 percent in the Layers palette, and a yellow diamond should appear in the timeline.

Press play to see your animation. You should have the words *The End* come up one word at a time while a cloud slowly drifts (Figure 9.22). Save the file as you normally would any other Photoshop file. You can use the shortcut **Ctrl+S**/⌘**+S** or go to **File** > **Save**.

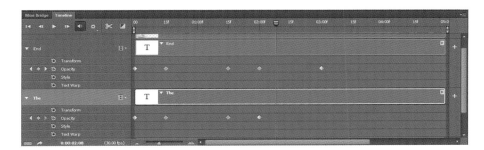

Figure 9.21

Your keyframed timeline.

Figure 9.22

Check out your moving picture.

Figure 9.23

Your final video.

Saving When Using Video Files

The Photoshop project saves the edits, text, graphics, and pretty much all the information—except the original video footage. All footage is referenced, so you need to choose a location to save the video files and do not move them. Changing the name or location will result in a nuclear winter. OK, maybe not a nuclear winter, but it'll feel like it when you go to your file intending to render and you can't.

Now let's render out our video. Go to **File** > **Export** > **Render Video…**. In the ensuing dialog, name your video, then click the **Render** button. Congratulations! You are the proud parent of a bouncing baby video (Figure 9.23).

This is just an introduction to get your feet wet. For more tutorials involving motion, check out Chapter 10.

Power User

Disintegrating Dancer
Pre-Vis Fly-Through
Surreal Painting

Disintegrating Dancer

This is a fun tutorial, and it has been popular. No doubt, you will recognize the effect, sometimes called the dispersion effect, sometimes fractal disintegration. Everyone does it a bit differently, usually concentrating on brushes or scanning paint drops, but as advanced users, we want to be able to make *exactly* what we want, which might mean bending some noncompliant source materials to our will.

We'll start with a stock photo of a dancer on one leg (Figure 10.1). I like the pose, with the hair flowing across the face and the street clothing, but I wanted a jumping photo of someone flying through the air on a white background. Luckily, we can make that happen.

Duplicate the layer by pressing **Ctrl+J/⌘+J**. You should automatically have the new layer selected. Next, I want to have more space for my dancer to leap. Choose **Image > Canvas Size…**. The Canvas Size dialog appears. By default, the canvas measurement is shown in inches. Click on the drop-down menu to switch to either percent or pixels.

Figure 10.1

Original stock photo of dancer on gray background (Photo from Sanches 1980/123rf).

I prefer pixels (Figure 10.2). Increase the size of the canvas. I made my canvas 3500 × 2500 pixels. By default, you can choose whatever space works for you, but make sure you have enough room for the disintegration to spread. It is better to make it larger than not large enough. You can always crop later. You may have noticed that I have the anchor set to the middle bottom square. I did this because my original vertical dimension was 2508 pixels, and in resizing, I wanted Photoshop to trim off the top rather than evenly trim top and bottom. It wouldn't have mattered in this case, as it does not affect the dancer either way, but habits die hard.

The background will fill with whatever color is currently in your background, but don't worry about that right now. First, let's get rid of the gradated soft blue background in the duplicated layer. Hide the background layer by clicking on the Visibility/Eye icon 👁 and make sure you are on the duplicated layer.

Press **W** to access the the **Quick Selection Tool** . If pressing **W** gets you **Magic Wand Tool** , just press **Tab+W** to obtain the **Quick Selection Tool** . Adjust the brush size to be large enough to easily select the dancer, but not so large that it accidently samples from the background. I made my starting brush just slightly smaller than her wrist, then started brushing away in her body. As this occurs, the **Quick Selection Tool**

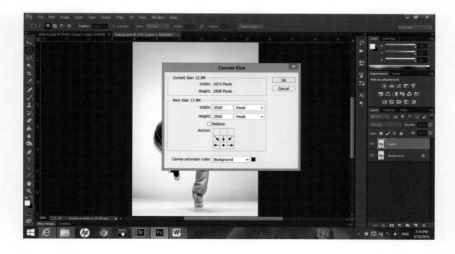

Figure 10.2

Canvas Size dialog. I like resizing in pixels, but I could have done this with any other setting.

Figure 10.3

Refining the selection around the hair.

smartly guesses what to select and creates a selection. By default, after the first swipe, the tool automatically goes to Add to Selection, so you can continue to brush away and create your selection. Adjust the brush size as necessary to include the entire dancer and zoom in and out to get to the smaller spots.

But, what about the hair, you ask? Have no fear! We'll refine the edges by activating the Quick Selection Tool's superpowerful **Refine Edge**. Zoom in to the area you want to refine, then click on the **Refine Edge** button in the Options bar, and a dialog box like the one in Figure 10.3 appears.

Adjust the settings to something similar to mine, and with the dialog still open, brush on the hair area. You will see the "crawling ants" adjust to a more refined mask. When you think you are done, click **OK**.

With the selection still active, click on the **New Layer Mask** ◙ at the bottom of the Layers palette, and a new layer mask will be applied to the new layer. For ease of this tutorial, rename this layer ExDance for "extracted dancer." You can do this by double-clicking on the name of the layer and changing it.

Hold **Ctrl/⌘** and click on the **New Layer** button ◪ on the bottom of the Layers palette to obtain a new transparent layer under your current layer. Click on the new layer and fill with white using the **Paint Bucket Fill** ◙. You should see your dancer on a white background, as Figure 10.4 shows.

We want to create a copy of the dancer without the mask or background, so **Ctrl+Click/⌘+Click** on the matte of your ExDance layer to create a selection, then click back on the thumbnail of the dancer.

You will see the selection around your dancer. Press **Ctrl+C/⌘+C**, then **Ctrl+V/⌘+V** to copy and paste the selection to a new layer above. If you get a new layer with a white

Figure 10.4

Make sure you filled the empty layer and not the matted layer.

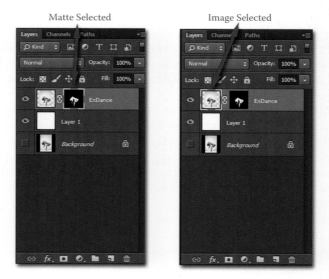

Figure 10.5

Loading the mask as a selection; make sure you **Ctrl**/⌘ click on the matte.

silhouette, you had the mask/matte selected when copying instead of the image. Undo your actions and make sure your layer image thumbnail is selected when performing the copy and paste commands. (see Figure 10.5 for clarification of the distinction).

Hide the ExDance layer and name your new layer New Pose. Then, move your dancer into a more dynamic position. There are many ways you can do this, but this time, we'll use the **Move Tool** . If you want to rotate your image, as I do, make sure your Show Transform Controls is selected in the Options bar and you can access all the transform tools (Figure 10.6). But, beware! You don't want to warp or deform the figure—yet.

Once you use the Transform Controls for anything other than moving the dancer, it activates the Transform function. If you use the Transform, even from the Move Tool, you still have to click the check mark or hit enter to accept the transform and move on (Figure 10.7).

Now, I have the dancer lunging through the air in the pose that I wanted—well, almost. I feel that her arm is too low for this kind of high leap. We could just cut and paste her arm onto a new layer and move it to the angle that I want, but then I have to manually paint in the joining areas or use the healing brush, which could lead to an even more awkward join.

So, we will use the Puppet Warp instead. Make sure you still have the New Pose layer selected and choose **Edit > Puppet Warp**. A mesh should appear around the dancer like

Figure 10.6

Checking Show Transform Controls in the Options bar will allow you to rotate and deform the selection in addition to moving.

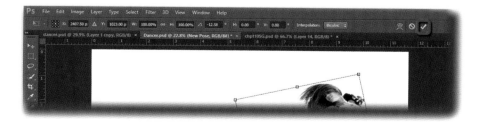

Figure 10.7

Make sure to accept the transform if you want to move on.

that in Figure 10.8. If you do not see it, make sure Show Mesh is checked in the Options bar. By default, the expansion is a mere 2 pixels. I want this mesh to be a little larger than that, so I've increased it to 10. Now, we'll need to pin down some areas we don't want to move or to act as pivots. Click on the armpit, chest, hip, knee, and foot first to pin them down. Small circles appear to indicate pins.

Next, click on the open palm to put a pin in the dancer's hand, then click and drag the hand up to the position you want her to be in (Figure 10.9). Voila! Notice how her head and body respond, and we can obtain natural lifting of her hand with no touchup required. Hit **Enter/Return** to accept the changes. We now have our dancer in position for the disintegration effect (Figure 10.10).

Figure 10.8

Introducing Puppet Warp.

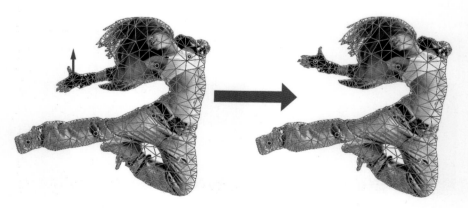

Figure 10.9

Click and drag on the pin to raise the dancer's hand, and the arm follows naturally.

You might have noticed that I haven't done any cleanup on the matte of the dancer, and there are artifacts from both the Puppet Warp and the matte pull. It's not that I don't see it or realize it—it's that it won't matter for our end product. We don't want to waste time cleaning up an area that isn't going to be seen.

That said, make a copy of your New Pose layer by pressing **Ctrl+J/⌘+J**. Next, we'll use the Liquify filter by pressing **Ctrl+Shift+X/⌘+Shift+X** or by using the top menu, **Filter > Liquify…**.

The Liquify dialog will open with the **Forward Warp Tool** 𝄞 set to a very large brush size; I click dragged on the image to obtain a very warped and wide image of the dancer (Figure 10.11). This is the part where I can't tell you exactly what to do because it will differ for every photo, but the basic gist is that you are creating the content for the disintegrating material. Imagine in your head where you think your "splash" or "debris trail" will be and push the photo into those areas. The one point I *can* confirm is

Figure 10.10

The dancer is ready to be dissolved/disintegrated.

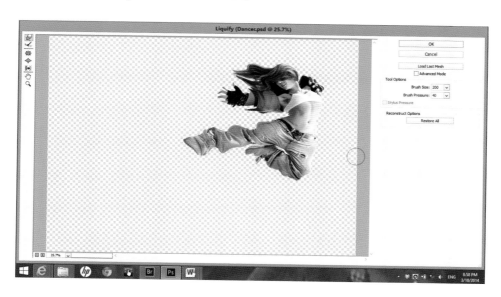

Figure 10.11

Liquify dialog: make it crazy and try to cover the blast radius.

that your end result should be larger than the original (Figure 10.12). This is one of those things that you really won't know how to do until you just do it. So, just do it.

Next, we'll need another duplicate of that Liquified layer. Press **Ctrl+J/⌘+J** to obtain a duplicate layer, then *hide this new layer* for now by pressing the **Visibility/Eye icon** 👁 of that layer. Click on the layer below. Go to **Filter > Blur > Motion Blur...** to apply a directional blur to the image (Figure 10.13). In the dialog box, greatly increase the distance and adjust the angle to an appropriate angle to match the motion of your subject.

Before we continue, we need to think about the direction and what parts we want to emphasize. Figure 10.14 shows the general direction of force that I want to get a feel for in my finished product. I also have decided that I want a splashing water effect; I could have chosen a disintegrating smoke effect, an ashy disintegrating effect, a pixelizing effect—having a vision before you begin will help avoid muddy artwork that tries to be too much at the same time. With the water effect, I want to feel that there is force and strength in the front, not just a trailing falling drop of water.

With all this in mind, the next step will be to create the water effect. It would be great if there happened to be a big splash stock

Figure 10.12

Approximate relationship of original to Liquified version.

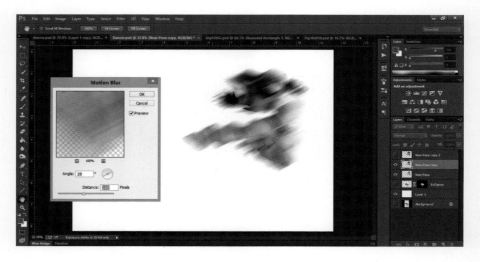

Figure 10.13

Applied motion blur.

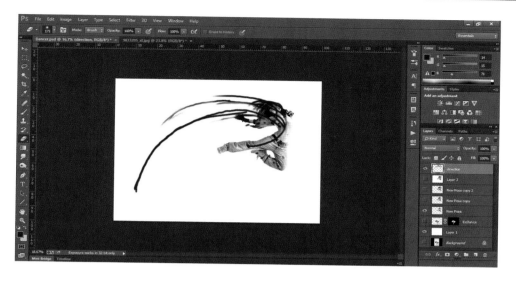

Figure 10.14

Direction of force.

photo of water that was shaped exactly like my dancer, but we know the chances of that are about as likely as my father admitting that the art I do is a "real job."

I found a stock photo of multiple splashes all in one document (Figure 10.15). Use the Lasso Tool 🔲 to select one of the splashes, then copy (**Ctrl+C**/⌘+**C**) and paste (**Ctrl+V**/⌘+**V**) on a layer above the dancer. I renamed this first one "water splash" just so I know that all the layers above it are water splashes. Change the Layer Blend Mode to Multiply so you can see how the water splash looks concerning the dancer's pose. Resize and transform the splash as you see fit (**Ctrl+T**/⌘+**T**) (Figure 10.16).

Keep cutting, pasting, and transforming water splashes until you have something that follows the form in the way you want. Don't forget that you don't have to just stick to transformations. You can use the Puppet Warp we used for her arm or the Liquify filter—bend the water to *your* will (Figure 10.17). As you are working, either matte out or erase overlapping sections.

Figure 10.15

Stock photo of water splashes.

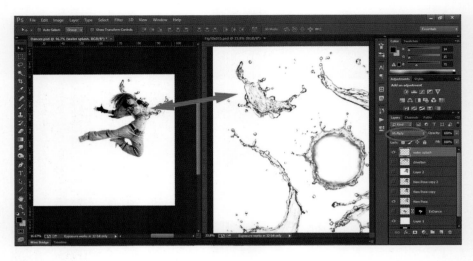

Figure 10.16

Transforming the splash to fit.

Figure 10.17

Use multiple means to create a shape that works for you.

When you are ready, create a white fill layer below the water splashes so that you have what looks like a blue water splash on a white background. You can do this by clicking on the New Fill button ◉ on the bottom of the Layers palette and choosing the solid fill layer in white. **Shift**+ select all the water layers, along with the white fill layer, and from the Layers palette's drop-down menu ▤, select Merge Layers (notice that you could have just pressed **Ctrl+E/⌘+E**).

Next, go to **Image > Adjustments > Black & White…**. Adjust the settings so you have some nice dark blacks and gray tones in the water. Once you are happy with the toning, click **OK**.

We will be using this as a holdout matte, so we need to inverse the image. Pressing **Ctrl+I/⌘+I** will invert the image, and you should have something that looks like Figure 10.18.

Click over to the Channels palette behind the Layers palette and click on one of the channels—any one of them will do because we are dealing with a pure black-and-white image. With one channel selected, go to the pull-down menu ▤ and choose **Duplicate Channel…**. Name your alpha with a descriptive name and click **OK** (Figure 10.19). Make sure you click back to RBG when you are done.

Now, we need to be able to fill all the droplets of that alpha with color information. Start with the warped but not blurred image, then place one of the blurred poses on top and

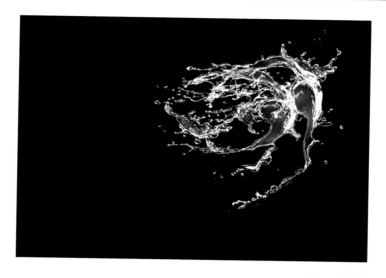

Figure 10.18

Invert the grayscale image.

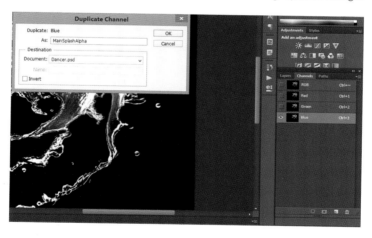

Figure 10.19

Creating an alpha channel.

just to the left (Figure 10.20). Use the most blurred pose for the leftmost side. Play with the layer blend modes to make all the layers blend together.

Let's check how we are doing. Make sure your black-and-white splash is above your dancer layers and change the layer mode to Multiply (don't forget to turn on its visibility with the Eye icon 👁). Check to see if all your droplets have color. To truly sell the effect, you want to have the liquid be the same color as the area that is melting off. As you can see in Figure 10.21, I need to fill in some areas that are white. Some of the white areas are purposeful—her white top, for instance—but the spray emanating from

Figure 10.20

Placing the blurred images over the water areas.

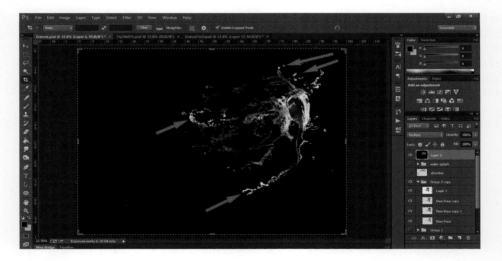

Figure 10.21

Checking your droplets for color.

her knee should have some of the color from her jeans, and some of the white spots on top should have her red hair color.

Turn off the visibility of the water splash and press **Ctrl+Shift+Alt+E**/⌘+**Shift+ Option+E** to obtain a merged copy on a new layer. Select the Clone Stamp Tool ▦ and set the settings in the Options bar so that it samples the current layer only. Then, turn back

10. Power User

the visibility of the water splash and reduce the opacity so you can see more of the blurry dancer. Make sure you are on the dancer's layer, hold **Alt**/**Option** to set the clone source, and clone to fill in the areas that need filling. Remember that anything showing up as white splashes will not show up on the white background. Let's see how our current incarnation will work with the splash.

Load the splash selection by going to **Select > Load Selection...** and load your saved alpha as a new selection. Make sure you are on your merged blurry dancer and press **Ctrl+C**/⌘**+C** to copy and **Ctrl+V**/⌘**+V** to paste onto a new layer. See how your pasted selection looks on a white background. Then, add your clean dancer on top (I made a copy of the New Pose dancer layer by pressing **Ctrl+J**/⌘**+J** and dragging it above the pasted layer) and take a good look (Figure 10.22).

It's not bad, but I feel like the hair isn't looking like it's splashing off, so I select some of the deeper red color in her hair and

Figure 10.22

Checking our progress.

paint it into the splash area around her head and darken some of the splash coming off the legs so it gradates from darker to lighter as it goes away from the body. Once I do that, the next step is to "melt" away some of the dancer so it truly feels like she is dissolving into liquid.

I already made a copy of the dancer. If you were working with your original, make a copy first by pressing **Ctrl+J**/⌘**+J**. Next, we'll use Liquify to blend out some of the edges and make her seem to flow into the water a bit more. Go to **Filter > Liquify...** and use the Forward Warp Tool 🖌 to push some of the edges around. You can see how I have pushed her hair to blend more with the motion of the water (Figure 10.23). Do not worry about the blurring as we will be erasing out a good part of her.

Once you are at a good point, click OK.

In the Layers palette, add a layer mask to your Liquified dancer. Making sure you have the matte selected, use a black brush to melt away sections of her. You may find it helpful to go back and forth between the Liquify and the matte and using the smudge tool in the layer. It doesn't take long to get a cool-looking splash effect (Figure 10.24).

This is so much fun I think we should do another dispersion effect. This time I'll make it a big more geometric. First, let's make a square brush. I'll make a new white fill layer in our dancer PSD by going to the Layers palette and clicking on the New Fill Layer button 🔘. Now, choose the Square marquee tool 🔲, create a small square, and fill it with black. Deselect by pressing **Ctrl+D**/⌘**+D**, then select around the square so that there

Figure 10.23

Painting and blending details.

Figure 10.24

Our final dancer.

is a bit of white around it. Go to **Edit > Define Brush Preset...**. Name your brush, click OK, and then choose the brush preset you just created; it should be at the bottom of the presets.

This simple square becomes much more with some specific brush settings. Open the Brush palette and first adjust the spacing so that the squares are distinctly separate. Then, crank up the Size Jitter in Shape Dynamics, followed by some scattering so that brushstrokes seem to be more flowing and less linear. Last but definitely not least, add in foreground/background jitter and pump up the brightness jitter. Make sure the hue and saturation jitters are at zero. This is going to be used as a matte, so we want shades of gray. Figure 10.25 shows the brush settings.

Now, to prep our trail, take the multiple dancer variations from the previous incarnation of the dissolving dancer and create an arc of dancers in her wake, with the clearer dancers near her and the blurrier ones near the tail of the trail. You should have something like Figure 10.26.

Make a merged copy by pressing **Ctrl+Shift+Alt+E/⌘+Shift+Option+E**, then duplicate that a couple more times with either the same keystrokes or by **Ctrl+J/⌘+J**. Assign a layer mask to each one by clicking on the Layer Mask button ▣ while having the layer selected, then invert the masks to black so that we don't see the trails of dancers.

Figure 10.25

Creating a custom brush for the effect.

Figure 10.26

Arranging the blurred duplicates on the trail of dispersion.

Make sure your brush is set to black and white by pressing **D** and in each layer brush a few strokes to make some trailing pixels You will have something that looks like Figure 10.27. I've put the dancer on top at half opacity to help me visualize and know where to put the trails.

Now, give each of the trail layers a slight drop shadow. Click on the layer fx button ƒx and choose Drop Shadow. Use your own aesthetic to determine how much shadow to give.

Finally, add a layer mask to the clean dancer and use the same square brush in black to take out chunks from her so that she blends in with her trails.

Voila! You have disintegrating dancer 2 (Figure 10.28).

Figure 10.27

Using the brush on the layer masks.

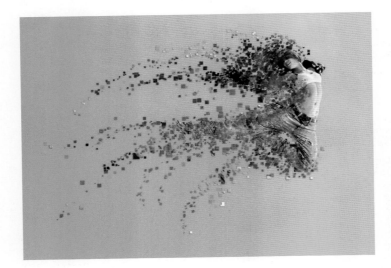

Figure 10.28

Disintegrating dancer 2.

Pre-Vis Fly-Through

One of the easiest and hardest Photoshop tasks is to create a displacement map. It is easy because it is simply a black and white image that reflects a numerical displacement along one vector. It is hard because saying what it is is easy, but visualizing it is not quite so easy. AND, not only do you need to visualize it, the person receiving the displacement map needs to know what you intended and what to expect and it needs to work in 3D, which means it has to work from multiple angles, and usually in motion. Then there are the technical specifications. Is ground zero 50% gray? Or is it black? Because of the way texture map creation straddles both 3D and traditional 2D, the texture painting often referred to was working in 2.5D. Usually the texture painter would have to go to a 3D package and create a whole separate file that calls in the textures and go between Photoshop and the 3D application.

This next tutorial will not only have you working with Photoshop tools in 2.5D, but also show a way you can pre-visualize the motion without having to learn another program. Pre-visualization is used extensively in the creation of movies, and is often just referred to as 'Pre-Vis.'

For this project, we want to keep everything small and quick – the pre-visualization will help us determine where to put our efforts. Create a new 1K document by going to **File > New…** and entering **1024** into the pixel dimentions for both the width and height.

Create a new layer by pressing the New Layer button ▢. Make a perfectly circular selection by selecting the Elliptical Marquee Tool ⬭, holding **Shift** and click-dragging across your canvas. Next, press **D** so that the default colors of black and white are set for your foreground and background, then go to **Filter > Render > Clouds**. With a brush ✎, carefully add some black down the middle for a canyon, and a few white high points to signify mountains (Figure 10.29).

We can now create a 3D mesh from this. Switch your workspace mode to 3D, or bring up your 3D palette by going to **Window > 3D**. In the 3D palette, select **Mesh from Depth Map** and choose **Plane** from the pulldown menu options. Our layer is now a mountainous mesh (Figure 10.30).

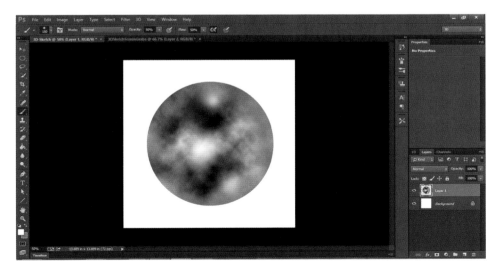

Figure 10.29

The Clouds Filter with hand-painted areas.

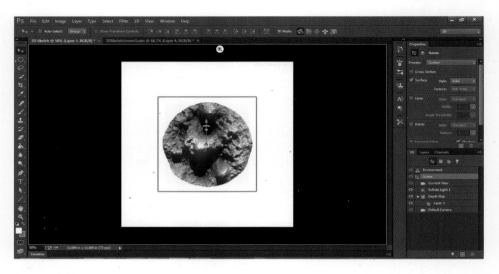

Figure 10.30

Mesh from Depth Map.

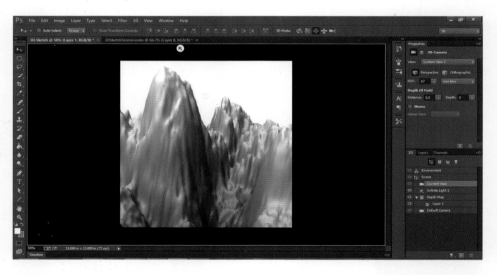

Figure 10.31

Setting your camera.

In your 3D palette you will see that you have several layers. Select the camera (by default it is named 'Current View') and make sure you have the Move Tool selected ▶⊕. You will see in the Options Bar at the top that you have a few 3D move tool options at the far right. Hovering your mouse over the tool icons will let you know what each one is. Select the movement type of your choice and click-drag in the window to move around until you have a good view of the canyon (Figure 10.31).

Figure 10.32

Save the view or create a fly-through.

You can save the view by **right-clicking**/**ctrl+clicking** on the 3D axis and choosing **Save**…. (Figure 10.32). Once you have a view saved, **right-clicking**/**ctrl+clicking** on the 3D axis will show your saved view in the popup menu. Clicking on any saved view, including the pre-set orthographic views, will animate your camera into that view. You can save many camera angles this way, and pre-vis your Pre-Vis by clicking through them in the order you would like.

While we are in the 3D Palette, let's take a moment to rename our geometry. Double-click on the layer called 'Depth Map' and rename it 'Landscape.' You'll see why a little later.

Before we start animating in our timeline, let's add one more component. Say that there is a UFO going through this landscape, and we want to know where it is in relation to the landscape and camera via some type of path indicator. **Right-click**/**Ctrl-click** on the 3D axis and choose Top so the view swings to a top-down orthographic view of our landscape. In the Layer's Palette, create a new layer by clicking on the new layer icon. Select the Pen Tool and draw a path to indicate our UFO's flight path. You can create a custom brush and choose **Stroke Path** from the paths palette pulldown menu, but Photoshop CC also has the ability to do this via Scripted Pattern and Fill.

Download my special DepthMapArrow.psd (Figure 10.33) from our site. The particular black and white pattern on this arrow will allow you to see it in 3D when combined with extrusion. But first, you need to make it a pattern.

Ctrl+A/**⌘+A** to select all.

Go to **Edit > Define Pattern**… and give your pattern a name. In my case, I called it '3D Arrow.' (Figure 10.34).

Figure 10.33

DepthMapArrow.psd can be downloaded from our site.

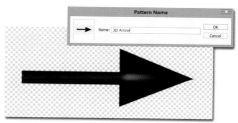

Figure 10.34

Naming your pattern.

Figure 10.35

The Fill dialog settings.

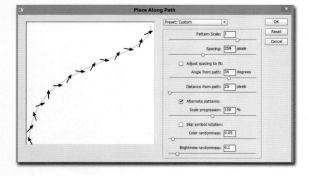

Figure 10.36

Place Along Path dialog settings.

Now comes the fun part. Make sure you have your path selected and that you are on a new layer above your 3D layer. Go to **Edit > Fill**…. In the Fill dialog box set Contents to 'Pattern' and in the Custom Pattern drop-down menu find and select your new 3D Arrow pattern. Make sure to check the check box next to Scripted Patterns and choose 'Place Along Path' from the Script pulldown menu (Figure 10.35). Click **OK**.

Another dialog box appears for you to adjust your settings. You can scale your arrow to be smaller or larger and give it the spacing you want. I'm also going to show the zig-zagging action of our UFO by adjusting the angle from the path to 37 degrees and give some distance from the path and check Alternate Patterns. You can see how my settings look in Figure 10.36. Click OK when you are ready, and you will see your new layer filled with our pattern.

At this point, our arrows are still a flat 2D layer. With the layer still selected, switch over to your 3D palette, and from the Create New 3D Object choices displayed in the 3D pallet, select Mesh From Depth Map and choose Two-Sided Plane from the dropdown menu. Click on the Create button and behold! You now have a 3D path!

This path is on a separate layer, so it isn't actually with the landscape. Go to the Layer Palette's pull-down menu ▤ select **Merge Down**. (If you don't see the option, most likely you are still in the 3D Palette rather than the Layers Palette.) Now when you click back to your 3D Palette, you should see that your scene now has both your landscape and your arrow path. And the method to my madness is revealed, as you can distinguish which depth map is the landscape, and which is the arrow right away.

You can select each geometry separately, so move around in your scene and place your path as you want it to be in the 3D space (Figure 10.37). You'll notice that you still have your saved views, since your views were attached to the bottom 3D layer. So now let's use them to create our fly-through. Set your 3D layers to be as you would want them to be in the beginning of your Pre-Vis.

Click on the Timeline tab on the bottom of your screen to bring up the timeline, or if you don't have the tab available just go to **Window > Timeline**. Click on the 'Create Video Timeline' button in the center of the Timeline window. Once Photoshop sets up your video tracks, click on the arrow ▶ next to your landscape layer and click on the small stop-watch ⏱ next to 3D Camera Position to set a key frame. Next, move the playhead to where you would like your next keyframe to be. You can either manually move the camera to where you want it to be, or you can choose your saved custom view and a keyframe is automatically generated, as indicated by the yellow diamond in the 3D Camera Position Track. When you are ready, render out your Pre-Vis (Figure 10.38)!

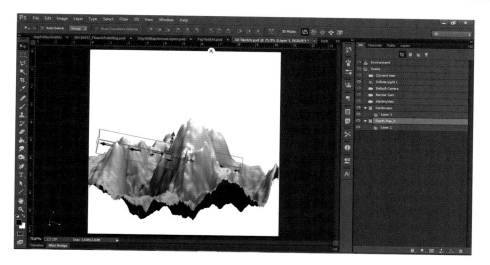

Figure 10.37

Adjusting the path in 3D space.

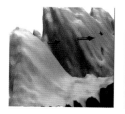   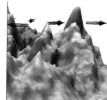 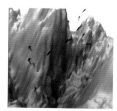

Figure 10.38

We've created a pre-vis video with full 3D in Photoshop!

Chapter 9 went over the basics of the video controls, so if you do not know what a playhead is or how to render, I would recommend checking out Figure 9.16 for interface nomenclature and reading the video section of that chapter.

Surreal Painting

When Photoshop came out with their Oil Painting Filter, people went hog-wild with it and created a lot of 'paintings' that looked like filtered photographs. The secret to getting something that looks closer to the real thing is to not rely on just one method, but to blend several methods and take the time to lovingly handcraft parts.

For this project, we will make a surreal painting. Let's start with the picture you see in Figure 10.39. You can download this image from our website, or choose a similarly composed image.

Press **C** to select the Crop Tool and crop out most of the foreground plant matter (Figure 10.39). Hit **Enter/Return** to accept the crop.

Figure 10.39

Cropping out unwanted areas.

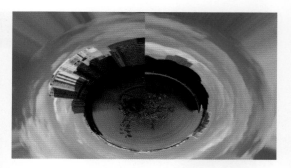

Figure 10.40

Our planet is formed.

Press **Ctrl+J/⌘+J** to create a duplicate layer above your current layer. Flip this new layer vertically by going to **Edit > Transform > Flip Vertical**.

Go to **Filter > Distort > Polar Coordinates**… and in the ensuing dialog box, select **Rectangular to Polar**. Click **OK** to accept.

You should get an image that looks like Figure 10.40. If your sky is in the center, then you skipped the flipping of the image. Undo by pressing **Ctrl+Z/⌘+Z** and make sure to flip the image and reapply the filter.

Use the Spot Healing Brush ▨ to clean up the visible seam, and clean up the vestiges of the foreground plant out from the center of the globe. Rename the layer 'Globe.'

Create a new blank layer above by pressing **Ctrl+Alt+Shift+N/⌘+Opt+Shift+N**. Go to **Edit > Fill**… and use **Pattern** for the Contents and check mark the Scripted Patterns and select **Tree** from the pulldown menu (Figure 10.41). Click **OK** and the Tree dialog appears.

In the Tree dialog, choose Tree Type #13 – Young Ash Tree, and set Leaves Amount to 0. You can see my settings in Figure 10.42. When you click **OK**, a bare tree appears.

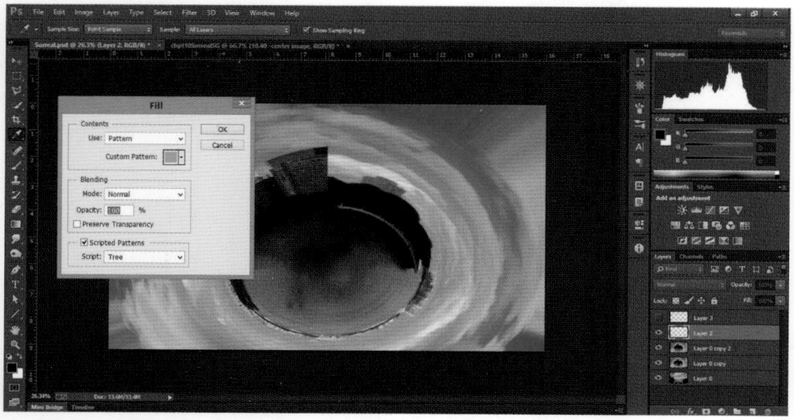

Repeat the process of creating a new blank layer and a new tree, but this time set the light to be in the opposite direction of the bare tree, and create a full tree with ample leaves. You can see that I have chosen a different kind of tree in my settings (Figure 10.43).

We'll need to increase our canvas space to complete our painting. Go to **Image > Canvas Size**… and double the height. Move the anchor from

Figure 10.41

Selecting the tree script.

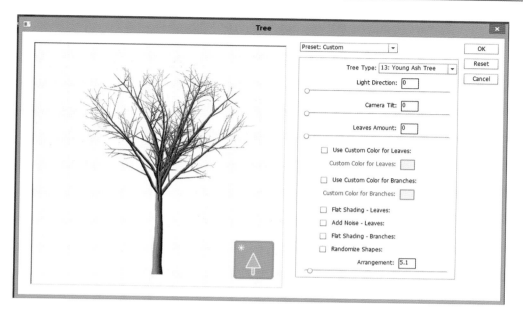

Figure 10.42

Tree dialog settings for first tree.

Figure 10.43

Tree dialog settings for second tree.

the middle to the lower middle spot so that the canvas is added to the top only. Hide all your layers except the bottom layer, and use the Rectangular Marquee Tool ▦ to select the blank new added area on top, with a bit of overlap into the sky. Go to **Edit** > **Fill**… and select **Content Aware** and click **OK**. Photoshop will do its best to fill in the sky. In this case, there is a little repetition, but I'll get around to fixing it after I assemble the rest of my contents.

Unhide your Globe layer and use the Elliptical Marquee Tool ◯ to select around your globe including all the buildings and some of the sky. With the selection still active, click on the Layer Mask button ▣. This should create a matte that holds out the rest of the layer.

Next, unhide your tree with leaves. Position it so that it is above the globe, like it is growing out of it. Move and resize the globe as needed for composition of your tree and globe with the extended background (Figure 10.44).

Now unhide your bare tree and apply the Spherize Distortion by going to **Filter** > **Distort** > **Spherize**…. Set the distortion amount to 100%. Reapply the filter a couple of times until the tree limbs look very rounded, like they are curving around a ball. Then go to

Figure 10.44

Placing our pieces together.

Edit > Free Transform and rotate the tree around so it looks like roots (that's why we made the lighting opposite of the top tree), and move and resize to fit over the Globe and under the top tree with leaves (Figure 10.45).

Painting in the layer masks of each element, you can blend the different layers together. When you have finished blending, it's time to apply the Oil Paint Filter.

To really bring out the oil paint filter, it helps to first apply some effects from the Filter Gallery. Go to **Filter > Filter Gallery**.... I chose **Brush Strokes > Accented Edges** and applied it before going to **Filter > Oil Paint**. In the dialog box, zoom in close and take a look at the details as you adjust your settings. Figure 10.46 shows a detail of how my leaves look with the two filters applied.

I like to make a few different layers with different filters such as the canvas texture and other brush strokes and use a layer mask to blend between the different layers to get a less uniform feel. But the final coup d'etat is the layering of a hand-painted canvas.

Figure 10.45

Creating 'roots.'

Figure 10.46

Filters update the image interactively as you adjust values.

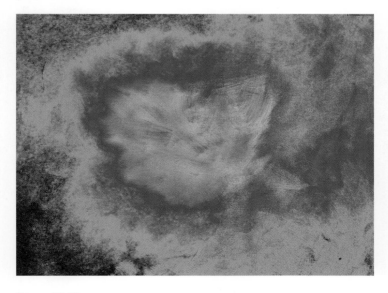

Figure 10.47

The coup d'etat for creating a more realistic 'painting.'

Figure 10.48

Our final 'painting.'

Download the BWbrushstrokes.psd file from our website (Figure 10.47). Drag the image on top of your composition or copy and paste on top. Set the layer mode to Multiply, and move the layer around until you find a spot that works with your image, adjusting the opacity if needed.

Tada! Your final surrealist painting (Figure 10.48)!

11

Efficiency and Display

They say all inventions are a result of a genius' inherent laziness.

Customizing Shortcuts

You have probably noticed that I tend to favor hot key shortcuts. When working on a project, it's just so much more efficient to use the hot keys over the menu navigation. Even the simple click of selecting a tool adds up to a lot of navigation time. As an example, imagine that you were constantly sampling a color and painting. You *could* go to the eyedropper tool, then go back to the canvas and select the color, then go back and select the brush, then go back to the canvas—or you can simply press the **Alt/Option** key while in Brush Mode to select the color and continue brushing on release.

But, what about the tools or menu options that don't have shortcuts? I was a bit upset when a Photoshop update included the negation of a shortcut for the Blur/Smudge/Sharpen Tool. I kept hitting the *R* button to no avail. Luckily, we can set our own hot keys—even if they are already assigned to something else.

Customizing Keyboard Shortcuts

Go to **Edit** > **Keyboard Shortcuts....** This brings up the Keyboard Shortcuts dialog window as seen in Figure 11.1. Notice that there is a drop-down menu that allows you to choose between Tools, Palettes Menus, and Application Menus. To edit keyboard shortcuts, simply click in the Shortcut column and assign a shortcut. If the shortcut is already assigned, a warning will appear to let you know that you will be overriding the shortcut and what the shortcut was for. You can choose just to click **Accept**, or you can change the shortcut keystroke to a different one at that time.

Automating Tasks

I'm lazy. I admit it. I am a strong believer in laziness; it fuels inventiveness and creates wonderful tools such as Photoshop's Actions palette. Why reinvent the wheel each time you deal with some type of image processing? If the steps do not involve brushstrokes or necessitate eyeing something, you can probably create an action for it. Photoshop even has Conditional Actions—small miniprograms or applications that can respond to different scenarios or conditions. If the condition is met, Photoshop runs a certain action. If it isn't, then Photoshop runs a different action.

The Actions Palette

By default, the Actions palette is in List Mode. By going into the palette's submenu, you can change this to button mode, which turns each action into a button but doesn't give you the option of tweaking the actions. See Figure 11.2 for a look at the two modes.

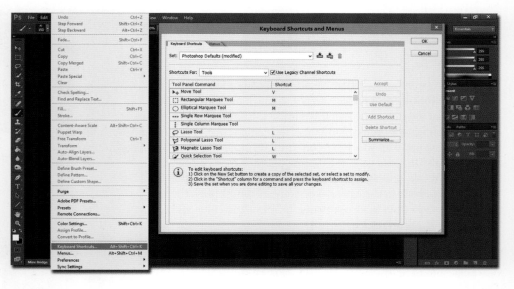

Figure 11.1

Keyboard Shortcuts dialog window.

11. Efficiency and Display

Defining an Action

What is an *action*? It is a set of instructions that repeat in a particular order. I had to create a few rocks for the movie *The Rundown* that needed the same treatment done to each texture map. I created an action and simply batch processed them.

How do you use these actions? More important, how do you make your own customized actions? And, what is batch processing, anyway? Patience, young grass-smoker—er, I mean grasshopper—Daniel-san. Ah, forget it; I'm just dating myself anyway. What I'm trying to say is: one thing at a time.

Using an Action

First, you need to know what the action does. You can get an idea by looking at the Actions palette in List Mode and expanding each of the action's steps. To do that, click the triangle next to the action itself and then each step. But, to really understand it, you just need to plunge in to the pool and press a button. I'll show you using the ActionsSample.PSD file from this book's site, but you can use your own file to follow along.

In the Default Actions, there is a cool-sounding action called Water Reflection. Let's give it a try. This action requires a selection, so I'm going to **Ctrl/⌘-Click** on the thumbnail in my top selected layer to have it create a selection. Open the Actions palette (if it is not up, you can go to **Window > Actions** to bring it up), scroll down to the Water Reflection Action and select it. Then, hit the Play button ▶ on the bottom of the Actions palette. Just sit back and watch as the actions automatically create a watery reflection for you (Figure 11.3).

Figure 11.2

The Actions palette in default List Mode and Button Mode.

Figure 11.3

Watery reflection in one click.

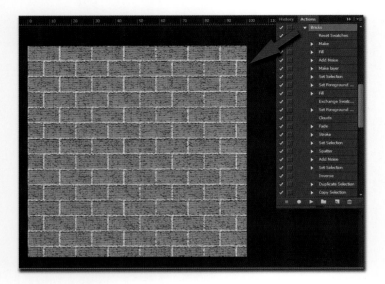

Figure 11.4

A completely procedural brick pattern programmed in as an action.

Let's try one more example. Not all the preset actions are listed by default. In the Actions pull-down menu  located at the top-right corner of the palette, select **Textures**. The Textures Action Set will load and be visible on the bottom of the Actions palette. Let's take a look at the Bricks Action.

Select the Bricks Action and click the Play Selection button ▶ at the bottom of the Actions palette. It will take a while for this to run because it is a bit more involved than the Water Reflection Action.

Photoshop goes through the series of steps, and voilá! You can see the results in Figure 11.4.

Figure 11.5

There are more action presets available, and you also can add your own.

Other Action Presets

As we have just seen, Adobe provides you with additional action sets beyond the default actions. To load the other action sets, click the Actions palette's pull-down menu. You see the other presets at the bottom of the menu in Figure 11.5.

If you had created and saved your own action sets to the Photoshop Actions folder, they would also show up at the bottom of this menu. Should you need to load a set that's saved elsewhere, use the Load Actions command in the palette menu.

Creating Actions

Now, of course, you want to know how to make your own actions and presets.

1. Start by making a new set. Go to the Actions palette's pull-down menu and select **New Set**. It's a good idea to keep your own created actions separately in their own set.

2. In the New Set dialog box, give your new set a name. I called the new set Speedy; I just didn't want to name it something as droll and predictable as MyPresets and wanted to make the point that you can name your presets anything you want.

3. Once you click OK, your new set is located at the bottom of the Actions palette (see Figure 11.6).

Now, add an action to your set. As an example, make one that reduces the image to 50 percent of its size and then converts it to grayscale. You probably do not want the Open command recorded as that will make the action open that *specific file every time* to perform the action. So, before you start, open a file that is a good candidate for the action.

1. Go to the Actions palette's pull-down menu ▪▪ and choose **New Action**.

2. In the New Action dialog box, name your action and make sure it's going to your new set. As you can see in Figure 11.7, you can create a hot key for this action by assigning a function key to it. You can also assign a color. The color helps you visually organize all your presets, so choose a color if you wish.

Caution

Any shortcut you assign overrides any default assignment, and there is no warning letting you know if you are reassigning a key. The only hint is that Photoshop tries to avoid your assignment and modifies it with a **Shift+** or ⌘+. It does not warn you if you deselect these options and overwrite another hot key. You can assign a hot key for the action in the Keyboard Shortcuts dialog mentioned in the beginning of this chapter.

---

3. Click Record ▪, and you're ready to roll. From this point, Photoshop will record your actions until you tell it to stop recording.

4. It is recording, so go to **Image > Image Size**.

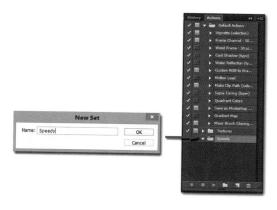

Figure 11.6

By default, your new set comes in at the bottom, but you can click and drag it up to the top.

Figure 11.7

The New Action dialog box.

---

5. In the dialog, change the units from pixels to percent. Enter 50 percent and click OK.

6. The image is resized to 50 percent of its size. Now, go to **Image > Adjustments > Black and White** to desaturate the image. Whatever settings you use here will be applied every time you use this action, but you *can* make changes later, so it's not set in stone. You'll learn how to make those changes a bit later in the chapter.

Why Not Change the Mode to Grayscale?

You may have noticed grayscale as a mode under the **Image > Mode** menu. I recommend against this because how color management deals with grayscale modes will differ from how it deals with RGB modes. Transfer between programs, conversion to other formats, and implementation in three dimensions (3D) can be affected by this "simple" mode change. So, unless you are working in a pipeline that specifically addressed using the grayscale mode in their color management, stick to RGB. Advanced texture artists will actually take advantage of using the RGB mode by putting several mattes together so that they can have three or four mattes in one file. So, just because you know a file is to be used as a matte does not mean that it is grayscale.

Figure 11.8

Your newly created action; you'll only see the color in Button Mode.

7. Stop recording by clicking the Stop button ■ at the bottom of the Actions palette. Now, you have your new action listed in your new set (Figure 11.8). If you change to Button Mode, you see that the button for your new action is the color that you selected. Had I saved and closed the file before stopping the recording, the action would have included it. Sometimes that is useful, as we can override the place and name of the save when batch processing, but because this is an action that I might use in the middle of my workflow, I kept it to the actions only.

Adding a Conditional

As a fairly new addition to the Actions, you can now set a conditional for your action. So, let's say you are batch saving a bunch of documents, but if there are layers, you need to have each layer saved as a separate document. The problem is that you don't know which of your PSDs are layered and which ones are not—and you have 120 images to go through. You can tell Photoshop to save all the files to your Delivery Folder, and if a file has layers, to save each layer as a separate document.

The conditions that Photoshop can recognize are specific. If you go to the Actions palette ▦ and choose Insert Conditional, you will see your options as displayed in Figure 11.9. You'll also notice that to make the conditional, the two actions you wish to use must be in the same action set (Figure 11.10).

So, for my example, I chose the following settings:
If Current: Document Has Layers
Then Play Action: Flatten Image
Else Play Action: None

Notice that "None" is a valid selection. I want to make sure that my document has only one layer in this part of the action, so I insert this conditional to ensure that happens. Because the action has to be in the set where it is being inserted, you might need to copy the necessary actions into the set where you are working. For example, the Flatten Image action is in the Commands Action Set, so if I were inserting this conditional in a new action in my new Speedy Action Set, I would need to copy the action into the Speedy Action Set first.

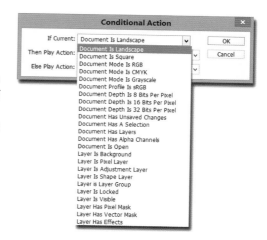

Figure 11.9

The choices available as a Conditional.

Editing or Changing an Action

The brick pattern action was a neat little trick, but it's hardly a finished-looking product. The good news is that it is easy to adjust or fine-tune any action. First, make sure you have your Actions palette in List mode. Then, you can implement changes in the following ways:

Figure 11.10

Insert Conditional Sample.

- You can move any part of an action to another part of an action by clicking and dragging it to wherever you want it. If you want to copy a step to an action, hold down the **Alt**/**Option** key, then click and drag it.
- You can add steps anywhere within the action by simply clicking the step after which you want your new steps to start, click record, perform the steps you wish to add, and click Stop when you are done. The new steps will integrate into the action.
- To change the name, function key, or an assigned color of an action, hold down the **Alt**/**Option** key while double-clicking the action. The dialog box will pop up. (This option is also available via the palette pull-down menu.)
- Want to get rid of a step within an action? Simply drag the step to the Trash 🗑 or highlight the step and click on the Trash button 🗑.
- Like your action but want to tweak some of the settings? Highlight the action, then use the Record Again feature. The Record Again feature is in the Actions palette menu and will run through each step, pausing at each dialog box so you can tweak values.
- You can program in a stop that stops an action and either puts up a message that the user has to confirm or just pauses and lets you perform a task that cannot be recorded, such as painting or selecting. After you complete the task or read the message, you click **Continue** to finish the action. To insert a stop, simply go to where you want to stop/pause, select **Insert Stop...** from the Actions palette pull-down menu ▣, and type your instructions or message.

Saving Your Set

You have these wonderful actions all under your new set. Then, your brother comes by and reinstalls Adobe Photoshop. Guess what? It's all gone. Yup—lost forever. You just have to start over. Before you go too far, make sure to save your set. This allows you (or anyone you decide to give it to) to load the set—and it doesn't even take up much time.

1. Select the name of the set and choose Save Actions from the palette pop-up menu.
2. Save the set in the Photoshop Actions folder if you want it to appear on the Actions palette menu.

However, you can save it anywhere as long as you remember where it is. Simple, isn't it?

Adobe Photoshop remembers your newly created sets and actions, even if you do not specifically save them. The actions are there the next time you open Photoshop. However, if you reinstall Photoshop without saving your new set of actions, you lose them.

Batch Processing

I have had friends who had to texture a creature with scales, and they had *hundreds* of scales they needed to paint and track. Luckily, Photoshop has *batch processing*. That is, Photoshop runs an action on a whole bunch of files for you. Go through this with me, using the example action just created:

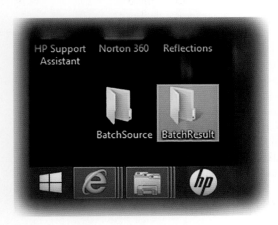

Figure 11.11

Set up your source and results folders before beginning batching.

1. Create a folder somewhere and copy a bunch of images into it.

   I created a folder on my desktop called BatchSource. Personally, I like to have a destination folder so the originals in the source folder aren't overwritten. I've created one called BatchResult, which you can see in Figure 11.11

2. Go to **File** > **Automate** > **Batch**.
3. In the Batch dialog (Figure 11.12), make sure you have selected your actions set and the action you want performed.
4. Under Source, select Folder. Use the Choose button to select your source folder.
5. Select any of the options that pertain to the action you are batching:
   • *Override Action Open Commands*. If your action has an open command, select this so the action processes the chosen images rather than the originally programmed images.

- *Include All Subfolders.* If you want to process folders within folders, select this option.
- *Suppress File Open Options Dialog.* Select this option to have Photoshop ignore any opening dialog boxes.
- *Suppress Color Profile Warnings.* Select this if you want Photoshop to use its default color profile rather than any embedded color profile when running the batch process.

6. Under Destination, select Folder. Use Choose to select your destination folder.

Should your action contain a Save As command, select the Override Action Save As Commands option. Once this is selected, you can use the boxes in the File Naming area to name the processed files. Because your action doesn't have a Save As command, the files are saved with the same name to the BatchResult folder that you created.

7. Click OK and watch the show.

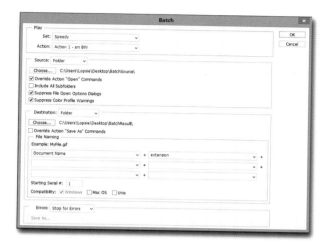

Figure 11.12

The Batch dialog box.

You cannot suppress a saving dialog box, so if you're saving as a JPG, for example, the batch waits for you to confirm the JPG dialog box. Because JPG is a *lossy* format (which means information is lost in compression each time the file is saved), I recommend *against* saving any master files as JPG. That way, you won't have to worry about having a semiautomatic batch process.

Creating a Droplet

Droplets are like little apps that you can put anywhere (on the desktop or in a folder) and just drag and drop files onto (hence *droplet*). Stand alone may be a bit misleading as an adjective because you still must have Photoshop on the computer on which the droplet is located because it accesses Photoshop to complete its actions. Think of it more as a shortcut to a prerecorded action. The only complaint I would make about droplets is that I wish they didn't have to open the Photoshop GUI (graphical user interface) when activated. It defeats the purpose a bit.

Let's take our previously made action and create a droplet.

1. Go to **File** > **Automate** > **Create Droplet**. The Create Droplet dialog box will pop up, as shown in Figure 11.13. Take a look at the options and adjust to fit your circumstance and needs.
2. Save Droplet In. This asks you where you would like to save the droplet. You would click on the Choose button and navigate to the location of your choice. It doesn't

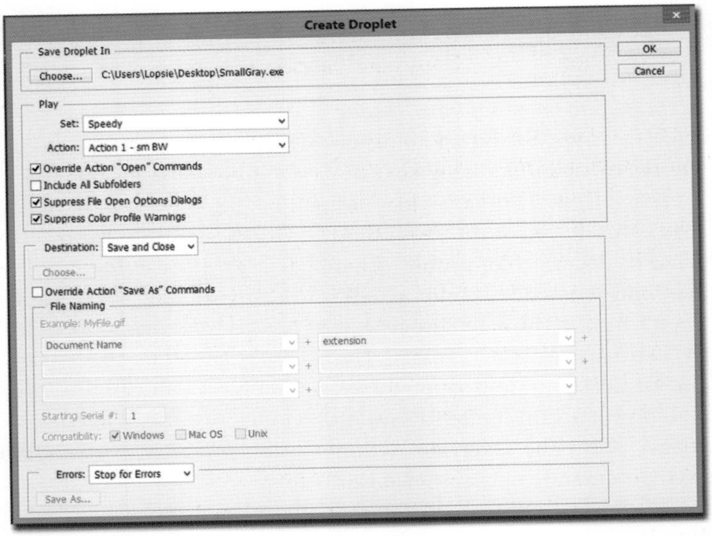

Figure 11.13

Create Droplet dialog.

matter where the droplet is saved because you can just move it anywhere that's convenient for you. I want to just save it to my desktop, so I click Choose and navigate to my desktop.

3. **Play.** Select the set that contains your action and choose the action for your droplet. In this case, go to Speedy (or whatever you named your new set) and use the new action we created in the previous section (in my case, it is named Action 1–sm BW).

The next few options are for specific circumstances; if you are creating a droplet that you know you will be using with folders of images, then you would want to make sure that Include All Subfolders is checked. Take a look at the following options and see if they apply to your circumstance.

- *Override Action "Open" Commands.* Select this option if your action specifically indicates opening and working on a file in a specific folder. This way, the action works on the files you're putting onto the droplet instead of just going to the specified folder. Because my action does not have an Open command, I won't select this option.

- *Include All Subfolders.* This option allows the droplet to process any subfolders that might be within a folder that I drop on it. I know that with the pipeline in which I work, this is a desirable trait for this droplet, so I select it.

- *Suppress File Open Options Dialogs.* A new option added in Photoshop CS, this option has Photoshop disregard any opening dialog box.

- *Suppress Color Profile Warnings.* If the color profile of the image being processed isn't the same as Photoshop's default profile, then a dialog box asks what it should do. Should you decide to suppress these warnings, Photoshop forgoes asking and uses its default color profile.

> If you have any other Open commands, like opening a file to use as a matte, Override Action "Open" Command negates that command.

4. Review the rest of the options for the dialog box:
   - *Destination.* Options include None, Save and Close, and Folder. Destination lets you choose where your processed images will be saved. Most of the time, I recommend that you save all to a new folder to avoid overwriting the originals. But, in this case, I want to choose Save and Close because I know I'll be dropping copies onto the droplet. If my action had included a specific Save command, I would have selected Override Action Save As Commands so I could also add frame numbers or file extensions.
   - *Errors.* Options include Stop for Errors or Log Errors to File. This comes down to what you consider more bothersome. If you like to have everything set to go and leave your desk, you should probably have errors go to a log file. That way, all other images are processed. But, if you don't want the process to continue if there's an error, choose Stop for Errors.
5. When everything is done, click OK. You should get a small icon that looks like Figure 11.14. To use it, just drop a file or folder onto the icon; it performs the processes you set up for it.

Figure 11.14

You can move this newly created droplet anywhere within your computer and drop files onto it to process.

Cross-Platform Compatibility

One of the great things about a droplet is that it is cross-platform compatible. You can create your droplet on a Windows machine and share it with someone on a Macintosh and vice versa. Of course, there's a bit of fine print here (beyond my previous mention about having Photoshop installed).

- If your droplet was created in Mac OS, you must append .exe, the executable file indicator, to its name for it to work on a Windows machine.
- If your droplet was created on Windows, drag and drop it onto the Photoshop icon once it is on a Mac. This updates and recognizes the droplet.

In both cases, once you have made it recognizable, the icon changes from an unidentified system file icon to the droplet icon.

> You don't need the same action set or even the action itself saved on each machine where the droplet is. It is self-sustaining in that sense.

Display

There are no display devices that can display the entire range of colors the human eye can see. The Commission Internationale de l'Eclairage (International Commission on Illumination) tried to give us a way to declare all visible colors, but the fact is that having a device-independent color profile does not negate the fact that for every device there will be colors that are out of the gamut.

Color Spaces

Photoshop provides a few different color spaces to which you can set it (Figure 11.15). Color spaces can be the colorimetric measurements of a specific device or artificial constructs defining a particular gamut of colors. Here is basic information on some of the color spaces:

sRGB (Standard RGB): Unfortunately, sRGB is still the default setting for many devices. The sRGB color space was designed for low-end consumer electronics in the 1990s. Some believe that this is the best for general monitor display, but our current monitors and tablets are more sophisticated than this old color model. However, most web browsers do not make use of color profiles, so sRGB ends up being the best option for images that are to be viewed on the web. What it comes down to is that the sRGB profile is the smallest and therefore "safest" default—or lowest common denominator. Most modern digital cameras, high-end monitors, and high-end printers can work with the wider-gamut profiles, so if you want richer, more accurate images, you'll need to work with a more complex color space.

Adobe RGB (1998): You can probably figure out that this color space was developed by Adobe in 1998. Despite that this was developed in the 1990s, this color space has long been a favorite as it encompasses 50 percent of the visible color space and most of the colors achievable on CMYK (cyan-magenta-yellow-key) color printers (Figure 11.16). Viewing the cyan and green hues would show some of the benefits of Adobe RGB (1998) over sRGB. If working with 8-bit images in Photoshop, Adobe RGB is still the preferred profile to obtain the most out of the image.

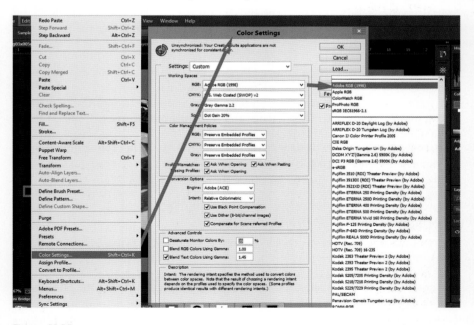

Figure 11.15

Color spaces.

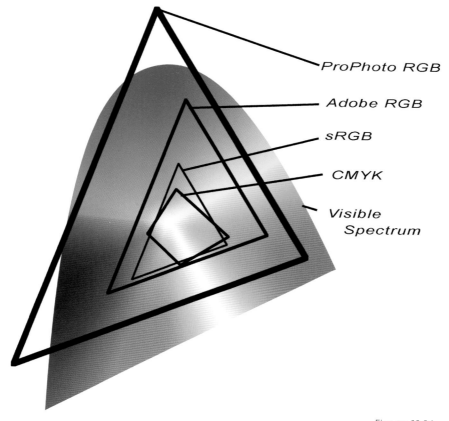

Figure 11.16

Notice that ProPhoto has areas outside of the visible spectrum.

But, images encoded in Adobe RGB will look washed out when displayed on an sRGB device.

Monitor RGB: Monitor RGB is just that: the monitor profile of your monitor's video circuitry. This is fine for you—if all you plan to do is use Photoshop on your computer and never let the art see the light of day on any other device. Like sRGB, if you were to print an image created on this profile on a CMYK printer, you would probably see the yellows, oranges, greens, and cyans get clipped.

ProPhoto RGB: ProPhoto RGB was developed by Kodak and has a much wider gamut designed for photographic output; it is now supported by most modern ink-jet printers. This profile uses blue and green primaries that are outside human vision to capture some of the tonality and colors of digital dye-sublimation printers and ink-jet printers. Personally, I try to keep my color space at ProPhoto RGB, but because the space is so wide, some 8-bit images will suffer from out-of-gamut colors mapping to the destination space in unwanted ways. For example, bringing 8-bit sRGB images into a 16-bit ProPhoto RGB space will sometimes remap into oddly saturated images.

Soft Proofing

So, now you know that any color we see is interpreted by a device—even if it is a professional's specialty matched to either a particular print or movie workflow. Even these displays cannot display every color that a printer can print or precisely predict a feature film output. The best you can do to predict the color output of those colors that exceed the gamut limits of your display is to have a tested soft-proofing workflow in place and just get used to the particular shifts that you know will happen.

Generally, the colors you see on the display appear brighter than those you see in print; this is no surprise considering that a display is lit electronically and therefore will not have the same tonal contrast range of ink. Photoshop has soft-proofing capabilities that simulate the output characteristics of print output devices on the display.

Go to **View** > **Proof Setup**, and you'll see a list of proofing options. We'll assume you are working diligently on a book and need to proof your images for print. (Hypothetically, of course, because we don't know anyone who is actually writing a book right now, do we?) Selecting Custom will bring up a dialog box with a list of profiles for different printers, devices, movie film print, standard Broadcast—you name it, you can find it. Of course, selecting Working CMYK will allow you to soft proof an RGB image using the current CMYK space established in your Color Settings.

Once you have that set up, you can press **Ctrl**/⌘ to toggle between views. The switch will be reflected in your document title/tab showing the color mode. To see the out-of-gamut colors, press **Ctrl+Shift+Y**/⌘+**Shift+Y** to toggle the view. Any colors unreproducible by the device being simulated will turn to gray.

12

Concepts, Definitions, and Terminology

Introduction

"We want to use these HDRIs for an IBL setup."
"We're delivering one-six-six, but work on it full ap."
"Hard mask it at two-three-five."

If all of that sounded more like a military launch code than anything related to Photoshop, this chapter will help you translate and understand some of the different high-end formats and terminology. The world is a lot less confusing with some basic image essentials.

Image File Formats

Each Photoshop book I ever picked up had a section on file formats. Each time I browse through one, I am disappointed to realize that they never discuss the formats I use every day in the movie/entertainment industry. EPS (Encapsulated PostScript), one of the most used and arguably important formats for print and advertising, is almost never used in visual effects (VFX) work. If well-known formats used in

Figure 12.1

What does your image need?

the postproduction industry are mentioned at all, they have a little blurb that reads "extremely high-end formats used in 3D animation."

The list in this section is derived from my experience of the formats commonly used. Some of these formats need special plug-ins to open or save the file formats, so don't be surprised if you don't have a particular option on your version of Photoshop (Figure 12.1).

PSD

Of course, the first option on the list of supported file formats is Photoshop's native format, PSD or Photoshop Document. You are probably saving your working file as a PSD. Photoshop's native format is the best lossless format to use while working because you are assured that it can support every program option, whether it is a channel, transparency, vector mask layer, a layer effect, or an annotation, and store all the structure and information that makes Photoshop so valuable. In addition, the PSD format is generally more efficient at applying lossless compression to the file than any other format. Now, with the more widespread acceptance of PSDs, you can often drag and drop them into other applications with full support for at least layers and some other features. If you are in an Adobe workflow, you can keep the image in the native Photoshop PSD format because there is a tight integration between Adobe products.

PSB

PSB (Photoshop Big) is Photoshop's large-document format for documents measuring more than 30,000 by 30,000 pixels or larger than 2 gigabytes. You *can* save a smaller file as a PSB, but if you want to interface with other programs and you don't *need* to have it be a PSB, then there really is no reason to save as anything other than a PSD.

12. Concepts, Definitions, and Terminology

TIFF

TIFF (Tagged Image File Format) supports layers and can sometimes do better compression, but you give up the ability to save certain Photoshop functions. It supports both lossless (LJW and ZIP) and lossy (JPEG [Joint Photographic Experts Group]) compression.

Arguably the most popular image format, TIFF can be suffixed as .TIFF or .TIF. Although well known across the gamut of digital artists, it is misleading to call it a format; TIFFs are an *extensible format*, which means that others can modify the original specifications. The TIFF standard was developed at Aldus and is now controlled by Adobe Systems. Adobe has a variant image file format supported by Photoshop, which can include layers, clipping paths, and adjustment layers, much like a native Photoshop file. You can also bring this TIFF that has a clipping path into page layout programs and maintain a transparent background. Then, there are the various lossless (LZW and ZIP) and lossy (JPEG) compression options available. Of course, the problem is that not all the options available in the TIFF format are supported by other programs. Despite the seemingly endless caveats, it is by far the most popular exchange format and is supported by countless third-party applications and devices. This may be because of its prior years of being the safest bet on transferring images between platforms and programs, that TIFF caters to both RGB (red-green-blue) and CYMK (cyan-yellow-magenta-key) data, and is accepted by virtually all professional printers. The icing on the cake is that TIFF is also capable of high dynamic range imaging (HDRI is discussed further in this chapter and in Chapter 5).

Oh, and one last thing: TIFFs support image files up to 4 gigabytes. That is much larger than many other formats that only support up to 2 gigabytes (even PSDs).

What is LZW? It doesn't really help you to know that LZW stands for Lempel-Ziv-Welch, but it *does* help to know that it is a lossless compression (which means that no information is lost) that is widely accepted and saves much space on storage media. ZIP can make smaller files but is less well supported. I don't recommend the JPG compression because it is a lossy compression (read: *deleted information*) and can lead to image degradation.

TGA

Although the TGA (Targa) format was designed for systems using the Truevision video board, this stable and commonly supported format is always 8 bit. This means that each channel is no more than 8 bits. It is a bit confusing because the images are referred to as 16-, 24-, and 32-bit images. This means Targa supports the following:

- 16-bit RGB images: 5 bits × 3 color channels + 1 unused bit
- 24-bit RGB images: 8 bits × 3 color channels
- 32-bit RGB images: 8 bits × 3 color channels + an 8-bit alpha channel

The Targa format also supports indexed-color and grayscale images without alpha channels. This was the file format of choice in many studios where I worked in the early days, but with the increased bit depth of the current image-processing world, TGAs are being seen less and less.

CIN

Developed by Kodak, CIN (Cineon), used interchangeably with DPX (Digital Picture Exchange), is a 10-bit-per-channel logarithmic digital format used mostly by compositors. The 10-bit log file emulates 16- or 12-bit images that capture the dynamic range of film. (A 10-bit linear file lacks the range.) Of course, this means that this format is often used to save a matte painting for a compositor. Despite increased support for other formats, and with 16-bit-per-channel capabilities being more prevalent, this format is used often in transferring film to digital and is still prevalent in the VFX world.

IFF

Most commonly associated with Autodesk or Alias/Wavefront (or with Amiga, for you old-school people), IFF (Interchange File Format) is a general-purpose data storage format that has extensions that support still picture, sound, music, video, and textual data. Most of the time, however, IFF is for opening a Maya-rendered image or saving an image for use in a Maya pipeline.

Filmstrip

The Filmstrip format is used for RGB animation or movie files created by Adobe Premiere. I haven't used this format in any of the studios where I have worked, even the small, boutique shops. Premiere is used by a few smaller shops, so I assume a few request this format. Photoshop does caution that if you resize, resample, remove alpha channels, or change the color mode or file format of a Filmstrip file in Photoshop, you cannot save it back to Filmstrip format. This makes me wonder if this is useful after all. But, as Creative Cloud becomes more popular as a full subscription, I can see more integration and more companies switching to use Premier because it is included in the suite. Only time will tell.

PhotoCD

Another format developed by Kodak, the PhotoCD (PCD) format allows five resolutions to be contained in a single file. Often, reference CDs are in this format, and you simply read it in and save it as a different format for your use. Although Kodak may now be defunct, the format and its later versions are still in circulation as reference photos.

Open EXR

The .EXR format was released as an open standard by Industrial Light and Magic (ILM), one of the premier VFX faculties in the world. It supports HDRI (high-dynamic-range imaging) with over 30 stops of exposure. Its multiresolution and multichannel format makes it appealing for three-dimensional (3D) rendering and compositing because it can store specular, diffuse, normal, and other channels in one file. EXR is also a deep data file format; a pixel can store variable values at different depths, supporting volumetric representation requirements for deep compositing workflows. So, it's no surprise that EXR supports 32-bit floating point, 16-bit floating point (called "Half"), and 32-bit integer pixels—you can't get that kind of functionality from 8 bits. Since its original release by ILM, other key industry leaders, such as Weta Digital, Pixar Animations Studios, and Autodesk, have embraced and expanded on the format.

PXR

Do you work at Pixar? Then you know this format and know when you are supposed to save this way. Everyone else? You don't work at Pixar and won't be using this format.

RAW

There is no such thing as a single .RAW file format. RAW is a bucket term used for every camera manufacturer's supposedly unprocessed raw data from the image sensor of a camera or scanner (hence, "raw"). What adds to the confusion is that Photoshop, Casio, and Leica all have a file format called raw with the .raw file suffix extension, and none of these three are actually the same file format. Generally, each camera manufacturer has its own proprietary formats that have their own file extensions; Cannon's RAW files are CR2s or CRWs, Nikon is NEF or NRW, and RED is R3D, for example. Most of these also have what is called a "sidecar" file, such as an .XMP sidecar with Photoshop .raw files and .RMD sidecars with R3D files. This file contains information about editing performed on the photograph and camera-specific data and allows for nondestructive editing because the raw captured data are still intact.

The problem is that most of the camera manufacturers are not trying to make their proprietary format compatible with anyone else's; they are just creating the file format based on the sensor. So, even within a single manufacturer, these unstandardized formats can change from one camera model to the next. That begs the question of how long you will be able to access your files. Photoshop supports most camera RAW formats, and there seem to be updates from one manufacturer or another all the time, but Adobe saw the writing on the wall; in 2004, it introduced an open source Digital Negative (DNG) format. Note that we discussed RAW in Chapter 5, so if you would like to understand and learn more about RAW files, return to Chapter 5.

DNG

DNG (Digital Negative) is Adobe's open source, publicly available archival format. More software programs can read DNG file formats than proprietary RAW file formats. Some companies, such as Leica and Hasselblad, have adopted this standard and use it as their native RAW format. One of the distinguishing properties of the DNG format is that there is no sidecar, so there is no fear of dislodging the data.

The Adobe DNG format contains raw image data from a digital camera and metadata that defines what the image data means. DNG is meant to be an industry-wide standard format for raw image data, helping photographers manage the variety of proprietary raw formats and providing a compatible archival format. (You can save this format only from the Camera Raw Dialog box.)

JPG

JPG is one of the most popular formats used—period. Named for the Joint Photographic Experts Group (JPG) that developed it, this format is effective at compression and lets you choose the level at which you wish to compress. The problem with this is that it uses a lossy compression; a JPG compresses information by looking at an 8 × 8 block of pixels and combining similar-color pixels. This means there is an irrevocable loss of data, which is especially apparent after multiple saves. However, the reduction in file size is dramatic.

This format is used mostly in nonprofessional settings, such as social media and other Internet-related sites, but also has its place in the workplace to show clients in-progress work or nonfinal reviews because its compact format is ideal for teleconferences and rough viewing. JPG delivers good continuous-tone images in a small file size. Other than degradation, the reason why it has not taken over the world is that it does not support transparency. So, as more information is delivered in our everyday lives on a variety of media and image capturing has developed more integrity, we are seeing professional services such as newspapers actually use JPGs despite the drawbacks.

Note that just opening and saving a JPG causes loss. Because JPG is lossy, you shouldn't save a JPG as a master but keep the original as a PSD and save a copy of the edited file as a JPG.

There are now other forms of JPG, such as JPG Stereo and JPG2000. JPG2000 has a lossless compression option, supports 16 bit, and has a feature called ROI for Region of Interest. This allows you to define a region (via alpha channel) that has a lower compression rate than the rest of the picture. This sounds intriguing, but despite being available for over a decade, JPG2000 still has not caught on. My guess is that having a different form of JPG and the worry that it will not be supported by all the other JPG-supporting systems has kept users shy. Future use will decide its viability.

GIF

One of three most common formats for the web, the Graphics Interchange Format (GIF) is highly compressible, but it is 256 colors, which is much too limiting for most other forms of display. Designed for minimal file size in the early days of the Internet and computer graphics, the GIF format supports transparency; the fewer colors used, the smaller the file size will be. It is terrible, however, at smooth transitions and antialiasing. The JPG format is still smaller in size, but the GIF is not a lossy format and will not degrade with multiple savings. One other aspect of GIF that keeps it alive is its ability to have "animated" forms that read as normal still images but do a limited small animation. Social media abound with all sorts of animated GIFs.

PNG

The Portable Network Graphic is a lossless compression format like GIF but supports antialiasing and continuous tone beautifully like JPG. In addition, it can support 256 levels of transparency. This means you can specify an image to be 50 percent transparent and have it show overlap with a background.

PNG-8 is too much like a GIF to give you any advantage, and PNG-24 can be too large a file with its 24-bit images that people would prefer just to save as JPGs. But, if you have a continuous tone (read: photo) image with transparency, then PNG is for you. Web developers have caught on to the benefits of PNG, and more savvy consumers are also starting to use it. I wouldn't be surprised if a few years down the road PNG becomes as ubiquitous as JPG.

EPS

Encapsulated PostScript is an essential interchange format commonly used in the publishing world. EPS files support duotone, clipping paths, bitmap images, and vector graphics, and content can be set up with special PostScript commands that govern how it will reproduce and that cannot be altered by prepress systems or software (ergo, "encapsulated" PostScript). It is not a very compact file format, so between PDFs and TIFFs, you can accomplish most of the features of EPS without the larger file size. That said, for the pre-press world, EPS still rules for all of its press-specific features. You can adjust the settings in the EPS options dialog box to custom printer calibrations and set specific screen rulings (lpi, or lines per inch). If you like to use Adobe Illustrator, this file format allows you to save clipping paths and link to your Photoshop file rather than embedding the clipping paths. However, PDFs are slowly creeping to the forefront and EPS may not have much longer to rule the pre-press world.

EPS-DCS

The Photoshop DCS (Desktop Color Separation) 1.0 and 2.0 formats are versions of EPS that enable you to save color separations of CMYK or multichannel files. Some workflows require this format, but if you have implemented spot color channels in an image, using the DCS file format is required to maintain them.

PDF

Adobe Acrobat's native format, PDF is the acronym for Portable Document Format. PDFs are an increasingly common standard for the distribution and viewing of complete documents, including images, page layout, typography, fonts, and vector graphics. Based on Adobe PostScript, the PDF format now supports transparency and vector graphics and is widely used as a digital master for media-agile color production workflows. PDF files are supported by more than a dozen platforms when viewers use Acrobat or Adobe Reader (Adobe Reader is available for free at http://www.adobe.com). Saving a file in the Photoshop PDF format supports your ability to edit the image when you open the file by choosing **File > Open** in Photoshop.

BMP

The bitmap (BMP) format is the standard Windows graphics file format.

PICT

PICT, short for Macintosh Picture, is the native Mac graphics file format.

By now you may be wondering what happened to all the pretty pictures. Didn't I say I was going to put in as many pictures as possible? Well, my young grasshopper, take a look at Figure 12.2 to see some of the differences between the formats.

A Word about HDRI

Generally, all of the "normal" formats mentioned are *low-dynamic-range images* (LDRIs). A scene's *dynamic range* is the contrast ratio between its brightest and darkest parts. An HDRI can be captured with specific equipment, rendered in CG (3D Computer graphics), made by combining multiple normal images of the same scene taken with different exposure levels; each end result pixel in an HDRI stores the amount of light in a floating-point number with no upper limit. Compare this to the RGB image integer values of 0 to 255, and you can imagine the difference. Figure 12.3 shows you one of the key benefits of HDRI. The HDRI contains a greater dynamic range of luminosity and radiance,

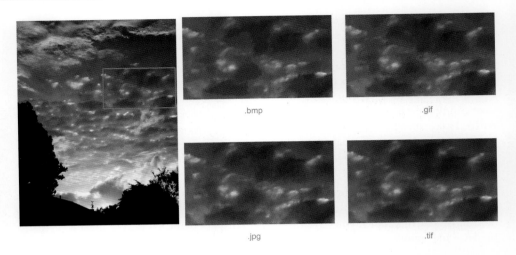

Figure 12.2

There are differences in how an image will look with different formats.

Figure 12.3

The difference between HDRI and LDRI.

portraying the full real-world levels of illumination. While standard image formats utilize 8 or 16 bits with applied gamma and color space, the HDRI format extends the bit depth up to 96 bits in a linear color space.

The beautiful luminance resulting from the use of HDRI is absolutely stunning. Fortunately, HDRI is becoming increasingly mainstream as our electronics are capable of processing more information at a faster rate. Companies such as RED and Arri have video recorders capable of capturing in a higher dynamic range. The increased sophistication of computer-generated imagery is also contributing to more HDRI. Most lighting setups now involve an IBL system that must use an HDRI as its lighting information source. This has contributed to faster and more sophisticated 3D VFX and animations.

Whenever an HDRI is shown, the image is limited to its display. When you watch a television program in HD, that is not the same as HDRI. HD on your television stands for high definition, and it is providing you with more pixels, not a higher dynamic tonal range. But, as HD popularity grows, companies are trying to find a way to display HDRI. For now, all HDRI has to be tone mapped to its display, whether that be print, projection, or screen.

12. Concepts, Definitions, and Terminology

Formats Supported for HDRI in Photoshop

- Photoshop native files: PSD, PSB
- TIFF
- LogLuv Tiff (read only)
- Radiance: HDR
- Portable Bit Map: PBM
- OpenEXR

Not all Photoshop functions can be used with 32-bit-per-channel HDRIs. Go to Adobe's help site to see the current list of functions that can be used. One of the benefits of Photoshop CC is that updates happen often and can change overnight. So, even if a function is not supported now, you might check back next week and find it available.

Vector Formats

As opposed to the raster image formats in which the data describe the characteristics of each individual pixel, vector image formats contain a geometric description. The difference in these methods is apparent when sizing an image. The rasterized image will begin to pixelate and lose detail, whereas the vector image can continue to be upsized indefinitely.

AI

Adobe Illustrator's native format is AI. It makes sense that Photoshop would accept its sister program's native file formats. Being an Adobe product, you know this vector file format is the best for Photoshop to import.

CGM

CGM (Computer Graphics Metafile) is a file format for two-dimensional (2D) vector graphics, raster graphics, and text and is supposed to provide a means of graphics data interchange for computer representation of 2D graphical information independent from any particular application, system, platform, or device. All graphical elements are specified in a textual source file that can be compiled into a binary file or one of two text representations. It has been adopted to some extent in the areas of technical illustration and professional design but has largely been superseded by formats such as SVG (Scalable Vector Graphics) and DXF (Drawing eXchange Format).

Gerber File Format (RS-274X)

The Extended Gerber File Format (RS-274X) is a 2D bilevel image description format. It is widely used in industries requiring high-precision 2D bilevel images and is the de facto standard format used by Printed Circuit Board (PCB) software.

SVG

SVG (Scalable Vector Graphics) is an open standard created and developed by the World Wide Web Consortium to find a versatile, scriptable, and all-purpose vector format for the web and is a key component in web applications (interactive web pages that act like applications). The SVG format does not have a compression scheme of its own but can be compressed using standard compression such as gzip.

3D Program File Formats

The 3D program file formats include Autodesk Maya, SoftImage, 3D Studio Max, or proprietary formats. I include here the "2.5-D" programs such as Foundry's Mari or Pixologic's ZBrush. Just about every 3D program has a Photoshop plug-in that allows you to save an image in its native image format, whether that be RLA, PIX, or 3DS. More often than not, wherever you're working has a pipeline that optimizes this, and you work with that format because your supervisor tells you so.

In regard to Photoshop, there are limited formats that are accepted.

OBJ

As the name would suggest, an OBJ object file format is used to store object code. You will get a model but no texture or other information. This is the JPG of objects in that it is the easiest and most accepted format for 3D models among all the 3D programs.

3DS

3DS is one of the native file formats used by Autodesk's 3D Studio Max 3D modeling, animation, and rendering software. Having been around since 1990, it is popular as a standard for transferring and storing models.

DAE (COLLADA)

The COLLADA file format has a DAE file extension that stands for Digital Asset Exchange. COLLADA (from collaborative design activity) files are 3D image XML (Extensible Markup Language)-based managed by the nonprofit technology consortium, the Khronos Group, and has been adopted by the International Organization for Standardization (ISO) as a publicly available specification, ISO/PAS 17506.

U3D

Universal 3D (U3D) is another attempt at another standardized file format. Put together by a special consortium called the 3D Industry Forum, U3D is a compressed file format that has the added benefit of being able to be inserted into PDFs and interactively visualized using Acrobat Reader.

KMZ

KMZ stands for Keyhole Markup language Zipped (the uncompressed file would be KML for Keyhole Markup Language). KMZ is a placemark file with a root KML document used by Google Earth and allows the inclusion of custom data such as COLLADA 3D models, overlays, and images.

DICOM

DICOM isn't really a 3D file format in the traditional sense. DICOM is an acronym for Digital Imaging and Communications in Medicine, and the format is the standard for receiving medical scans. Its extensions are .dc3, .dcm, or .dic. These DICOM files contain multiple "slices" of data and can be represented in Photoshop as layers or as a volume.

Aspect Ratios

An *aspect ratio* is a way of expressing an image's proportions, which are always stated as the horizontal size versus the vertical size. Therefore, 1.78:1 means that the width is 1.78 times as long as the height. You may also see this expressed as 16:9. The *normalized* ratio (1.78:1) is often used because it is easier to calculate the dimensions from this ratio. When speaking of the normalized aspect ratios, usually just the first number is recited without the decimal. In that case, 1.78:1 would be recited as "one-seven-eight."

You can see a graphical representation of some common aspect ratios and their relation to each other in Figure 12.4.

At one point, television and film shared the same aspect ratio. That is, the ratio of width to height was 1.33:1. This ratio was called the *Academy Ratio* because the Academy of Motion Picture Arts and Sciences had this ratio as its standard for film. When television was developed, the designers kept the same ratio for the screen. Makes sense, right?

As human nature would have it, people started staying home and watching more television, and fewer people saw any reason to go to a movie. The movie industry decided to make movies "grander" than television by making the aspect ratio different, and now we have to deal with the plethora of film formats. Of course, then television sets started to change, with flat screens and wide screens, and our lives started integrating other types of screens such as those on phones, tablets, and computers. At least for movies and television, we have started to settle into a few common ratios.

Figure 12.4

Common aspect ratios and their relationship to each other.

These three aspect ratios are most common today:

- 4:3 (full screen)
- 16:9 (wide screen)
- 2.39:1 (anamorphic: cinemascope)

Film Format Nomenclature

Shooting in film has almost become a novelty as the world has almost completely gone to digital. A lot of the nomenclature still comes from our film roots, however, so it's good to know not only the terminology but also some of the history behind the terms and numbers. Although easier to calculate, normalized ratios are a bit misleading. Generally, if a movie is shot on actual film and not digitally, then those movies are shot on 35-mm film stock; the width is common, and the height is reduced. But, the normalized ratios have the height constant and the width adjusted. In reality, when a wide-screen movie is shown in letterbox format on television (pixel resolution aside), the movie is not squeezed to fit the screen, but rather the film was masked in the first place. Take a look at Figure 12.5.

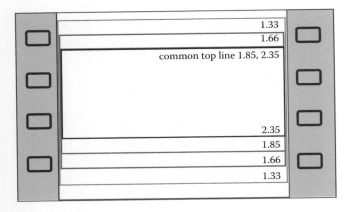

Figure 12.5

Ratios in relationship to film.

As you can see, each of these ratios shares a common width. The height is cut out to create its respective aspect ratio. Also, notice there are no lines for the soundtrack depicted in this diagram. This type of film is called *Super 35*. Sometimes, directors film with Super 35 to give leeway for shifting in the editing process, although the camera operator frames the picture with all of the action within a 2.35:1 rectangle. Of course, not having space for the soundtrack changes the aspect ratio of Full Aperture. Academy Full Aperture is 1.37:1 because of the sound strip on the film, but Super 35 Full Aperture is 1.33:1.

Table 12.1 associates common names to their aspect ratios. As you can see, often several names are associated with a single aspect ratio. You can't deduce what ratio is associated with a name. You can copy this table and memorize it, but luckily, most people refer to the aperture numbers rather than the film format names (or at least follow up the name with its respective ratio).

Table 12.1 Common Aspect Ratios

Ratio	Film Type
1.33:1	Full Aperture 35 mm, 16 mm, 8 mm
	NTSC
	Standard Television
	Academy Standard
1.5:1	Classic 35-mm still film (not for motion pictures) (3:2)
1.66:1	European film standard (5:3)
1.78:1	Digital HDTV
	US digital broadcast TV standard (16:9)
1.85:1	Academy flat
	Matted spherical
	VistaVision
	US wide-screen cinema standard
2.35:1	Current wide-screen cinema standard
2.39:1	Anamorphic
2.4:1	Scope
	CinemaScope
	Panavision
1.6:1	Common computer screen ratio (8:5)
1.25:1	Common computer screen ratio (5:4)

12. Concepts, Definitions, and Terminology

File Resolution

Knowing the terms and their implied aspect ratios, how do you determine what size your matte painting or texture should be?

Resolution is actually a misnomer because, in the strict sense, *resolution* refers to the pixels per unit length. Often, artists also refer to resolution as a document's pixel dimensions.

Common resolution terms for textures are 1 K, 2 K, and 4 K. *K* stands for kilo or 1000, but because you are dealing ultimately with binary digital machines, K is actually equal to 1024 (or 2 to the power of 10).

- 1K texture is 2^{10} or 1024 × 1024 pixels
- 2K texture is 2^{11} or 2048 × 2048 pixels
- 4K texture is 2^{12} or 4096 × 4096 pixels
- Half-K texture is 2^9 or 512 × 512 pixels

You may be asked to make things to half-K for small textures or television. Or, you may have to make something 256 × 256, which is usually just called 256 (not quarter-K) and 128 × 128. These are all powers of 2: 2^9, 2^8, and 2^7, respectively.

Occasionally, you hear someone refer to a 3-K map, which is a break in the math. You don't obtain 3 K from a power of 2. This just means that someone wants a 3072 × 3072 map. It won't be optimized because it is not a power of 2, but it is still a common texture size.

That all seems clear until you hear someone asking for a 1-K render or comp, and you are supposed to know that you are to deliver a 1024 × 778 image. If you are a genius, you probably looked at that and realized, "Hey, that's a 1.32:1 ratio based on a 2^{10} image width, so it's probably because we're working with Academy Full Aperture!" (Show of hands, how many of you *immediately* thought of that as soon as I said 1024 × 778?) The rest of us have to resort to memorizing the most common resolutions. Better yet, make a copy of Table 12.2 and keep it near your desk.

But not everything is about display on TV or movies. Unfortunately, there are so many forms of devices, from smartphones, to tablets, to wide-screen 3D TVs, that it really depends on what you are developing. And, we haven't even discussed other display media like YouTube or factors such as Retina Display (with a 2:1 pixel ratio) or other considerations that affect the pixel count. Wikipedia has a list of displays by pixel density that you can look up for other device dimensions.

Efficient Texture Size

Even with these resolutions memorized, determining texture map dimensions takes a bit of calculation. You must know how close to the camera your 3D object will be or how much of the frame your rendered object will occupy. Take a look at the two images in Figure 12.6.

The texture for the left insect must be larger than the texture for the right insect. You can make a guesstimate for the texture size needed for a 2-K render by figuring out the proportion of the texture map seen in the context of the render, then apply the size to obtain the final texture dimension. This is a bit easier to understand with pictures. Take a look

Table 12.2 Common Image Ratios and Resolutions

Format	Aspect Ratio	4 K	2 K	1 K
CinemaScope	1.17		2048 × 1743	1024 × 871
Full Ap 1	1.32	4096 × 3112	2048 × 1556	1024 × 778
Full Ap 2	1.33	4096 × 3072	2048 × 1536	1024 × 768
Academy	1.37	3656 × 2664	1828 × 1332	914 × 666
Euro	1.66		2048 × 1234	1024 × 617
HDTV	1.78	4096 × 2304	2048 × 1550	1024 × 575
UHDTV	1.78	7680 × 4320	3840 × 2160	1920 × 1080
Flat	1.85	3996 × 2160	1998 × 1080	1024 × 554
Digital cinema	1.9	4096 × 2160	2048 × 1080	1024 × 540
Scope	2.35	3656 × 1556	2048 × 872	1024 × 432
Scope 2	2.39	4096 × 1716	2048 × 858	1024 × 429

Format	Aspect Ratio	Pixel Dimension	
6K	1.94:1	6144 × 3160	
IMAX digital	1.37:1	5616 × 4096	
Red Epic 617	3:1	28000 × 9334	

UHDTV, ultra-high-definition TV.

Figure 12.6

Calculating texture sizes based on output expectations. Two insects are identical but require different levels of detail.

at Figure 12.6 and approximate the pixel size of what is showing. Then, take a look at the portion of the map that is seen in the render in Figure 12.7 and approximate what ratio of the entire map is seen.

Correlating these values, you can safely guess that a 2-K map works fine in this case. And, in the other case, there is no real need for calculations because you'll never see the logo at that size and in motion. "But," you say, "I can't read the Nanny Bug logo on the bug in the left picture!" Remember this is a 2-inch image. On a 70-foot-wide movie screen, that bug is about 7 feet across. So, the logo would be about 2 feet long. If it's always in motion, you just need enough of the logo there to register. Plus, you have to take into account the people who buy the DVD and look at it frame by frame. If you are one of those people, then I have no idea how all the generators in the movie *Serenity* have what looks like "LOPSIE" stamped on their fast-moving arms—no idea—must be coincidence.

Matting

Even if the film you are working on is going to be 2.35:1, you have to work in a larger aspect ratio if it is *not* going to be hard masked (sometimes called *soft matted* or *soft masked*). *Hard masked* means there is permanent black padding added to the image to fill in the rest of the Full Aperture frame. Therefore, you need not worry that something that isn't meant to be seen will somehow enter the cut in the final edit.

Figure 12.7

Texture map. Thorax section highlighted in yellow. At what size does the text have enough resolution?

It is common to give a little bit of leeway, so you may hear, "We're supposed to deliver 2.35:1, but we're protecting to 1.85:1." This means you should make sure everything within the 1.85 mask is clean, but that the final film is shown at a 2.35:1 ratio. The 1.85:1 matte still saves you from having to work at the 1.33:1 ratio of Full Aperture (see Figure 12.8).

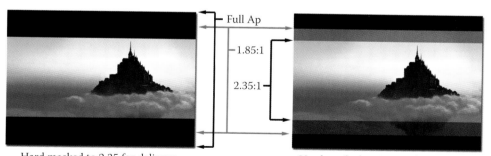

Hard masked to 2.35 for delivery

Hard masked to 1.85 and soft masked to 2.35 for internal visualization

Figure 12.8

The grayed area denotes a soft mask and is a "safety net" in case the shot is recomposed.

Index